learning in the

learning in the schools

Robert A. Davis

George Peabody College for Teachers

Wadsworth Publishing Company, Inc.
Belmont, California

Acknowledgments

Acknowledgment is made of the following for permission to use certain materials: Abrahams Magazine Service; American Educational Research Association; Balance Sheet; John Wiley and Sons; Macmillan Company; McGraw-Hill Book Company; National Education Association; Prentice Hall; Psycho-Educational Clinic, University of Wisconsin; Research Quarterly; School of Education Bulletin (University of Michigan); University of Chicago Press; University of Minnesota Press; University of Pittsburgh Press; Yale University Press.

L. C. Cat. Card No.: 66–19725

Printed in the United States of America

preface

The purpose of this book is to emphasize the general theme of learning in schools and to discuss problems that teachers confront in their day-to-day work. To achieve this objective the presentation is more descriptive than explanatory; emphasis is on conditions of learning rather than on theories. The various chapters draw on a considerable amount of research, but the research findings are not critically evaluated. Neither are the conflicting viewpoints resolved in the context of theory. The conclusions drawn, however, reflect the present state of knowledge on the various topics.

The book is intended primarily for prospective teachers who are meeting professional requirements in the broad area of educational psychology where either special courses or sections of more general ones emphasize the learning process. Much of the material may also be adapted to methods courses associated with apprenticeship teaching. Topics such as growth and development, mental measurements, individual differences, and other subjects commonly treated in educational psychology textbooks are omitted, the purpose being to include materials that are most directly related to learning and instruction.

Inasmuch as the materials are based, for the most part, on research or experience in school situations, their relevance to practical problems may be readily recognized. For the student who is already engaged in practice teaching or who has had teaching experience, the applications will be evident. It is hoped that school people in particular will be able to use some of the conclusions drawn from objective investigations in a practical way and be stimulated to conduct similar studies along the lines of their special interests.

The materials and problems considered here are selected for their relevance either to the planning of courses of instruction or to course supervision. They are organized into two parts: *Course of Learning* and *Improvement of Learning.*

The purpose of Part I is to describe the process of learning, with minimum consideration of the conditions under which learning occurs. This part illustrates learning situations, describes techniques of measuring learning gain, discusses the processes of learning and forgetting, and ends with a chapter on transference of learning. The title *Course of Learning* refers to the route learning characteristically takes. This route is marked by fluctuations that are characterized by gains and losses and, sometimes, recovery of losses. The net effect of learning is that some of it becomes permanent or is transferred to other learning situations.

Conditions contributing to learning efficiency are considered in Part II. The effectiveness of many of these conditions is appraised by the criteria of learning, retention, and transfer of training—the processes described in Part I. The conditions relate to the organization and presentation of course materials, direction of learning activities, the use of interests and incentives, and recognition of the learner's emotional and social needs. Many of these, which are largely within the teacher's control, may be anticipated when planning a learning program and they can be dealt with directly during day-to-day teaching. Because the conditions of learning afford the most practical basis for improving the learning process, this part ends with a chapter on implications of learning theories for teaching. These theories provide reference points from which a teacher may analyze his own philosophy in the light of experience. In time, it is expected that he will develop certain beliefs about the nature of learning and the conditions that affect it.

This book grew out of a course, Classroom Learning, designed for students who had limited background in psychology and education and who wanted assistance in preparing their own instructional programs. The interests and needs of this group are reflected in the organization as well as in the kinds of materials that are included. Certain parts of "Planning Learning Programs in Secondary Schools" (Peabody Bulletin, 1963), also originating in the same course, are used in Chapters 1, 5, and 6. Mr. D. F. Butler, graduate instructor in the Department of Science Education at Peabody, assisted on various occasions in surveying and evaluating research on the various topics. The task of readying the book for publication was made easier by the typing and editorial services of Mrs. John Procter of Nashville.

contents

introduction

School learning has been traditionally regarded as an applied field, applied in the sense that educational psychologists have applied general, theoretical psychological principles or generalizations to teaching situations. Since such adaptations of psychological knowledge have often been based on experimental studies employing artificial tasks, with either animals or human adults used as subjects, doubt arises as to their applicability to school situations. But even though laboratory studies are based on meaningful tasks and often use school children as subjects, skepticism over the applicability of laboratory techniques to the study of classroom learning still remains.

laboratory versus school techniques

A technique commonly employed by psychologists in a study of learning is to select or devise an unfamiliar task and determine the efficiency with which the learner masters it. The task, which may be verbal or motor, remains constant, and efficiency is measured by criteria such as correct responses, time, errors, or trials. The verbal task, for example, may consist of a list of nonsense syllables which are displayed one at a time on a standard apparatus at a specified rate. The learner is required, after each practice period, to reproduce as many syllables as possible. During the first few, he may be able to reproduce only three or four syllables; but with continued practice the number may increase to eight, ten, or even more, after which no further improvement occurs.

The laboratory task may also be a human maze, the purpose of the investigator being to study the learner's progress in tracing the pathways leading to a solution. For example, he may keep a record of the number of errors the learner makes on his first trial, his second, and so on. He may also keep a record of the time required for each successive trial. In addition to these, the measure may be the number of trials needed to meet a criterion of success, such as one errorless tracing of the maze.

An individual's performance in memorizing nonsense syllables and in solving maze problems always fluctuates during the several practice periods, but it tends to improve continually until physiological or psychological limits are attained. These limits are reached when the individual no longer is able to improve his score regardless of the effort he exerts.

Several important features are revealed by a study of learning in laboratory situations. The tasks selected for learning are usually novel in the sense the learner has not had any direct experience with them. As a result, he begins his practice at a point near zero efficiency; thus measurement of his gain is made more accurately than would be the case if the learner were familiar with the task. Laboratory tasks also make possible an analysis of the learner's efficiency at each practice period and thereby afford a basis for studying the *process* of learning.

One of the striking characteristics of learning in laboratory situations is the marked improvement produced within a short period of time. In such situations there are definite objectives, specific materials or tasks, and supervised practice. Also, the results of learning are analyzed objectively. The learner is made conscious of the need for attaining definite goals.

One can readily recognize the usefulness of laboratory techniques for determining the rapidity and accuracy with which spelling words can be mastered and reproduced without error, the number of arithmetical exercises that can be solved within a given time, the ease with which certain motor tasks may be performed, or the number of items that can be reproduced in a reading assignment. Such techniques, however, are mainly applicable to drill situations.

The task that confronts a learner in typical school situations is constantly changing. Instead of being required to seek improvement in performance in a constant task, which might be that of memorizing a list of words, he is continuously confronted with new material that requires him to make forward and backward associations before he makes advancement. In studying arithmetic, for example, the pupil first learns the number concept, then addition, and on the basis of these he builds other skills in subtraction and division. In history he studies material that is not only a separate unit but is also a foundation for other units to follow. Each element in his task eventually becomes part of another interrelated and interdependent task.

The steady presentation of new material requires progressive reorganization of subject matter as a course of instruction continues. Consequently, information learned one day may mean something different to a learner when subsequent materials are studied. The learning situation is broken down for study of its essential parts. In a course of instruction, however, reference must be made to material while it is in a continual state of reorganization. Instead of using laboratory techniques that stress the effect of practice on a constant task, the teacher must recognize and exploit the cumulative and progressive nature of learning as instruction continues. The evident need is for studies that are conducted in actual school settings employing techniques appropriate to classroom learning. Until this need is met, adaptations of laboratory techniques must be made.

Systematic study of learning in school situations requires certain steps in planning: define learning objectives, organize learning materials, select learning activities, devise testing situations, and provide a schedule for administration and use of tests. After learning programs have been prepared, there is a period of instruction and a period of testing. After these periods further instruction and study are required. The results of learning are then confirmed by some kind of evaluation. This follows consideration of difficulties and the elimination of errors. Throughout, effort is made to provide for practice of the responses suggested by the learning objectives, and tests are made to determine the proficiency acquired in making the responses.

In the laboratory, learning and testing are intimately related; it is possible to take measurements at all stages of practice. In the schools, however, there may be a period of instruction followed by a period of testing that is distantly removed from initial practice or study. The only practical means for studying the process of learning systematically is to give tests frequently enough to afford a basis for analyzing and tracing the learner's progress.

studying problems under school conditions

Substantial progress has been made in the study of learning under school conditions. In 1940, Stroud[1] surveyed 256 studies related to school learning. His list of descriptive and experimental investigations embraces a period of approximately 40 years. He found that the general quality of these studies was good. Many of them compared favorably with those conducted in the laboratory. In commenting on the results of this review, Stroud suggested that the educational psychologist was confronted with two needs—each pointed in different directions. One was the need to

[1] J. B. Stroud, "Experiments on Learning in School Situations," *Psychological Bulletin,* 37 (1940), 777–807.

solve immediate practical problems without recognition of the standards set in experimental psychology. The other was the need to discover, under school conditions, the generality of psychological principles and techniques. He felt the future of classroom learning would be particularly good if experimental psychologists would become better acquainted with classroom problems and adapt their techniques to the study of school learning.

In recent years, research on learning in school situations has continued to develop, indicating a trend toward less use of applications of general, theoretical psychology and a greater emphasis on studies of teaching[2] problems. Less evident, but paralleling this trend, are the efforts to test, under school conditions, the techniques and generalizations of laboratory research. Using the present state of knowledge, however, it is not possible to build a psychology of classroom learning on the basis of information developed in school settings. In a number of situations the needed information is not available. It is necessary, for example, to draw on the implications of laboratory studies if one is to consider principles of organizing course materials. The same situation exists when one considers the amount and distribution of practice as well as the conditions affecting the permanence and transference of learning.

Study of practical learning problems in school situations does not need to be elaborate. It can be done using simple research designs by anyone having limited technical knowledge; or it can be done using formal research designs that require some training in research techniques.

simple research designs

When using simple research designs, the investigator must observe and record the actual events during a course of instruction. No effort is made to compare one teaching method with another, the aim being to discover everything possible about the effects of one procedure. This kind of research requires a carefully prepared learning program. After its preparation there must be systematic study of significant events while instruction is in progress. The techniques include testing, interviewing, observing, and recording. From the information obtained one may revise his plans for further use. This type of research is described by Brownell[3] as follows:

[2] Marvin D. Sterrett and Robert A. Davis, "The Permanence of School Learning: A Review of Studies," *Educational Administration and Supervision* 40 (1954), 449–460. Also Lloyd Standlee and Edmund Mech, "A Brief Note on Trends in School Learning Research," *Journal of Educational Research,* 48 (1955), 355–367.

[3] W. A. Brownell, "Educational Research in the Decade Ahead" (Address at Annual Banquet, American Educational Research Association, Atlantic City, New Jersey, February 15, 1960).

My first concern is that in our growing preoccupation with the more complicated forms of research we shall not overlook the virtues of—indeed, the need for—simpler kinds. Note that I did not say *easier kinds.* To make clear what I mean let us suppose that our problem is to determine the effectiveness of Method A (whatever that is) in teaching a particular segment of subject matter in Grade 5.

In research simple in design we could select a reasonably large sample of Grade 5 children, determine their characteristics in detail, and teach them as planned. We should then note carefully what occurs from day to day—which children progress rapidly, and which slowly, and *why;* at what points in the sequence of subject matter topics learning difficulties arise, what they are, and why they appear; which instructional devices or aids are successful, which unsuccessful, and *why.* Our procedures would be those of testing, interviewing, and observing.

To get specific and accurate data at critical points, the testing would almost certainly have to be done with instruments especially prepared for the purpose. We would interview, probably, not all the children but those most likely to supply significant information. . . .

In the end we should have a large body of data on Method A, data both comprehensive and intensive. They would include measures and estimates over a wide range of phenomena, and they should enable us to get close to reasons, relationships, and explanations. We should have clues for the improvement of Method A, and we should be able to predict how well the method would serve in teaching other groups of similar children the same, or a very like body of subject matter. Of course, we should not know how Method A compares in effectiveness with Method B and C; but that, by assumption, was not our problem.

Other simple types of research include analyses of pupils' written work. A well-known educator once observed that teachers discard written material that could provide valuable information in directing the learning process. Such material, when analyzed, would reveal frequently recurring types of error, misunderstandings resulting from varied pupil backgrounds, and a host of other information that could be used to improve learning efficiency. Valuable information may also be collected by means of questionnaires or checklists designed to discover special interests, hobbies, and vocational goals. Also of value is background material on the student's family and home life. Such information, even though analyzed roughly, provides clues to learning problems.

controlled-group experimentation

An investigator may prefer more formal research designs. The procedure most applicable is controlled-group experimentation. This type of design requires precise definition of problems, formulation of hypotheses, selection of learners to be used as subjects, and the establishment of controls. The particular aim may be to discover which methods are effective in learning; but more generally the purpose is to determine the conditions that enhance learning efficiency.

The steps in initiating controlled-group experiments are illustrated by Swenson.[4] As an educator, she became interested in the problem of retroactive inhibition, and this interest led her to a review of research as reported in psychological periodicals and monographs. Almost all of the research on this topic at the time had been conducted under laboratory conditions, but the results were sufficiently definite to suggest what might happen if comparable studies were made in school situations. This review of research on retroactive inhibition resulted in her identifying a number of implications for directing the learning process. These indicated the need for testing in the schools some of the generalizations growing out of experimentation in the psychological laboratory. At the end of her review she outlined five major problems, which she stated in the form of questions to be answered through experimentation. She also suggested possible procedures for answering her questions.

Problems that may be studied by techniques of controlled-group experimentation are almost unlimited if one considers the varied activities associated with day-to-day teaching. The key to successful innovations lies in providing assistance to teachers as they begin to experiment with new approaches. Wherever new techniques are tried out the subjects usually show noticeable improvement in learning; almost anything new seems to work better than the old. In commenting on this situation Brickell[5] says:

> . . . the attention, encouragement, and recognition given to teachers by persons outside the classroom during the introduction of new programs are among the strongest causes of their success.
>
> . . . teachers normally work in such isolation that the kind of attention provided by the principal and others during major instructional changes can scarcely fail to have an exhilarating effect. The "Hawthorne" effect—higher production stimulated by a change that does not alter the original resources.

The educational psychologist should consider the possibility of trying out under school conditions any theories, hypotheses, or clues that hold promise of theoretical or practical application. Professional writings on instructional and learning problems in school subjects are already replete with adaptations of psychological theories as illustrated, for example, by the continuing controversy, *drill versus meaning theory* in arithmetic. The purpose of testing the practical value of such adapted theories should not be to determine whether or not one's results are in agreement with current psychological theory. Rather, the purpose should be to determine whether or not practice based on a particular theory facilitates school learning.

[4] Esther J. Swenson, *Retroactive Inhibition* (Minneapolis: University of Minnesota Press, 1941), pp. 52–54.

[5] Henry M. Brickell, "The Dynamics of Educational Change," *Theory into Practice*, 1 (1962), 81–88.

developing professional competence

Materials that are concerned with the general problem of learning and its direction provide a foundation for instructional improvement. Also necessary to the development of professional competence is a knowledge of problems that are peculiar to a certain area. Eventually, one must become familiar with learning problems in such fields as social science, natural science, and the language arts as well as individual subjects such as arithmetic or history.[6] It is in a study of the problems within specialized areas that one finds the most applicable information. These are sufficiently varied and challenging to provide opportunity for a lifetime of study and research. The study of special treatises on learning and teaching in particular areas helps one keep abreast of new techniques and principles. These sources within one's special field of teaching interest may be studied to gain awareness of instructional problems, or they may be studied to find answers to specific problems that already exist.

Sometimes a teacher may study writings and research merely to become aware of trends in education. For the moment he may not be considering his own specific teaching problems. In this case he may become conscious of problems he did not know existed in his own classes. As a result of studying the findings of sociometric investigations, for example, he may be made aware of possible cliques among his pupils. In reviewing the research on learning activities he may detect deficiencies in his own teaching methods. Keeping up with the thinking and research in one's field is one of the best ways to stimulate self-appraisal.

On the other hand, he may already be struggling with a problem in his teaching and decide to make a thorough study of the writings and research on it. Here again the books and periodicals in his teaching field are appropriate sources of information. Other sources include technical journals[7] in psychology and education. A review and synthesis of the writings and research on problems from such sources provide a basis for possible solution. Having such information, he may then adapt any techniques or principles relevant to his problem.

Finally, if educational psychology is to make any real difference in the thinking and teaching of teachers, the program of professional training should be a continuous one wherein the educational psychologist and the teacher on the job work together in a discussion and solution of teaching and learning problems. Organization for this purpose in some cases has

[6] See, for instance, *Mathematics Teacher, English Journal,* and *Science Education.*

[7] For instance, *Journal of Educational Psychology* and *Journal of Educational Research.*

taken the form of learning conferences conducted for teachers in service. At these conferences the teachers describe their own problems and present practical suggestions for their solutions. The attending educational psychologist describes applicable research trends and points of view. The workshop and other well-known forms of organization serve essentially the same purpose, especially if effort is made to blend research and teaching experience.

Many teachers desire assistance in planning their own courses of instruction. Among the advantages of planning is the opportunity to build learning principles into an instructional program. It is during the planning stage that certain questions may be asked and answered in the light of psychological knowledge and teaching experience. What objectives are appropriate for a particular situation and how may they be stated? How may learning materials be organized to form connecting links in a series of activities? What objectives are likely to be attained by certain kinds of learning activity? And what kinds of performance should the learner be able to demonstrate after completing a course of instruction? Inadequate planning may result in failure to unify *objectives, course materials, learning activities,* and *evaluation.* The learning objectives may suggest that certain abilities are to be stressed, but the course material may be inappropriate for their cultivation. Objectives may indicate particular kinds of performance, and the means of evaluation may emphasize others. The methods of evaluation may be geared to the objectives, but the learning activities may be unsuitable for their attainment.

This blending of research knowledge and teaching experience through learning conferences provides one of the most promising methods of putting educational psychology to work. In general, the educational psychologist knows little about the everyday happenings of the classroom; and the teacher knows very little about the scientific study of learning and teaching. As a result of cooperative effort the teacher is stimulated to take a more critical attitude towards his own practices and in some instances to conduct research in his own classroom.

part one

course of learning

gains of learning

1

The first requirement of an effective learning program is a clearly defined statement of the objectives to be achieved. What kind of response is the learner supposed to make? What is he supposed to get out of it? What is he expected to be able to do as a result of it? A second requirement is that testing situations shall measure the extent to which the objectives have been attained. Failure to recognize the interrelationship of these two elements in a learning program is responsible for much of the "cat and mouse attitude" prevalent in teaching situations. When learning objectives are carefully defined, they suggest the kinds of response to be cultivated and afford a basis on which to evaluate the learning that occurs.

learning situations

Since most learning takes place through the media of language and symbols, emphasis will be placed on verbal learning and intellectual skills.[1] The purpose is to outline certain illustrative types of learning that are applicable to a variety of subject matter and a wide range of educational levels. These may be classified broadly as those emphasizing

[1] B. S. Bloom, *Taxonomy of Educational Objectives* (New York: David McKay, 1956). Learning situations (objectives) are classified as *knowledge, comprehension, application, analysis, synthesis,* and *evaluation,* ranging from simple to more complex processes.

See also Leon Lessinger, "Test Building and Test Banks through the Use of Taxonomy of Educational Objectives," *California Journal of Educational Research,* 14 (1963), 195–202.

recall and those emphasizing *effective thinking*. Under the first classification, the learner is concerned primarily with acquiring information; under the second, he may continue to acquire information, but his major purpose is to use it.

situations emphasizing recall

Varying stages in the degree to which information may be regarded as learned may be described. The processes to be considered are: *rote memorizing, memorizing substance of the main points,* and *assimilating information.*

rote memorizing

The learner may memorize facts, principles, terminology, definitions, dates, axioms, or even the solution of problems by rote. During study as well as testing, he attempts to reproduce verbatim what he has memorized.

A high degree of accuracy in memorization is desirable in some learning situations. Multiplication tables and other number combinations must be reproduced accurately. In the study of a foreign language, certain rules must be memorized for progress in the subject, even though they may not be understood readily. Rote memorization may be desirable for quotations, dates in history, and locations in geography. Certain rules, facts, principles, and formulas in science may require exact memorization.

If the learner uses rote memorization when it is not required, it may be symptomatic of his lack of readiness to study a subject. If he is incapable of understanding the material, he may use rote methods in the hope of adjusting to requirements. When exact reproduction is stressed in tests, it is possible for a student to obtain high marks in subjects in which he has developed little understanding.

In examinations that stress exact reproduction, there is no way to know if the student has acquired an understanding of the subject. It may be assumed he studies for the purpose of reproduction and gives little thought to the meaning of information. His responses tend to be mechanical; he relies principally on continued repetition to achieve the accuracy that is desired.

The efficiency of the learner who uses rote methods may be measured by simple reproduction tests in which blanks are to be filled. His performance may also be evaluated by short answer tests that require listings such as names and locations.

memorizing substance of main points

In another kind of learning situation the individual may not use rote methods in acquiring information but attempt to memorize the substance of the main points or ideas. He selects significant items in material without regard to the outline of the teacher or the textbook. For example, the student might read an article in one of the popular magazines and select five major points that cover the discussion. Or he might list the major points made in a lecture. He does not study for exact reproduction but makes his own selection of important items and reproduces them in any order.

On this voluntary selection basis the individual is still operating on a low learning level, because his main effort is to reproduce material. But he is performing on a higher level than is the student who uses rote memorization, since it is he who makes the selection of material to be recalled. Also, because he is not expected to reproduce the material in any particular order, he is likely to gain more understanding than he would if he studied to reproduce it verbatim.

This kind of learning may be observed in many subject-matter fields where teachers are interested in determining whether or not students are familiar with a wide range of foundational material.[2] It may be measured by short answer tests that require listings or enumerations, such as stating three advantages or three disadvantages of some point of view or naming in any order the major causes of a trend.

assimilating information

The most common type of learning is the assimilation of ideas, viewpoints, principles, or facts presented in predigested form in textbooks or by teachers. The learner studies these materials with a view to their assimilation and recall. In a particular instance he attempts to understand the viewpoint of an author and to think thoughts in harmony with those expressed by him. In another he may follow the author's steps in reaching a conclusion or solving a problem. His major purpose is to understand and assimilate the facts, principles, or generalizations so that he may impart such information to others, particularly teachers.

This kind of learning is used in all subject-matter fields but is most readily observed in subjects that require extensive reading, such as English literature and the social sciences. The student, through his reading, class discussion, and "buzz" sessions, seeks to assimilate the major ideas, facts, principles, and viewpoints in a course of instruction. His efforts are likely to be evaluated solely on his ability to assimilate the materials—with no effort made to test his ability to analyze, apply, or evaluate the materials. Obviously, one who studies with such a purpose is

[2] Francis P. Hunkins and O. L. Davis, "Textbook Questions: What Thinking Processes Do They Foster?" as reported in *Ideas Educational,* Kent State University School, 3 (1965), 11–17. These authors, using Bloom's *Taxonomy* as a guide, analyzed questions from fifth-grade textbooks in the social sciences. Eighty-seven percent of the questions were concerned with *knowledge,* 78 percent with *knowledge* of *specifics.*

trying to prepare himself to answer only questions that are acceptable to teachers. He becomes primarily an assimilator of information and studies merely to recall what he has assimilated.

A foremost objective in every subject is to cultivate assimilation and require the learner to demonstrate it through recall. This ability involves primarily questions of *who, what, when,* and *where.* Recall of materials assimilated may be measured by objective tests, such as multiple-choice items; but the essay examination provides the best opportunity for the learner to demonstrate how effectively and completely he has assimilated basic subject matter. He can then proceed more competently to other types of learning, such as the ability to apply principles or to provide evidence in support of generalizations.

The essay examination affords the student an opportunity to describe, explain, or simply to narrate the information he has acquired. During study for such an examination, he organizes his information around cues that assist him in recall of significant items at the time of testing. He may form opinions and evaluate or apply the materials being assimilated; but his major objective is to recall the significant ideas, facts, or principles.

reproduction versus recognition as measures of recall

Experimental evidence suggests that recall is rarely literal[3] if the learner is permitted to follow his own inclinations. Where a testing situation provides opportunity for voluntary and spontaneous responses, as in some forms of the essay examination, the learner tends to make alterations in the original material—elaborating on certain parts of the material and omitting other parts. Thus, he does not duplicate the material in its original form but reworks it into patterns based on his own interpretations. In other words, he *recognizes* the material but does not *reproduce* it in its entirety.

The purpose of the recognition technique of testing is to encourage the learner to discriminate among various suggested answers; such items draw on his store of experience through aided reproduction. Reproduction items,[4] in contrast, require the learner to reformulate his responses. The effectiveness of reproduction and recognition techniques as measures of recall was studied by Postman,[5] who used nonsense syllables as

[3] F. G. Bartlett, *Remembering: A Study in Experimental and Social Psychology* (New York: Macmillan Co., 1932). See also R. C. Oldfield, "Memory Mechanisms and the Theory of Schemata," *British Journal of Psychology,* 45 (1954), 14–23; and Irving H. Paul, *Studies in Remembering* (New York: International University Press, Inc., 1959).

[4] Sutherland Davis and others, "Information Content in Recognition and Recall, *Journal of Experimental Psychology,* 61 (1961), 422–429.

[5] L. J. Postman and others, "Experimental Comparisons of Active Recall and Recognition," *American Journal of Psychology,* 61 (1948), 511–519.

learning material. Two groups learned the same material under identical conditions and served as their own control. His findings show that recognition is poorer after reproduction than before. On the other hand, reproduction is better after recognition. Items that fail to appear in reproduction often are recognized correctly. Total scores on the two types of measurement, however, are highly correlated. Postman believes the fundamental difference between the two techniques lies in the "minimal strength of associations" required for successful performance. The recognition technique is more sensitive, because it provides a better opportunity for a student to earn high scores on materials not thoroughly learned.

Courtney[6] compared the effectiveness of *oral reproduction, written reproduction,* and *multiple-choice recognition.* He used fifth-grade children as subjects, and selections from social studies and science as material. Written reproduction was measured after the children had been given adequate time for a single reading of a selection. After they had written all they could reproduce, a multiple-choice test was given. The oral-reproduction test was given individually, the examiner checking the items reproduced orally after each child had read the selection silently. After this, the children were given the multiple-choice test.

The multiple-choice (recognition) test was considerably easier than unaided reproduction, either oral or written. The coefficient of correlation between oral and written reproduction was .68; between written reproduction and multiple-choice recognition it was .76. Some of these fifth-grade pupils could express themselves much more readily in writing than in speaking. Others were low in both types of unaided reproduction; but all were superior on the multiple-choice test. Hulburt's[7] study shows that reproduction-completion and recognition-multiple-choice techniques for measuring word meaning have only a limited number of factors in common. On the basis of these findings it would seem that both reproduction and recognition techniques are needed if a test is to be an adequate measure of vocabulary.

situations emphasizing effective thinking

When not in learning situations that emphasize recall, the individual frequently must use information in answering questions or solving problems. The term "effective thinking" is loosely used to describe the mental activity one practices in such situations. This activity includes numerous abilities and skills, many of which overlap. Most of them,

[6] D. Courtney and others, "Multiple-Choice Recall versus Oral and Written Recall," *Journal of Educational Research,* 39 (1946), 458–461.

[7] Delphia Hulburt, "The Relative Value of Recall and Recognition Techniques for Measuring Precise Knowledge of Word Meaning—Nouns, Verbs, Adjectives," *Journal of Educational Research,* 47 (1954), 561–576.

however, may be classified broadly as those stressing *critical thinking* and *problem solving.*

critical thinking

The process of critical thinking, in terms of ability and skill required of the individual, stands somewhere between assimilating information and solving a problem. Consequently, its cultivation may be regarded as preparation for the more complex process of problem solving.

An objective of some investigators[8] is to analyze abilities believed to be associated with critical thinking. These analyses have resulted in the listing of a large number of abilities, including the following: (1) recognition of inferences, (2) evaluation of the reliability of evidence, (3) interpretation, (4) identification of causal relationships, (5) awareness of trends, (6) distinction between fact and opinion, (7) recognition of the assumptions implied by a statement, and (8) effectiveness in the use of informational sources.

The kinds of learning described in this section include, in one form or another, all of the abilities listed above. Each ability requires the learner to do something more than become *familiar with, understand* or *assimilate* information, and *demonstrate* his knowledge through recall. Instead, he is supposed to become actively involved in his learning and make various kinds of responses to information already acquired or in process of acquirement. The described learning situations require the abilities to *generalize* on the basis of given information, to *apply principles* to new situations, to *interpret tabular, graphic,* and *textual data,* and to develop a *logical proof.*

Drawing generalizations. Instead of assimilating generalizations that are presented in predigested form in a textbook or by the teacher, the learner is assigned materials that require him to derive his own generalizations.[9] The aim of this type of learning situation is to cultivate ability to draw generalizations on the basis of a body of uninterpreted information.

[8] Harold L. Herber, "An Inquiry into the Effect of Instruction in Critical Thinking upon Students in Grades 10, 11, and 12" (unpublished Doctoral dissertation, Boston University, 1959). See also Thomas G. Devine, "Critical Thinking in the English Class," *Peabody Journal of Education,* 39 (1962), 359–365; Velma I. Rust and others, "A Factor Analysis Study of Critical Thinking," *Journal of Educational Research,* 55 (1962), 253–260. One of these factors seems to be *general reasoning;* another, *logical discrimination* or *application* of *logical principles.* See also B. O. Smith, "Critical Thinking," *13th Yearbook* (American Association of Colleges for Teacher Education, 1960). In this study Smith found that only 30 percent of student activities were clearly related to the *reasoning* process.

[9] There is also *ability to infer* as differentiated from the *ability to generalize.* In drawing inferences the learner operates on a more subtle level than he does when making generalizations. He must "read between the lines." He must discover information in the material that may be obscure or not stated directly.

Opportunities to encourage generalizations exist in most school situations. In the early grades generalizations are stimulated by simple projects that require pupils to look up items of information, to collect objects, and to discuss possible reasons for events. In the senior high school the learner may develop a project on the basis of original source materials. In this situation his task may be to review and summarize varied kinds of information on a subject in which viewpoints vary. He may also perform laboratory experiments and draw generalizations on the basis of his results. But whether he is in the early or advanced grades, his primary purpose is to formulate his own generalizations rather than to try to understand those presented by a mentality other than his own.

In tests designed to measure ability to generalize, the learner no longer relies on recall of existing generalizations. He is expected to draw them on the basis of given information. What do certain data mean? What element is common among a number of different sets of facts? On the assumption the information is accurate, what generalizations may be drawn? One of the simplest methods for measuring this ability is to provide the learner with a list of statements and require him to formulate his own generalizations.

Applying principles. Ability to apply principles is a critical test of understanding. And the learner increases his understanding or grasp of a principle each time he applies it. Thus, it has been strongly argued, a student has not thoroughly learned until he can apply his knowledge to concrete situations. Before a principle can be applied, it must be understood; but, it should be remembered, understanding alone does not necessarily ensure successful application. In many cases the learner's understanding of a principle is limited. He can only apply the principle to the specific situation used when it was taught. His ability to apply principles, then, is best demonstrated when he confronts new situations or at least confronts those that have not been used during instruction.

The child's ability to apply principles begins to develop during the elementary grades and increases in complexity through the school years. During his early years, he learns to associate words with everyday objects and experiences in his home, neighborhood, school, and playground. A high degree of ability to apply principles is not expected during the "What's this?" and "What's that?" period. It is anticipated, however, that he will later detect organization in information and solve simple problems as he increases his understanding of relationships. Toward the beginning of the junior high school period the learner will have acquired ability to apply a great deal of information. At this time he is introduced to relatively simple principles in such fields as natural science, social science, and mathematics. As he advances through high school and into college, he is concerned more and more with complex principles and their application.

Testing situations designed to measure ability to apply principles should require the learner (1) to know what the result or effect of certain principles will be and (2) to give *reasons* to support his decision. He must give reasons for his conclusion to demonstrate his awareness of the principle being applied. The solution must include both the *principle* and the *reason*.

The technique for measuring ability to apply principles differs in one fundamental respect from that of the ability to generalize. When testing ability to generalize, the learner is presumed to be working on subject matter that is new to him. He must demonstrate his ability, for each immediate situation, without recourse to recall of any similar material. In applying principles, on the other hand, the learner supposedly studies his material with the advantage of being able to recall principles. In other words, the principle is already known; the situation in which it is applied is *new*.

Interpreting data. The ability to interpret data bears certain similarities to that of drawing generalizations. Like the ability to generalize, the ability to interpret requires situations that encourage the learner to study bodies of uninterpreted information and give interpretations. Opportunities to interpret data exist in many areas of subject matter. Particularly is this true of the natural and social sciences, because large bodies of information in these fields are presented in tables and graphs as well as in textual form. Through study of such material the learner is expected to become skillful in noting trends that may be evident in the data, in making qualified inferences from the data, and in recognizing their limitations.

When confronted by this kind of learning situation, the individual must operate on a high intellectual plane. It is different from the one on which he operates when he tries to comprehend or assimilate interpretations that have already been made for him. The purpose is to help him to cultivate an ability to think intelligently about materials as distinguished from an ability to understand or assimilate interpretations made by a textbook author or teacher. This ability, like the others in this section, suggests the importance of learning situations that encourage the learner to obtain answers and solutions through his own efforts.

In measuring ability to interpret data, the learner is presented with a body of material in textual, tabular, or graphic form. From these materials he is expected to make his own interpretations. The data presented should be new; or at least they should not have been treated in course materials or discussed in class. It is assumed that past experience and training in similar situations will be helpful to the learner, but not to the extent that they can be relied upon to meet test requirements.

Developing a logical proof. Each of the types of learning discussed in this section makes demands on the individual as he engages in critical thinking and the reasoning process. But none of the demands is so closely associated with critical thinking as is the ability to develop a logical proof. When the learner responds to a situation that requires a proof, he is concerned not only with the body of conclusions and principles of the subject matter he is considering. He is also concerned with the logical thinking processes of the recognized scholars in the field.

To develop the ability to make a logical proof, the learner must practice two[10] important elements of the reasoning process. One of these is the element of definitions and assumptions. The other is the relationship between conclusions and their antecedent definitions and assumptions. The learner is expected to analyze his material critically and discover the reasoning process that led to the conclusions. He must analyze ways of obtaining knowledge as well as assimilating it. For that reason the development of a logical proof brings into play a more penetrating and analytic kind of thinking than does any of the other types of learning previously discussed.

Measuring ability to develop a logical proof requires recognition of two problems: (1) the significance of definitions and assumptions, and (2) the relationship between the conclusions reached and the definitions and assumptions on which the conclusions depend.

problem solving

In problem solving, a high level of learning, the individual must draw upon and integrate varying types of learning with which he is already familiar: learning situations that emphasize recall as well as those that stress critical thinking. The best preparation for problem-solving procedures is, therefore, the acquisition and understanding of information pertinent to the problem situation and development of the techniques and skills that are needed in critical thinking. Failure of the student to recognize the relationship between efficiency in other types of learning and the steps in problem solving is a principal obstacle to problem-solving efficiency.

The steps in problem solving are stated in various forms, but all tend to conform to Dewey's[11] classic sequence as follows: (1) sensing the difficulty and its location and definition, (2) developing suggestions and hypotheses, (3) testing hypotheses and suggestions by reasoning, and (4) evaluating the solution by observation and experiment.

The procedure in problem solving includes both *inductive* and *deductive* processes. Induction is the process in which judgments pass from the specific to the general; deduction is the process in which judgments pass from the general to the specific. In problem solving the

[10] Gordon M. Dunning, "Evaluation of Critical Thinking," *Science Education,* 38 (1954), 191–211.

[11] John Dewey, *How We Think* (New York: D. C. Heath, 1910).

mind jumps so rapidly from one process to another that it is difficult to determine the point at which one ends and the other begins. When presented with a problem, the individual at once formulates some hypothesis of solution (deduction) then tries to fit the known parts together (induction) to determine whether or not the hypothesis is correct and the solution can be performed. Induction is a process of proving deduction; and deduction is an hypothesis upon which induction may work.

Problem-solving tests may be relatively simple or complex, depending on the number of variables to be considered. But regardless of their degree of complexity, they must provide relatively new situations so that the learner will be unable to meet requirements by recalling duplicative experiences. The most desirable technique in a testing situation is to provide all the specific information needed for solution. It is expected that the learner will recall any previous knowledge or experience that may be at his command.

uniqueness of learning abilities

Justification for defining abilities that are appropriate for cultivation is based on something more than logical considerations. Are abilities relatively independent or do they overlap? The answer to this question may be found in research on the relationships among certain abilities as revealed by testing situations.

Tyler[12] gave three types of tests to science students. One of these required recall of facts. A second required both *recall* of principles and their *application* to new situations. And a third was designed to measure ability to draw *inferences* from data not previously presented in class. The coefficient of correlation between recall and application of principles to new situations was .45 with a range of .27 in chemistry to .60 in zoology. The coefficient of correlation between scores on the recall test and those on the test of ability to draw *inferences* was .35. These findings suggest that recall of principles and their application is a mental function different from that of simple recall. They also indicate that ability to recall and ability to draw inferences are two reasonably distinct types of mental activity, one relatively simple and the other complex.

In another study, Tyler[13] reported a .02 coefficient of correlation between skill in the use of a microscope and recall of information; .35, between understanding of technical terms and the ability to draw inferences; and .40, between recall of information and ability to apply principles to new situations.

[12] R. W. Tyler, "Measuring the Results of College Instruction," *Educational Research Bulletin,* 11 (1932), 253–260.

[13] R. W. Tyler, "The Relation between Recall and Higher Mental Processes." In Charles H. Judd, ed., *Education as Cultivation of the Higher Mental Processes* (New York: Macmillan Co., 1936).

In this series of investigations Tyler determined the relationship between (1) ability to *recall information* and ability to *recall and apply principles,* (2) ability to *recall information* and ability to draw *inferences* from new data, and (3) ability to *apply principles* to new situations and ability to draw *inferences* from new data.

In general, none of these coefficients was relatively high, the highest being .58. Most of them clustered around .45. To show the significance of these relatively low coefficients, Tyler analyzed test results in a zoology course. He found that of seven students who were in the upper 10 percent of the class in *recall of information,* only three were in the upper 10 percent in *recall and application of principles.* Of the eighteen who were in the upper 25 percent of the class in *recall of information* only eight were in the upper 25 percent in *recall and application of principles.* Six of the eighteen who were in the upper 25 percent in *recall of information* were below average in *recall and application of principles* when considered together. Approximately 50 percent of the students who exceeded the average in *recall of information* were below average in *recall and application of principles.* On the basis of this analysis Tyler concludes:

> Many students develop . . . a high degree of ability in mere recall without acquiring great facility in application. Since the two types of test required recall of information and one required application in addition to recall, the relatively low correlations show clearly that application is a mental process different from mere recall.

These studies also show a lower relationship between *recall of information* and *inference* than between *recall of information* and *recall and application of principles.* In a botany course, of students in the highest 10 percent of the class in *recall of information,* 40 percent were below the average in *inference.* Of those who were in the upper 25 percent of the class in *recall of information,* 30 percent were below average in the ability to *draw inferences.* Approximately half of those who were above average in *recall of information* were below average in ability to *draw inferences.*

Considered at their face value, Tyler's results indicate that *recall of information* is at a lower level of learning than either the ability to *recall information* and *apply principles* or the ability to *draw inferences. Drawing inferences* seems to require a higher ability than does *applying principles.* The ability to *draw inferences* correlates less closely with ability to *recall information* than does any of the other abilities.

Horrocks and Troyer[14] found coefficients of correlation ranging from .31 to .54 between *knowledge* of human growth and its *application* to

[14] J. E. Horrocks and Maurice Troyer, "The Relationship between Knowledge of Human Development and the Use of Such Knowledge," *Journal of Applied Psychology,* 30 (1946), 501–507.

case studies. Dunning's study[15] showed that the abilities to *interpret data, apply principles,* and *develop a logical proof* were relatively independent. McFall[16] classified B. S. Bloom's objectives (as outlined in his taxonomy) into two major areas: (1) the ability to recall knowledge and (2) the ability to understand concepts, analyze principles, make judgments, and evaluate material relative to problems within a specific area. Special achievement tests were then devised to measure these abilities. The results of this investigation, like those obtained in the studies above, indicated low correlation between recall of information and the other abilities that were measured.

The results of the studies above cannot be fully interpreted in the absence of knowledge concerning the learning and teaching conditions under which they were obtained. It may be supposed they were obtained, for the most part, under conventional conditions where study practices as well as teaching methods favored recall of information, as distinguished from the use of information. Closer relationships among these abilities would be expected in teaching situations where both teacher and student seek purposefully to cultivate the higher levels of learning.

measuring gain

In appraising learning abilities we may measure the individual's state of accomplishment at a given time or we may measure the progress he has made during a given training period. We apply the term *indeterminate* gain when we use the first technique; and we apply the term *determinate* gain when we use the second technique.

indeterminate gain

In using the technique of measuring *indeterminate* gain, we obtain a measure of status, the performance of an individual or group at a given time. It is not known from this status how far the learner has advanced within a given period, because no reference point is yet established with which we can mark off his progress. This technique is illustrated by achievement surveys of individuals of varying age and grade levels, by tests covering topics or units, and by end-of-course examinations.

achievement surveys

The differences in achievement from one grade to another are shown by the ability of pupils to identify the meaning of life science concepts.

[15] Gordon M. Dunning, "Evaluation of Critical Thinking," *Science Education,* 38 (1954), 191–211.

[16] Robert W. McFall, "The Development and Validation of an Achievement Test for Measuring Higher Level Cognitive Processes in General Science," *Journal of Experimental Education,* 33 (1964), 103–106.

The results are presented in Figure 1, which indicates that as pupils advance from the first to the sixth grade, larger numbers are capable of recognizing a list of 35 concepts in the life sciences.

Studies such as this illustrate the results of surveys in which the same tests are given to different groups. The testing provides a measure of

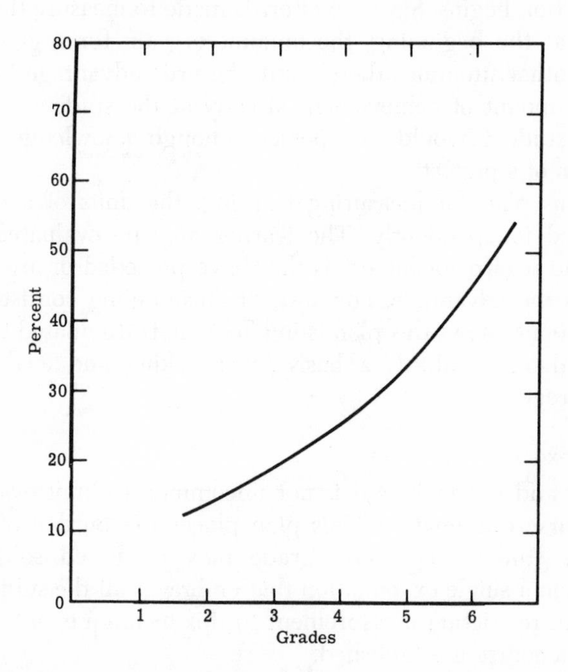

Figure 1. Percentages of pupils recognizing the meanings of 35 concepts in life science. From D. F. Butler, *A Test for Measuring Certain Life Science Concepts of Elementary School Children.* Unpublished doctor's thesis, Peabody College, 1965.

status. It also affords a basis for comparing the performance of separate groups as well as the performance of representative school populations.

testing over topics or units

One of the most common plans for measuring gain is to teach a topic or unit of material and then give a test to measure accomplishment. A unit of material may be studied for two or three weeks, for example, and be ended with a test that measures attainment. The learner's performance is then evaluated and a grade is recorded for his progress.

Another unit is then taken up and ended with a test. A grade is recorded. Another unit is completed. This pattern is followed throughout the course. At the end there may be a final comprehensive examination that is designed to include the significant material from the beginning of a course to its completion. A grade for this examination may or may not be assigned more weight than those of the individual units. Thus, as a result of all of this testing, the learner may have a number of scores on the basis of which the teacher establishes a term grade.

Under this plan there may be several measurements; but the gains are indeterminate. In certain instances it is possible for a number of students to have already acquired considerable knowledge and skill in a unit before instruction begins. Since no effort is made to measure the learner's achievement at the beginning, the amount of gain for a given time is unknown. In other situations there would be little advantage in trying to discover the amount of achievement already at the students' command. The typical student would not possess enough knowledge to justify administration of a pretest.

In using this plan for measuring learning, the units of a course are usually treated independently. The learner may be evaluated on each unit with little regard for materials that have preceded or are to follow. The plan has the advantage, however, of encouraging consistent study. When the student knows this plan is in effect, he is stimulated to keep his work up to date. It affords a basis for checking and evaluating his performance regularly.

end-of-course examinations

In colleges and universities it is not uncommon to limit evaluation to an end-of-course examination. This plan places the burden of responsibility on the student. His term grade may be based solely on his performance on a single examination that embraces all the subject matter of a course. In restricting measurement to this technique, only his status at the end of a course is established.

One of the most obvious limitations of this technique is that it provides no basis for determining the student's progress as he advances from one topic or unit to another. This is especially true where classes are large and the teacher is unable to make even informal checks of performance. Neither the student nor the teacher knows if progress has been consistent or erratic. The kinds of difficulties he may have experienced, likewise, are never revealed. The tendency to "cram" is encouraged, especially as the learner nears the end of a course. In addition to these limitations, there is, of course, the hazard of reliance on only one measurement as a basis for appraisal.

determinate gain

The technique of determinate gain provides a basis for measuring the amount of achievement made by students during a given training period. Instead of providing for only one measurement of different individuals or groups, the technique of determinate gain provides for repeated measurement of each individual. This technique may be illustrated by *two* studies: One shows progress in learning to typewrite during a ten-week course and the other shows gains on a standardized achievement test during a four-year period.

progress in learning to typewrite

The progress of two groups of students in learning to typewrite is shown in Figure 2.[17] The purpose of the experiment was to compare the

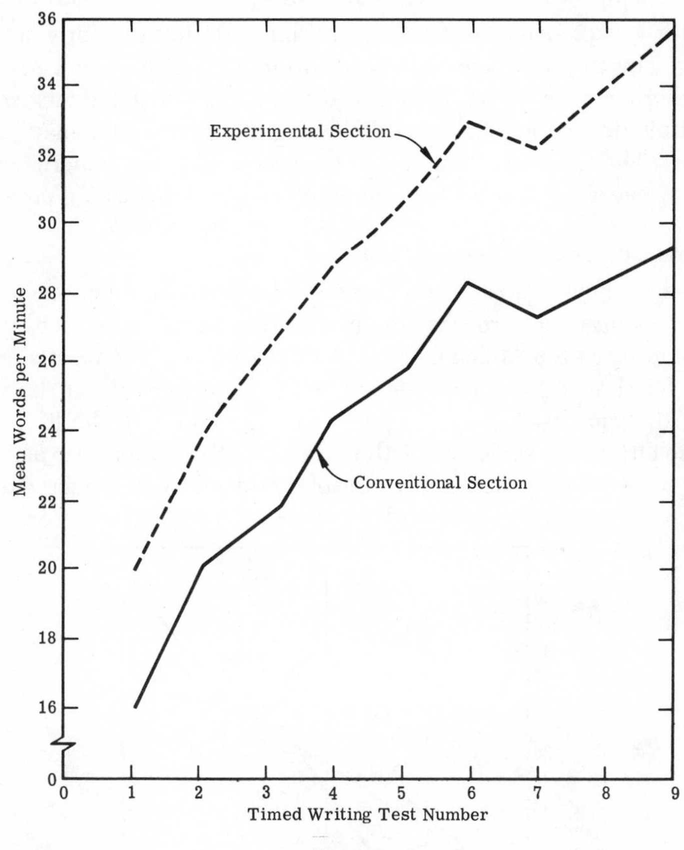

Figure 2

relative effectiveness of televised and conventional methods of teaching introductory typewriting. Students in the experimental group were paired with students in a control group. Both groups studied the same course, which included 48 lessons of 50 minutes each, and were taught by the same instructor.

After the students had been taught to typewrite all the letters of the alphabet, the experimental and control groups were given the same series

[17] William R. Pasewark, "Teaching Typewriting through Television," *Balance Sheet,* 40 (1959), 388–392.

of nine timed three-minute writing tests. One test was given each week, beginning with the second week of the ten-week course. At the end of the tenth week, both groups were given a production test, which consisted of a personal business letter and a tabulation problem.

Since the course was introductory, the students began their training at a low level of efficiency and the teacher was able to mark off a desirable reference point for measuring each student's progress. It should be noted that both groups made marked improvement during the early stages of training. This improvement continued through the fifth period. After that point there was a short period during which the students showed perceptible decline in efficiency. Following this period they made steady progress. The students taught by television did not experience this pattern. They showed superior progress throughout the testing periods.

gains on standardized achievement test

Figure 3 shows gains made from grades four through seven (four separate testings) on three sections of the Iowa Basic Skills Test by a girl of average IQ in the Abilene, Texas, public schools.[18] The results provide a basis for showing the achievement status of this girl when she was in the fourth grade as well as her gain from the fourth to the fifth grade, from the fifth to the sixth, and sixth to the seventh—a four-year period.

This study begins with a measure of status and shows increments of

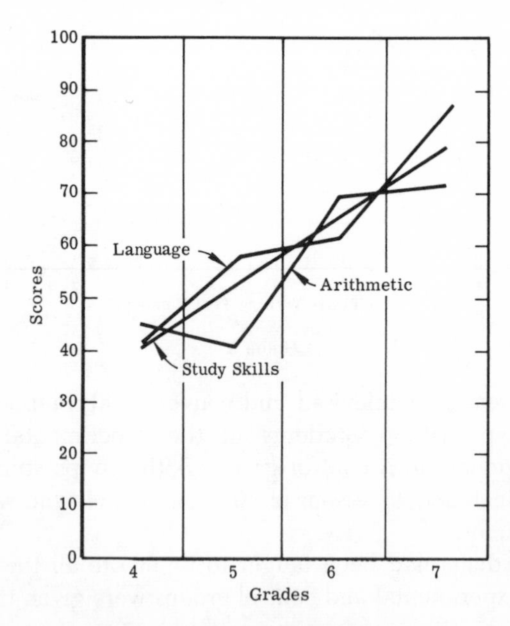

Figure 3. Educational growth as measured by the Iowa Basic Skills Test (repeated measurement over a four-year period).

[18] Data supplied by Alma Malone, Hardin-Simmons College, Abilene, Texas, 1964.

learning over an extended period of time. Repeated measurement made it possible to determine the rate of progress from one testing period to another. This study, like the immediately preceding one, is a "moving" situation as contrasted with the "static" situations illustrated in the techniques of *indeterminate* gain.

pretesting and posttesting

Minimum requirements for measuring determinate gain are two testing periods. The first measures the learner's performance at a given time; the second provides a basis for measuring progress. The difference between scores on the first and second testings represents the gain or loss that has occurred.

A standardized achievement test may be given to a group at the beginning of a school year and a duplicate form of the same test may be repeated in the spring, after the students have had a full year of instruction. The plan may be extended to include several measurements during a school year. For example, measurement may be made at the beginning and end of a semester. The plan may also be adapted to the subject matter of an assignment, a unit, or an entire course.

Whenever pretests and posttests are given, gain[19] is likely to be shown, especially for subjects in which there is normally a continuing development of skills and information. Gains may also be expected in any subject that is actively taught or where the learner has favorable opportunity to broaden his background through reading, work experience, or travel.

In analysis of test results, it is important to consider the nature and extent of gains made by different individuals or groups. Table 1 shows gains made by students on a series of standardized tests. The students were categorized into *low, middle,* and *high groups.* It should be noted that students in the low groups tended to make greater gains than did students in the high groups. It seems probable that students in these high groups already possessed considerable knowledge and skill at the time of initial measurement and, consequently, had less opportunity to improve their scores. On the other hand, students in the low groups may have been substandard in accomplishment at the beginning and, thus, had greater opportunity to improve. The table does not provide a measure of the initial status of the various groups whose gains are shown.

The manner in which classes are organized for instruction often affects the gains of groups possessing widely different ability. Where low, middle, and high groups are taught together as a single class, there is a

[19] Such gain may mean that the learner knows more of the same kinds of items—demonstrates more of the same kinds of learning. In other words, he is simply more proficient on comparable test items. On the other hand, a test may be constructed to include items of varying degrees of difficulty and complexity. When this is the case, a student's gains may represent qualitative as well as quantitative changes in performance.

Table 1. Average gains of students on posttests, classified according to pretest standing

Test	Low Group	Low Middle Group	Middle Group	High Middle Group	High Group
Critical thinking in social science	6.89	5.48	3.68	4.20	2.26
Science reasoning and understanding	6.26	5.16	2.93	2.04	0.31
Analysis of reading and writing	5.33	2.89	1.81	1.22	0.25
Critical thinking	6.68	4.65	3.47	2.60	1.59
Problems in human relations	3.19	1.67	1.31	1.51	0.36

Taken from Paul B. Diederich. "Pitfalls in the Measurement of Gains in Achievement," in *School Review,* 64 (1956), 59–63. © 1956 by University of Chicago. Reprinted by permission.

tendency to adapt instruction to the needs of typical students. As a result, high ability students tend to achieve less according to their potentiality; low ones tend to achieve more. Greater gains, both absolute and relative, are likely to be made where superior students, in particular, are taught as a separate class.

learning versus forgetting

An individual's gain depends on the manner in which learning and retention reinforce and supplement each other. Learning is the cumulative effect of training when first measured; retention is the sustained effect of training. These two processes are so closely related that, in reality, measurement of learning is also measurement of retention. If a student did not have the ability to retain the effect of previous training, he could not show progress from one practice period to another.

The processes of learning and forgetting may be illustrated by two studies: One is concerned with the meaning of new words, the other with detailed information in a course of instruction.

learning and forgetting the meaning of words

Courtis[20] measured learning and retention of new words in a ninth-grade "vocational civics" course. The design of the study provided a basis for comparing gains and losses of meaning of two classes of words: those

[20] S. A. Courtis, "The Scientific Analysis of Learning," *School of Education Bulletin,* University of Michigan, 7 (1935), 3–7.

specifically taught compared with those not taught. The "taught" words were studied one week. The pupils were tested seven times, twice before study of the "taught" words and five times afterward during a total period of approximately six weeks.

Figure 4 shows the curves on the "taught" and "untaught" words. Before teaching, the scores on Test B were 40.0 percent for the taught

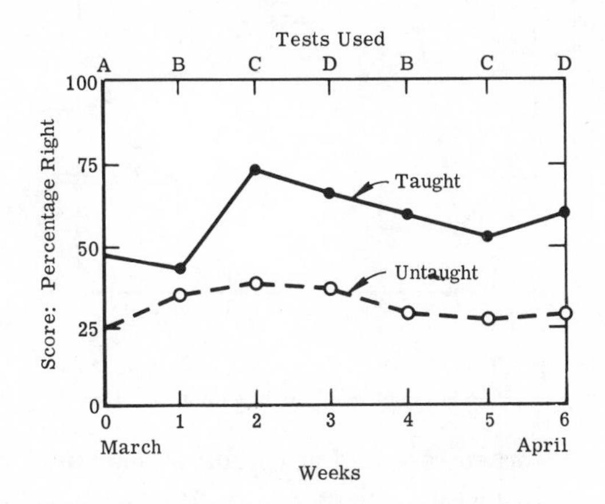

Figure 4. Curves of learning and forgetting of vocabulary (after Courtis, 1935).

words and 34.3 percent for the untaught. A week after teaching, the scores on Test C were 77.0 percent for the taught words and 44.0 percent for the untaught. But on subsequent testing the markedly decreased scores made on the taught words appear in sharp contrast with those on the untaught. Scores on the untaught words remain within a relatively narrow range during the total testing period.

The same results are shown in Figure 5 in the form of differences in scores. On Test B, before teaching, the difference in scores was 5.7 percent in favor of the taught words. On Test C, after teaching, the difference increased to 37.0 percent. This difference decreased, however, to less than 20.0 percent before the end of the testing period. The initial gain of 37.0 percent after teaching may be regarded as an index of learning efficiency achieved as a direct result of practice. But since these pupils lost a major portion of what they gained, their initial improvement lacks validity as an index of the effects of instruction.

learning and forgetting detailed information

In more typical school situations, initial learning is recognized formally when tests are first given to obtain tangible evidence of achievement. The results of tests given over the various units of learning material immediately following their completion may be regarded as *initial*

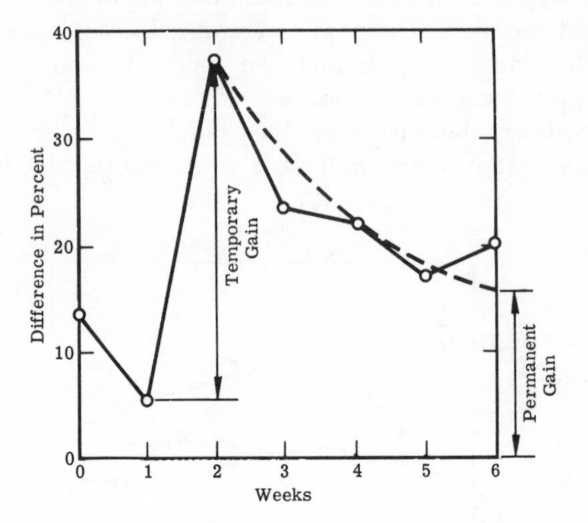

Figure 5. Curve of differences between taught and untaught words in Figure 4.

learning. Such tests when repeated at certain periods during a course of instruction provide a measure of retention. After a course is completed and the learner discontinues study of a subject, the long-term effects of instruction become evident.

Learning and forgetting may be illustrated by gains made in a course in seventh-grade general science,[21] achievement being measured by a test designed to measure ability to reproduce items of information (simple recall). The course was organized into nine units, each of two weeks duration, and was based on the contents of a textbook. The pupils were informed in a syllabus and by the instructor that they would be given such a test at the end of each two-week period of instruction—at the end of each unit. The dates for giving the tests were also stated in the syllabus. The pupils were not informed, however, that their retention would be checked at two-week intervals. Neither were they told they would be given a final comprehensive examination that would embrace all of the course material.

At the end of the first two-week period of instruction a test was given to measure *initial learning.* At the end of the fourth week (the second two-week period) the pupils were given an alternate form of the same test that had been previously used to cover the material presented during the first unit. Consequently, at the time of testing for the material

[21] A. H. Word and Robert A. Davis, "Individual Differences in Retention of General Science Subject Matter in the Case of Three Measurable Objectives," *Journal of Experimental Education,* 7 (1938), 24–31. See also A. H. Word and Robert A. Davis, "Acquisition and Retention of Factual Information in Seventh-Grade General Science during a Semester of Eighteen Weeks," *Journal of Educational Psychology,* 30 (1939), 116–125.

covered during the second unit, the pupils were required to demonstrate their retention of material presented during the previous unit. During the remainder of the course the same type of test was given at the completion of each unit. The tests at each testing period measured *initial learning* of the current unit and *retention* over the immediately preceding one. In measuring retention for each two-week period, items were arranged so that the pupils were not informed that they were also being tested for their retention of material presented during each of the previous two-week intervals.

reproduction of information

Progress of these seventh-grade pupils in reproducing information is shown in Figure 6. Here the average scores of the group are plotted

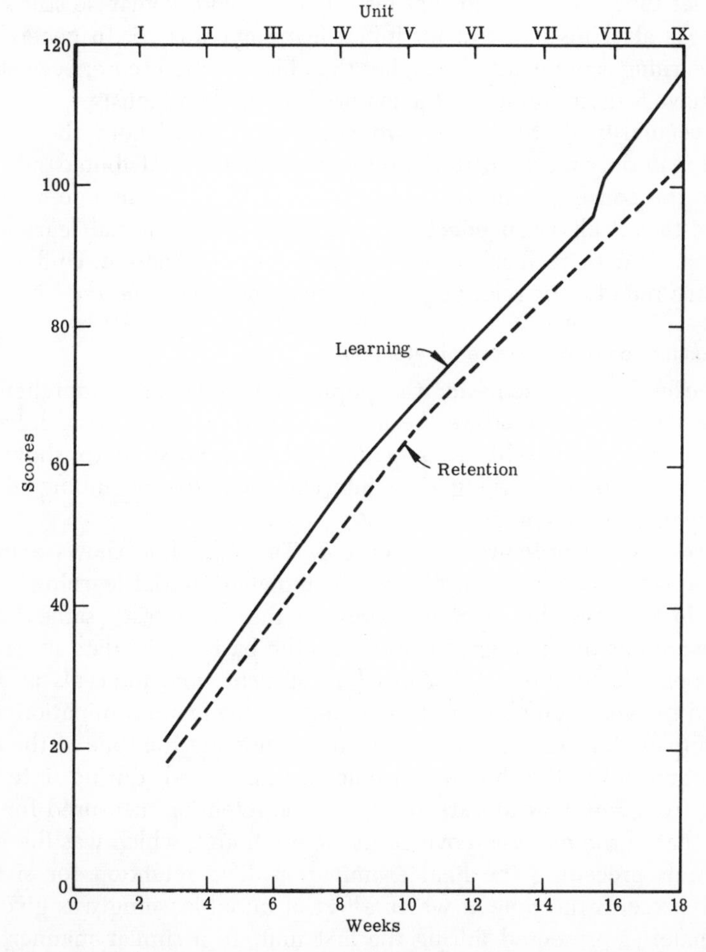

Figure 6. Learning and retention scores plotted cumulatively (tests measuring ability to reproduce information).

cumulatively. The solid line refers to initial learning (scores made on tests of current material at the end of each unit). The broken line shows average scores made on the retention tests for each two-week period. This figure shows that while the pupils are mastering the material of the second unit, for example, they are forgetting some of the material of the first unit; while they are mastering material of the seventh unit, they are forgetting part of the material of the sixth unit. Retention in each case was measured at two-week intervals.

By substituting the record of an individual pupil for average scores, Figure 6 has special meaning. A pupil, for example, would be able to determine his initial learning and retention scores at any particular stage during the course. He might be told at the end of the seventh unit that his initial learning score (expressed cumulatively—what he once knew up to that time) was 80 and that his retention score (what he still knew two weeks after his first test for initial learning) was 75. In general his initial learning score would be higher than his retention score, because he would have forgotten some of the material covered previously.

The regularity of testing at two-week intervals of both the newly-learned material and the material retained probably contributed substantially to the consistent gains the pupils made from one unit to another. Since testing itself is an effective means of practice, initial learning is strengthened with each successive measurement of retention. Under such conditions retention is relatively high throughout the semester.

final examination as a measure of retention

At the end of the semester the pupils were given a comprehensive examination that included all the items used to measure initial learning over the nine units. This examination made it possible to show the amount retained for varying time intervals from the beginning of the course to its completion.

The results are presented in Figure 7. The solid line shows average scores on tests given as each unit was completed (initial learning). The broken line shows the average scores on the same test (same form) administered as the final examination. On the basis of the data in Figure 7 it is possible to show the scores for different time intervals as they occurred between completion of each unit and the final examination. One may compare, for example, the degree of retention at the time of the final examination with the initial learning demonstrated during intervals ranging from five days to sixteen weeks. The retention measured for five days is that of the material covered in the ninth unit, which was the most recent unit preceding the final examination. The retention for sixteen weeks represents the time at which a test of initial learning was given to cover material presented during the first unit. In a similar manner, the test of initial learning of material covered in the second unit is fourteen weeks removed from the final examination.

The retention scores shown (as measured by the final examination) in Figure 7 may be compared with the initial learning scores made on corresponding units. One may see at a glance whether the pupils' retention scores for a given unit are higher or lower than are their initial learning scores. Gains in retention may be noted for some units; losses may be noted for others. High initial learning and retention scores on

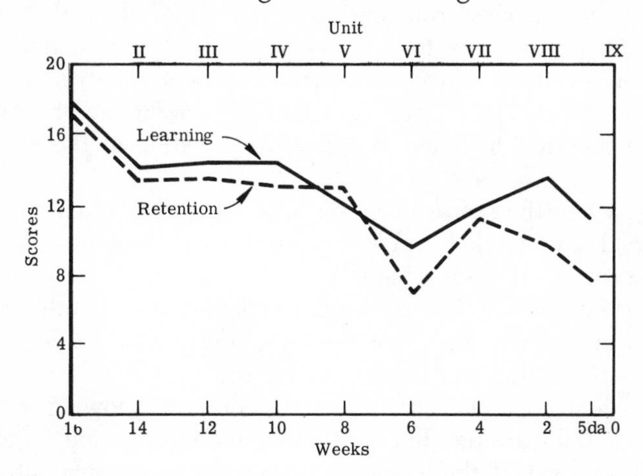

Figure 7. Retention scores compared with initial-learning scores on tests measuring ability to reproduce information.

some units and low ones on others reflect, in most cases, the varying difficulty of the material. Exceptionally low scores were made, for example, on the seventh unit. This unit covered a section in the textbook that presented formulas, equations, and technical information similar to that prepared for more advanced students.

Relatively high retention scores may be observed for the first unit, which occurs in point of time farthest from the final examination—sixteen weeks. The marked loss in the last two units probably is due to the nearness of this material to the end of the course and the lack of opportunity to assimilate it thoroughly. In general, the losses in units studied at short-time intervals preceding the final examination are fully as great as losses in units studied during the early part of the course. And even greater losses occur in the case of the last unit. In other words, there is no definite relationship between the amount retained on the final examination and the recency of instruction.

The double testing program that was followed up to the time of the final examination probably affected favorably the degree of initial learning as well as the amount of retention for varying time intervals. The testing program itself was a significant aspect of the instruction the pupils received. Even though some pupils may have studied little, frequent testing probably resulted in their learning considerable information.

predicting results of the final examination

Measuring *initial learning* and *short-term* retention throughout a course, as was done in this particular study, provides a basis for predicting the results of the final examination.

When average initial learning scores for all units are totaled and compared with average scores on the same form of the test given as a final examination, a close relationship is found. Pupils with high total initial learning scores make high scores on the final examination when it includes identical items. If we know that a pupil once knew a great many items, we can be reasonably sure that he will know many of those same items when they are included in a final examination at the end of the course.

Similarly, when the scores made on tests measuring retention at two-week intervals are totaled and compared with the scores made on an alternate form of the same test, given as a final examination, the agreement is even closer. When a pupil has demonstrated ability to retain information even for a short time, he may be expected to do well on a final examination based on the same materials.

These facts suggest the importance not only of knowing something once (as in initial learning) but of retaining the information acquired for a two-week interval. If the learner is to look forward confidently to the final examination, it is important that he know something once. It is even more important that he know something once and, a short time later, demonstrate that he still knows it.

The two studies reviewed above indicate two conflicting processes in learning. In the first study the amount of forgetting is pronounced, probably because the words were isolated for study and were not in the context of the *vocational civics* course. A considerable amount of the practice was also limited to testing situations. In the other study the information was learned in a course of instruction and was an integral part of other learning objectives. The learning program also made provision for measuring earlier learning while testing current materials. The double testing program during the semester was a means of ensuring thorough learning.

The results of both studies suggest, however, that while the individual is learning he is being thwarted by a tendency to forget, and this conflict continues during all of his learning experience. An optimistic aspect of this situation is that he gains more than he loses. If this were not true, there would be no basis for progress within subjects or from one subject or grade level to another. There is also the fact that anything once learned can be more easily relearned—a subject to be considered in a later chapter.

study questions

1. How is learning usually defined?
2. What aspects of learning are generally measured in learning experiments?
3. Evaluate the reproduction and recognition techniques (a) as means of measuring learning and retention of various abilities and (b) in the light of their adaptability to classroom use.
4. Give examples from your own experience to show that recall tends to be reconstructive rather than reproductive. Under what circumstances, if ever, should recall be reproductive?
5. How do the recall techniques differ from the plan of presenting the learner with a problem situation in which the information needed for solution is provided as a part of the test?
6. How does the technique of *indeterminate* gain differ from that of *determinate* gain? What barriers stand in the way of using the technique of determinate gain to a greater extent in the schools?
7. Describe any of your learning activities that gave you the impression your teacher hoped to cultivate abilities other than recall of information.
8. From your own experience give evidence of uniqueness or differences in learning abilities.
9. Analyze an examination you have taken recently from the standpoint of the kinds of mental process (memory, reasoning, etc.) brought into play.
10. What means other than tests may be used to evaluate a pupil's progress through a course?
11. How do you account for the fact that learning is characterized by fluctuations in performance?
12. Discuss certain advantages to be derived from continuing to measure retention of earlier materials while measuring learning of current materials.
13. What evidence is there for the belief that the best assurance for successful performance on a final comprehensive examination is consistent, diligent study from day to day and week to week?

losses of learning

2

Retention that accompanies the learning process should be distinguished from retention that occurs after a training period has ended. We have already discussed retention as the concomitant of learning, indicating that gains result from the combined effects of acquiring and remembering. It is obvious, however, that we cannot leave retention at this point. In school, future use or application is the primary purpose of subject-matter mastery. Immediate recall is only a secondary purpose.

retention studies

In retention studies one encounters the same problems that prevail in learning studies. First, one must consider the kinds of tests that may be used to measure loss or gain of knowledge; and then one must consider the techniques of administering the tests. Techniques usually applied in retention studies are remeasurement of *indeterminate gain* and remeasurement of *determinate gain.*

The first technique includes (1) measurement—for example, at the end of a course, (2) allowance for a lapse of time, and (3) remeasurement, by a second testing, of the amount retained following the first measurement. When using this technique, the examiner cannot know whether the items answered correctly are dependent upon specific training or previous experience. The measurement may show the results of learning in a previous course rather than gain made during a certain training period.

The second technique requires (1) initial testing, (2) a period of instruction, (3) a second testing to measure the gain that has occurred, (4) allowance for a lapse of time, and (5) a final testing to determine the extent to which the gain has been retained. This more refined technique provides for testing at the beginning of a course. The difference between the scores on the first and second testing constitutes the gain and rules out the knowledge pupils may possess at the beginning of a learning period.

With this technique, the remeasurement of *determinate* gain, it is possible to compute *three* scores for the delayed or final test. One of these scores represents what the students retained from their precourse learning. Another represents what they retained from learning during the progress of the course. The third represents what they acquired after the course was completed.

In computing retention scores in this manner, Little[1] found that frequently students answered questions correctly on a pretest and answered the same questions incorrectly on the posttest. While taking a course, students often forget part of what they had previously known. He also found that on a delayed or final test frequently they correctly answered questions that they had answered incorrectly on both the pretest and the posttest. This indicates that learning occurs after a course is completed.

When items for the testing periods are analyzed, a distinction may also be made between *true* and *apparent* retention. Freud and Cheronis,[2] using the technique of remeasurement of *indeterminate* gain, gave a comprehensive objective test in physical science to a group and repeated it one year later. They made an analysis of each item for each student to determine how each had responded to various possibilities on the two administrations of the test. These possibilities were as follows:

Item 1   RR   RW   RO   WR   WW   WO   OR   OW   OO

These letters, which represent *Right, Wrong,* and *Omit,* indicate the different ways of responding to Item 1. It was possible for a student to get RR (right on both administrations of the test), RW (right on the first and wrong on the second), and so on, through the other combinations. The following formulas were used:

1. True retention—(RR) divided by score on first testing.
2. Loss—(RW + RO) divided by score on first testing.
3. Gain—(WR + OR) divided by score on first testing.
4. Apparent retention—score on second testing divided by score on first testing.

[1] Ellis B. Little, "Pre-test and Retest Scores in Retention Calculation," *Journal of Experimental Education,* 29 (1960), 161–167.

[2] Henrietta Freud and Nicholas D. Cheronis, "Retention in the Physical Science Survey Course," *Journal of Chemical Education,* 17 (1940), 289–293.

When test results are analyzed in this manner, the difference between true and apparent retention may be marked. In their study, Freud and Cheronis found that *true* retention was 59.8 percent whereas *apparent* retention was 75.6 percent. Unless detailed analyses of items are shown in retention studies, it may be assumed the results yield *apparent* rather than *true* retention.

retention under varying degrees of opportunity for practice

Retention studies may be classified into three categories according to the varying degrees of opportunity the learner has for practice between stages that measure his initial learning and remeasure his retention of knowledge. In one, the learner discontinues formal study but continues to use certain abilities and skills that were developed during the course of study. In a second, he discontinues the learning of certain subject matter for varying time intervals. These interruptions may include the summer vacation. In a third, his retention is measured after long periods of time have elapsed. During these periods, the learner is denied an opportunity to practice the abilities or skills he has learned in the course. The purpose is to review findings with minimum consideration of the conditions under which the findings were obtained.

retention of abilities and skills that continue to be used

The situations to be described here are illustrated by retention of certain arithmetical abilities and by specially developed reading skills.

retention of arithmetic abilities while continuing study of arithmetic

During the school years, certain conditions make the revival of earlier learning possible. As a result, each time the use of an ability is required, the ability is further fortified against loss. Such influence is significant when a sequence of courses is taken in the same subject-matter area.

Learning and retention progress of 56 pupils through the seventh and eighth grades was traced[3] for a period of twenty months while the students continued study in arithmetic. During this time, their abilities in this subject area were measured regularly on the same standardized test. The purpose was to determine the extent to which pupils retain certain basic skills while they are engaged in studying increasingly complex, but

[3] Robert A. Davis and E. J. Rood, "Remembering and Forgetting Arithmetical Abilities," *Journal of Educational Psychology,* 38 (1947), 216–225.

new and related, material. The basic skills they used were those they had acquired previous to the beginning of the investigation.

During the twenty-month period, pupils reviewed fundamental operations as provided in the textbook; but the teacher made no effort to keep such abilities alive. Pupils continued to study arithmetic in grades seven and eight. They were not informed they would be given tests regularly on material they had studied during their early elementary-school grades, material they had practiced during a greater part of grade seven. Testing was repeated at intervals of approximately four months. The same test (A and B forms rotated) was given during the twenty-month period.

Progress in arithmetic during a twenty-month period. The results shown in Figure 8 are based on scores obtained on the six sections of the

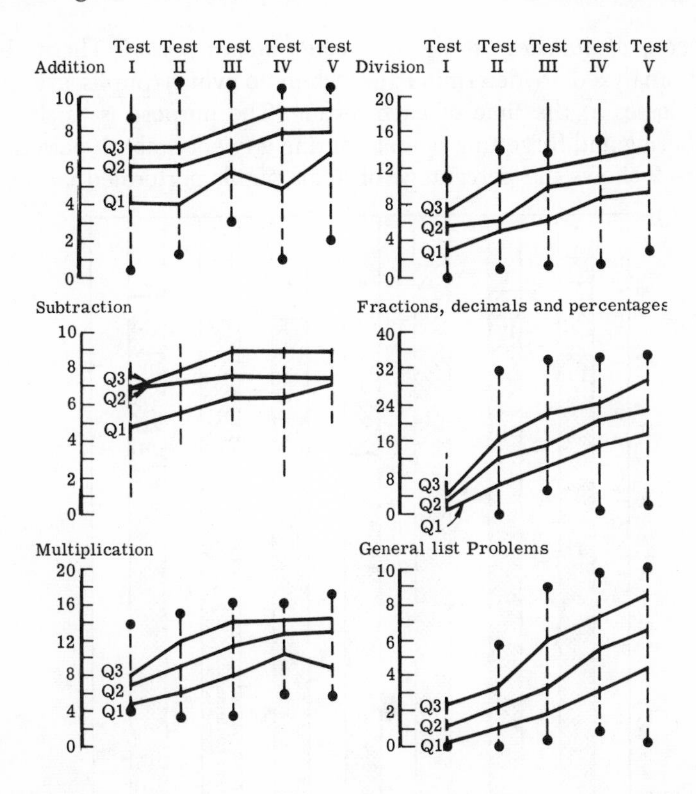

Figure 8. Progress in separate aspects of arithmetic (in medians, quartiles, and ranges).

standardized test. The skills measured are those of addition, subtraction, multiplication, division, fractions (including decimals and percentage), and problems. The scores shown are the median (charted as Q2) and the upper and lower quartile points (Q1 and Q3). These scores are connected by solid lines on the graph to trace the results of testing during the twenty-month period. Vertical broken lines indicate the range of scores obtained for different sections of the test.

Pupils tend to demonstrate increased power with the several testing periods. Some aspects of arithmetic, however, permit greater improvement than others. Scores in subtraction, for example, level off at the third testing period and multiplication at the fourth. Those of division, fractions, and problems increase irregularly throughout the testing program. Such variations reflect operational difficulty of the processes. They may also be influenced by the varying opportunity that exists for use by the students in seventh- and eight-grade arithmetic. The results suggest that one cannot assume that abilities once demonstrated will remain at the same degree of efficiency, even during a four-month period.

Recovery of abilities during the twenty-month period. These abilities may be analyzed to determine the extent to which pupils are able to recover losses at the time of each testing. The purpose is to show how remembering and forgetting operate during a twenty-month period.

Figure 9 shows the percentage of items pupils performed *correctly* on

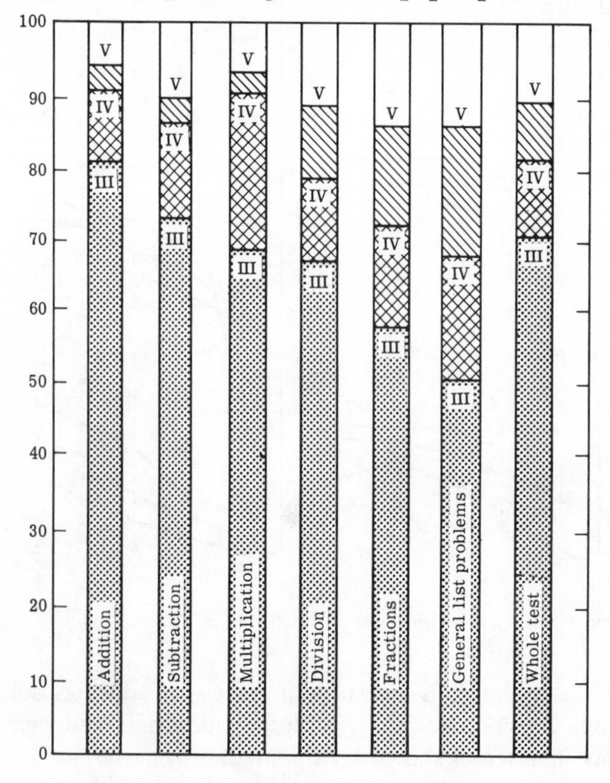

Figure 9. Percentage of problems or exercises (correct on first testing and incorrect on the second) regained during subsequent testing.

the first testing, *incorrectly* on the second, but performed *correctly* on at least one of the remaining testing periods. Each recovery is credited to the particular testing period at which it was first made. On the section dealing with addition, for example, the exercises that were *correct* on the first testing and *incorrect* on the second were selected for special study during the remaining periods. Of this group of exercises, 82.5 percent were correct on the *third* testing, 8.8 percent were not regained until the *fourth* testing, and 2.9 percent not until the *fifth*. The pupils eventually regained a total of 94.2 percent. The loss in addition, therefore, was 5.8 percent at the end of the testing program.

A similar situation is shown in Figure 10. Here, the exercises and

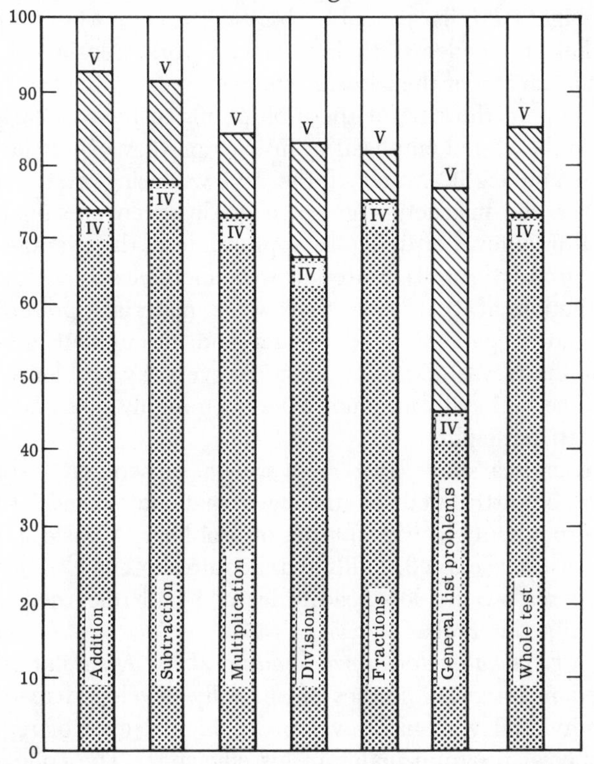

Figure 10. Percentage of problems or exercises (correct on second testing and incorrect on the third) regained during subsequent testing.

problems *correct* on the second testing but *incorrect* on the third are analyzed to determine the success made on the fourth and fifth testing periods. The pupils regained a total of 84.4 percent of this material and failed to recover 15.6 percent. It should be noted, however, that they had one less testing period on which to recover.

Of the problems and exercises *correct* on the third testing but *incorrect* on the fourth, the total recovery for all types of operation was 65.3

percent. The fifth testing period was the only remaining opportunity the students had to demonstrate recovery. Addition showed the highest recovery, 74.4 percent; problems showed the lowest, 57.4 percent.

A significant trend is that in each case greater recovery is made on a test that follows a test containing incorrect responses than is made on all succeeding tests. In other words, if a pupil works an exercise correctly in one test and misses it in the second, he is more likely to work it correctly in the third in the series than in any that follow.

This finding may be due to the demand for particular arithmetical skills. Relearning is stimulated to a high degree but not completely. A majority of skills appear to be required consistently throughout grades seven and eight. Pupils probably have little opportunity to forget operations that are needed in their advanced work. Because of this, they regain a major portion of their losses quickly.

The tendency on the part of these 56 pupils to recover early may be due in part to the varied emphasis of instruction they experienced during grades seven and eight. Much of the review during grade seven was incidental. Yet, the instruction given in grade seven presumably began with material on a level of difficulty appropriate to the average ability of the entering group of pupils. Materials were more closely integrated with earlier instruction at that time than were materials presented later. During the latter part of grade seven and throughout grade eight, increased emphasis was placed on practical everyday problems. Probably possession of certain skills may not have been highly essential to success in grades seven and eight.

Problem exercises show least recovery on subsequent testings. This finding may be attributed to the fact that no specific formula is applicable throughout the varied types of problems. A basic skill appears to be more easily relearned. Skills that require higher abilities, such as the ability to reason, are less readily learned and relearned, especially during short time intervals.

Retention of specially developed reading skills. A similar situation is demonstrated in retention studies of specially developed reading skills. Does the individual who has developed a high degree of reading skill through a special program maintain his efficiency? The college student would be expected to use reading skills in his academic program. The out-of-school adult would probably continue his reading on a voluntary basis.

Weber[4] determined the effect of two types of special training on reading skills of college freshmen and the extent to which the results of such training are retained. Two comparable experimental groups were formed. One of these groups used the *Pressey Manual of Reading* as a

[4] C. O. Weber, "Acquisition and Retention of Reading Skills by College Freshmen," *Journal of Educational Psychology*, 30 (1939), 453–460.

means of training; the other group used the *tachistoscope*. Both groups were given six once-weekly periods of remedial training in reading. The gains in reading skills of these two groups were measured immediately following the six-week period of training and again one year later. These special training programs produced greater gains on speed than on comprehension of reading. And there was virtually no difference between the gains of the two groups on either speed or comprehension. Retests after the lapse of a year indicated that the gains made by both groups during the remedial reading program were substantially retained.

Cosper[5] found that undergraduate students who enrolled in a course in developmental reading retained, after a fourteen-month interval, approximately 60 percent of the speed they had gained. Mullins and Mowry[6] conducted a reading program for out-of-school adults at the Monsanto Chemical Company in Texas City, Texas. Its purpose was to improve reading speed and comprehension. Machines such as the rate-of-reading controller and the opthalmograph were used in training. One year following this program, the authors retested as many of the original participants as possible. The results showed that when the number of words comprehended per minute is used as an index of efficiency, approximately 57 percent of the gain was retained.

The results of all three of these studies just described were influenced by the motives of the participating students, the opportunities for continued practice, as well as the measures of efficiency that were used. Because of the intense nature of this type of training, marked improvement is often experienced within a short period. But the learning that occurs is not always thorough learning, because it is dependent on massed practice, a short-lived substitute for true motivation. Consequently, the learner tends to regress following a training program. Obviously the best way to assure maintenance of specially developed skills would be to design a program that encourages the consistent and continued use of the skills. Equally important to success would be the learner himself, who must have a strong desire to improve himself.

retention after discontinuing instruction for varying time intervals

Most retention studies are designed to determine what happens to learning when training is discontinued or when the individual is subjected to a different influence. Such discontinuity and change in influence is commonly imposed by summer vacations. In the psychological laboratory, a high degree of control may be exercised over these

[5] Russel Cosper and others, "Retention of Reading Skills," *Journal of Educational Research,* 49 (1955), 211–216.

[6] Cecil J. Mullins and Harley W. Mowry, "How Long Does Reading Improvement Last?" *Personnel Journal,* 32 (1953–54), 416–417.

factors through use of meaningless material. Thereby, the investigator reduces the possibility of further practice during the time intervals he uses in his retention studies. To use meaningful material in the school, however, requires the exercise of a different kind of control, especially for the time interval. Since summer vacation is very close to a total learning "blank out," being a period during which little or no formal study takes place, this interval of approximately 90 days is frequently used. Investigators, naturally, are interested in the retention that occurs during summer vacations, because any effects of loss are felt when the learner returns to school in the fall. This is an important field of study. Therefore, several such studies are reviewed here, being classified into: (a) elementary-school subjects and (b) high school and college subjects.

elementary-school subjects

Retention studies of elementary-grade subjects follow a simple pattern. The pupils are given a standardized achievement test toward the end of the school year and this is repeated during the opening week in the fall. The first testing provides a measure of achievement at the end of the school year; the second, when compared with the first, shows the amount that is lost or gained during summer vacation. Most of the elementary-school subjects have been studied at one time or another in this manner.

Brueckner and Distad[7] measured reading retention of three groups of first graders and found that all showed a slight loss. Coefficients of correlation between June and September scores ranged from .58 to .81. Sister Irmina[8] reported a slight loss in reading ability each year from the first through the eighth grade. Elder,[9] in a study of third-, fourth-, fifth-, and sixth-grade pupils, obtained the following results: 59 percent improved in reading, 15 percent received the same scores on both testings, and 27 percent showed a loss. Seventeen percent of his pupils advanced from below average in reading to approximately standard. Kramer's[10] study showed a slight increase in reading efficiency of fifth-grade children; and Nelson[11] found a marked loss in reading in the third,

[7] L. J. Brueckner and H. W. Distad, "The Effect of Summer Vacation on the Reading Ability of First Grade Children, *Elementary School Journal,* 24 (1924), 689–707.

[8] Sister M. Irmina, "The Effect of Summer Vacation on the Retention of the Elementary-School Subjects," *Educational Research Bulletin,* Catholic University of America, 3 (1928), 99.

[9] H. E. Elder, "The Effect of the Summer Vacation on Silent Reading Ability in the Intermediate Grades," *Elementary School Journal,* 27 (1927), 541–546.

[10] G. A. Kramer, "Do Children Forget during the Vacation?" *Baltimore Bulletin of Education* (1927), 56–60.

[11] M. J. Nelson, "Difference in Achievement of Elementary-School Pupils before and after Summer Vacation," *Bureau of Educational Research Bulletin,* University of Wisconsin, 10 (1929), 47–48.

fifth, and seventh grades. In Morrison's[12] study, however, first-, second-, and third-grade pupils made, during summer vacation, one third of the gain they normally make for a similar period during the academic year.

Retention studies on arithmetic yield reasonably consistent results. Kramer[13] obtained a median score of 39.7 for fifth-grade pupils in June; the median for the same group in September was 37.0. Garfinkle[14] administered a standardized arithmetic test, stressing fundamentals, to fifth-, sixth-, and seventh-grade pupils in June and repeated it in September. His results showed a loss that was equivalent to almost two years of work for all groups, the greatest loss occurring in the seventh grade. Patterson,[15] using a battery of tests in grades one through eight found the greatest loss was experienced in arithmetic. In Sister Irmina's[16] study of retention in grades one through eight, a marked loss in rate and accuracy of arithmetic computation was noted, but there was a gain made in exercises that required reasoning and problem solving. Gagne and Basler,[17] using the technique of determinate gain, found that sixth-grade pupils forgot from 60 to 80 percent of their knowledge of elementary nonmetric geometry after a nine-week period.

Since retention studies in the elementary school are often based on the results of test batteries, subjects other than reading and arithmetic are included. Bruene[18] gave the Stanford Achievement Test to fourth-, fifth-, and sixth-grade children in May and again in September. Language usage showed a loss of .31 of a school year; spelling .29; history and literature .26; and arithmetic reasoning .07. In contrast, he reported a gain of .22 of a school year for nature study and science. Irmina noted a loss in spelling in all grades from the first through the eighth. In a study by Josephina,[19] using the technique of determinate gain, fifth-grade children forgot approximately 20 percent of religious knowledge during the summer.

Certain trends are evident when the results of these studies are reviewed as a whole. Skills in the arithmetic fundamentals, such as

[12] As reported in Nelson.

[13] G. A. Kramer (10).

[14] M. A. Garfinkle, "The Effect of Summer Vacation on Ability in the Fundamentals of Arithmetic," *Journal of Educational Psychology,* 10 (1919), 44–48.

[15] M. V. W. Patterson, "The Effect of Vacation on Children's Mental Ability and on Their Retention of Arithmetic and Reading," *Education,* 46 (1925–26), 222–228.

[16] Sister M. Irmina (8).

[17] Robert M. Gagne and Otto C. Basler, "A Study of Retention of Some Topics of Elementary Nonmetric Geometry," *Journal of Educational Psychology,* 54 (1963), 123–131.

[18] E. Bruene, "Effect of Summer Vacation on the Achievement of Pupils in the Fourth, Fifth, and Sixth Grades," *Journal of Educational Research,* 18 (1928), 309–314.

[19] Sister Josephina, "Retention of Religious Knowledge," *Religious Education,* 54 (1959), 372–373.

addition, subtraction, and multiplication, almost always show a loss during the summer; but there may be improvement in problem solving. Spelling efficiency also declines. In contrast, gains are frequently noted for reading. Gains also are sometimes observed in nature study and science.

Some teachers recognize a loss during summer and review the work of the preceding year. Others launch immediately into new subjects on the assumption the learner is ready to go forward. The net effect of these studies, however, is that definite assumptions about the efficiency of elementary-school pupils cannot be made at the beginning of a school year.

No effort was made in these studies to take into account the conditions under which the original learning occurred nor were they reported in the investigations. During a summer, both facilitating and inhibiting conditions exist. Facilitating conditions include increased pupil maturity and opportunities for continued practice[20] of subject matter. Inhibiting conditions include varied kinds of pupil activity as well as the absence of formal practice.

high school and college subjects

Retention studies of high school and college subjects are reviewed here together, because similar abilities are measured. These include abilities to apply principles, to explain data, to generalize, to make interpretations, as well as to recall information. The tests given are generally not standardized (as contrasted with tests given in the elementary schools); they are usually constructed locally for a particular purpose. Also, the time intervals over which both high school and college subjects are taught vary widely, and investigators seldom include the summer vacation exclusively as a means of control. In most instances, the students who are used as subjects in experiments discontinue their study of subject matter under consideration and yet remain in school. Retention, therefore, is frequently computed on the basis of the gains made during a single period of instruction. As is true of studies made in elementary schools, very little is known about the conditions under which older students acquire their original learning nor is much known about the nature of the activities that follow the period of original learning.

High school subjects. Layton[21] gave the New York Regents examination to first-year algebra students and repeated it twelve months later.

[20] K. M. Parsley and M. Powell, "Achievement Gains or Losses during the Academic Year and over the Summer Vacation Period," *Genetic Psychology Monograph*, 66 (1962), 285–342. These authors found that when the skills learned during the school year are practiced while on summer vacation, as in reading, there may be only slight forgetting. In some cases there may be pronounced gains.

[21] E. T. Layton, "The Persistence of Learning in Elementary Algebra," *Journal of Educational Psychology*, 23 (1932), 46–55.

These students were given a month of intensive drill at the end of the course in an effort to prevent loss, but their retention was only 33⅓ percent. Lahey[22] measured retention of algebra students who continued instruction in geometry. She gave computational and problem-solving tests in May and September of one year and repeated them in January the following year. Loss in fundamental operations was ten percent during the summer vacation and an additional ten percent during the next semester. The average for problem-solving ability in September, however, was slightly above that of the initial test. Worcester[23] used the results of standardized algebra tests that were given to a small group in February, March, and May and repeated the following December. Some items on the initial tests were retained by 100 percent of the students; others were forgotten by 100 percent. The California Advanced Achievement Test was given to college sophomore and junior students,[24] the aim being to determine the amount retained in fundamentals of subject matter that were presumably learned in the elementary and secondary schools. Reading efficiency was fairly well retained. Fundamentals of mathematics, however, were not retained at the functional level. English fundamentals also seemed to have been forgotten or never learned. These fundamentals included parts of sentences, kinds of sentences, and parts of speech.

Several retention studies in the sciences were designed to measure various abilities. Smeltz[25] gave a chemistry test three times to eleventh-grade students. This test, which supposedly measured various abilities, was first given at the beginning of the school year; it was repeated after these students had completed two semesters of chemistry and still again after one year. The gain was calculated by the differences in scores between the first and second testing; retention was determined by the difference between the second and third. Computed on the basis of total scores, retention was 68 percent. Frutchey,[26] also using a chemistry course, measured the amount of gain that was retained, after a one-year period, in application of principles and knowledge of terms, symbols, formulas, and valence. He found that 92 percent of the gain was retained in application of principles and 66 percent in knowledge of chemical terms, symbols, formulas, and valence. Ninth-grade students who had

[22] Sister M. Florence Louise Lahey, "Permanence of Retention of First-Year Algebra," *Journal of Educational Psychology,* 32 (1941), 401–413.

[23] D. A. Worcester, "The Permanence of Learning in High School Subjects—Algebra," *Journal of Educational Psychology,* 19 (1928), 343–345.

[24] Glenn W. Durflinger, "The Fundamentals Forgotten by College Students," *Journal of Educational Research,* 49 (1956), 149–154.

[25] John B. Smeltz, "Retention of Learning in High School Chemistry," *Science Teacher,* 23 (1956), 285–305.

[26] F. P. Frutchey, "Measuring the Ability to Apply Chemical Principles," *Educational Research Bulletin,* 12 (1933), 255–260.

completed eighth-grade general science in June were tested by Tyler[27] in September and again the following May. He tested their ability to recall information, to explain data, and to generalize. A standardized test was used for measuring the first ability; specially prepared tests were employed to measure the others. On the information test, the loss was 40 percent; and on tests of ability to explain data and generalize the losses were eight and six percent, respectively.

College subjects. Like those in high school, some college studies emphasize recall, whereas others stress functional abilities. Cedarstrom[28] retested students one year following the completion of a zoology course. These students, who apparently had not had any opportunity to review, retained approximately 60 to 80 percent of the material. Freud and Cheronis[29] devised a comprehensive objective test in physical science which they gave students at the end of the course and again after a one-year interval. The materials the students retained best were those that consisted of principles, theories, and their applications. The materials the students retained least were those of a detailed factual nature.

Other studies that consisted of varied kinds of subject matter and stressed recall were made by Greene, Myers, and Weitman. Greene[30] gave final examinations to classes in zoology, chemistry, and psychology. Each of these classes was retested after four-, eight-, and twenty-month intervals. The results showed a 50 percent loss in general information for these subjects during the first four months—from June to October. At the end of the twenty-month interval, retention had leveled off to a point where between one tenth and one fifth of the initial learning was retained. Myers[31] tested a group of college girls one year after they had completed a course in American history. A list of 50 important historical names was prepared, and the students were instructed to write one important fact about each name. Approximately 40 percent of the initial learning was forgotten. Fifty-four percent of the answers were correct, 15 percent were wrong, and 17 percent were not attempted. As a test of retention, Weitman[32] used approximately one third of the multiple-choice items (which presumably stressed recall of information) included in a final examination

[27] R. W. Tyler, "What High School Pupils Forget," *Educational Research Bulletin,* 9 (1930), 490–492.

[28] J. A. Cedarstrom, "Retention of Information Gained in Courses in College Zoology," *Journal of Genetic Psychology and Pedagogical Seminary,* 38 (1930), 516–520.

[29] Henrietta Freud and Nicholas D. Cheronis (2).

[30] E. B. Greene, "The Retention of Information Learned in College Courses," *Journal of Educational Research,* 24 (1931), 262–273.

[31] G. C. Myers, "Delayed Recall in History," *Journal of Educational Psychology,* 6 (1917), 275–283.

[32] Morris Weitman, "A Study of Long-Term Retention in Medical Students," *Journal of Experimental Education,* 33 (1964), 87–92.

for students in an introductory physiology course. This test was given fifteen weeks after these students (medical) had completed the course. Retention on this surprise posttest was 80 percent, but the correlation between performance on the two tests was only .60.

Retention studies of college subjects, studies stressing measurement of functional abilities, include those made by Tyler, Wert, and McDougall. Tyler[33] gave a zoology test at the beginning and end of a course and repeated it after a period of fifteen months. The percentage of gain or loss on the different parts of the test (stressing different abilities) during the fifteen-month interval was shown in relationship to the initial gain. On the test requiring identification of organs from pictures, the loss was 22 percent; recognition of technical terms showed a loss of 72 percent; recall of detailed information showed a loss of 80 percent; application of principles showed neither loss nor gain; and on interpretation of new experiments there was a gain of 126 percent. Wert,[34] also using a zoology course, computed the percentage of loss or gain over a three-year period in relationship to the amount of initial gain. During this period, there was a gain of 60 percent in ability to apply principles to new situations and a gain of 20 percent in ability to interpret new experiments. In contrast, there was a loss of 50 percent on tests measuring the meaning of terminology, functions of structure, and identification of main ideas; and there was a loss of 80 percent on tests that required the matching of names with structures. The results of McDougall's[35] study of gains and losses on a measurement unit in educational psychology resemble those reviewed above. His tests were designated as *factual knowledge, translation, interpretation,* and *extrapolation.* The greatest loss (relatively) during a four-month period was made on the test of factual knowledge.

Retention studies of high school and college subjects often show marked forgetting of specific facts, names, formulas, terminology, and detailed kinds of information as measured by tests stressing recall. Such material is forgotten quickly. Sometimes as much as 50 percent is lost within a one-year period. The retention curves for these types of information resemble those for meaningless laboratory materials.

Although the studies show that unrelated facts and mere information are forgotten easily, they indicate that abilities requiring application of knowledge have a relatively high degree of permanence. Some of these abilities also show gains after instruction is discontinued. This is particularly true of learning that exercises the higher mental processes—

[33] R. W. Tyler, "Permanence of Learning," *Journal of Higher Education,* 4 (1933), 203–204.

[34] J. E. Wert, "Twin Assumptions," *Journal of Higher Education,* 8 (1937), 126–140.

[35] William P. McDougall, "Differential Retention of Course Outcomes in Educational Psychology," *Journal of Educational Psychology,* 49 (1958), 53–60.

the abilities to apply principles, to draw inferences, and to interpret information. These abilities tend to persist over long periods and are maintained even though they are often superficially stressed during instruction.

retention after long periods with little practice

One of the best ways to study the sustained effects of training is to check the efficiency of persons who have had little or no opportunity to practice their learning over an extended period of time. A review of the results of several such studies follows.

Wall[36] measured achievement of 83 girls and 47 boys (average age of sixteen years) who were employed in two large Army centers in England. These adolescents had been reared in agricultural and industrial areas and were the children of skilled and unskilled workers, minor clerical employees, shopkeepers, and casual laborers. The formal education of these adolescents was limited to the elementary grades. At the time of testing they had been out of school five or six years.

In arithmetic (the four fundamental processes) the scores of these adolescents indicated a retardation between one and a half and three educational years as evaluated by achievement norms in the elementary grades. There was also retardation of approximately one year in spelling. Of the subjects tested, however, arithmetic tended to suffer most.

From her eighth to thirteenth year, Smith[37] memorized the answers to 107 questions in the *Westminster Short Catechism*. Much of this material was overlearned through continued repetition and a considerable part of it had a pleasant connotation. Her ability to recall this material was first checked after a period of 24 years. A second check was made sixteen years after the first check, when she had passed her 60th birthday.

In a study of recall made after a period of 24 years had elapsed, she discovered that she could still remember 50 percent of the initially learned material and that she required minor prompting on only 8 percent. In commenting on these results she stated, "Frequency of repetition during the period of original learning, either on account of more frequent reviews, incidental outside contact, or special stress at the time of learning . . . was an important factor in determining which answers could be recalled." In the second study, which was repeated sixteen years after the first, the results were not markedly different. She found that there was a "slightly lessened accuracy in retention after the

[36] W. D. Wall, "The Decay of Educational Attainments among Adolescents after Leaving School," *British Journal of Educational Psychology*, 14 (1944), 19–34.

[37] M. E. Smith, "Delayed Recall of Previously Memorized Material after 24 Years," *Journal of Genetic Psychology*, 47 (1935), 477–481. See also M. E. Smith, "Delayed Recall of Previously Memorized Material after 40 Years," *Pedagogical Seminary and Journal of Genetic Psychology*, 79 (1951), 337–338.

lapse of 16 years, as compared with the greater loss during the first 24 years."

Worcester,[38] also using himself as the subject, measured retention after varying time intervals over a period of more than 40 years. The materials consisted of prose from the writings of Matthew Arnold and Thomas Huxley. In one case he had the materials read aloud to him and in the other he read them silently to himself. When he attempted to relearn the materials by the use of both the passive and active methods, he found that he made substantial savings in the amount of practice he required for accurate memorization.

Hill[39] made two studies in which he remeasured himself on typewriting skills. The first was conducted after a period of 25 years, during which time he had virtually no practice on the typewriter. The second was made under similar conditions 25 years after the first, representing a total of 50 years of elapsed time after his initial learning. In both studies the results were analyzed according to the criteria used in the original investigation.

The significant finding in these studies was the relative ease with which the author could regain typewriting efficiency with comparatively small amounts of practice. In the first study, after a period of 25 years, his efficiency had declined 75 percent; in the second study, he was able, at the age of 80 years, to recover most of his initial skill within a short time. In this type of task, high efficiency cannot be maintained without consistent practice. It is relatively easy, however, to regain skill that has been lost.

The observation is frequently made that knowledge of verbal materials, such as prose, seems to be forgotten quickly; whereas motor skills, such as those required in typing, are retained over long periods. Several suggestions have been proposed to explain the apparent difference in retention of motor and verbal habits. It is suggested, for example, that in learning the motor skills of typing the individual is compelled to pursue a plan of continued practice to attain proficiency. During this process he may check his efficiency at each stage of progress and correct errors. In learning a motor task he also uses several sensory avenues and thereby must form a larger number of associations than he would in performing tasks that require only a response to sight and sound. Motor tasks require response to both ideational and motor stimuli. Verbal tasks frequently require response only to ideational stimuli.

The results of the studies reviewed in this section indicate that there is little, if any, difference between the retention value of motor and verbal

[38] D. A. Worcester, "Learning Ability and Retention after Long Periods," *Journal of Educational Psychology,* 48 (1957), 505–509.

[39] L. B. Hill, "A Second Quarter of Century of Delayed Recall or Relearning at 80," *Journal of Educational Psychology,* 48 (1957), 65–68.

tasks. Controlled experiments[40] also show that when such tasks are mastered to the same degree of proficiency they will be retained equally well, provided the experimental conditions and the activities following original learning do not favor one type of response at the expense of the other.

additional observations

The first and most obvious observation is that forgetting in varying degrees is likely to occur after instruction ends. Second, although the learner might be unable to recall effectively, he still might recover some of his losses with relatively small amounts of practice. Third, he might continue to gain, thus earning higher scores on retention tests than on those of initial learning. In these studies the stability of learning is associated with kinds of subject matter and types of abilities as well as with opportunities for continued practice.

Relatively high degrees of retention are noted for arithmetic and reading in situations that afford opportunities for continued use. Elementary-school pupils who continue study of arithmetic tend to maintain, with only slight loss, the abilities in addition, multiplication, division, and subtraction they first acquired in earlier grades. They frequently demonstrate forgetting at various testing periods while they continue their study of arithmetic; but they quickly regain much of their loss. Likewise, students who have developed special reading skills retain their abilities with a relatively high degree of permanence if they consistently use their skills.

Retention studies of elementary-school pupils made during summer vacation show large losses for some subjects and small ones for others. Such pupils often show pronounced forgetting of the arithmetic fundamentals of addition, multiplication, and subtraction and the fundamentals of spelling—all abilities that involve skills. The losses of these students tend to be less evident in the social and natural sciences and in reading.

Less is known about opportunities for maintaining or improving gains made in high school and college studies. Students used as subjects usually discontinue study of the subject matter under investigation but often remain in school and are influenced by many undetermined conditions. For retention studies in high school and college it is necessary to base the discussion mainly on the kinds of abilities measured by the tests. The studies show marked forgetting of facts and detailed kinds of information as measured by tests that emphasize recall. They also show relatively high degrees of retention on tests that stress the use of

[40] Frances Van Dusen and Harold Schlosberg, "Further Study of the Retention of Verbal and Motor Skills," *Journal of Experimental Psychology,* 38 (1948), 526–534.

information. In measuring such abilities the usual procedure is to provide the learner with most of the information he will need to answer the questions or solve the problems in the test. The fact that the results of such tests cannot be compared with the results of recall tests, either on the basis of functions measured or techniques applied, would account for some of the differences in revealed retention ability. It would seem, however, that the higher retention of functional abilities may be attributed in part to "overlearning" and to the significance the abilities have in the successful completion of a course of instruction. These types of ability are frequently practiced by the learner when, for example, he relates a principle in chemistry to life situations or relates a theory in biology to experimental results. The learner continuously cultivates these abilities. He continuously uses the learned principles and theories as reference points, either consciously or unconsciously, around which to build his knowledge of a subject. Such principles and theories are the bases of significant thinking in a subject and they consistently command the learner's attention.

Perhaps the most significant findings are those based on persons who have discontinued study of a subject for long periods and, in the interim, have not practiced their previously acquired abilities and skills. Young adults show marked forgetting in arithmetic and spelling after they have been out of school several years. Studies that use mature adults as subjects show similar results. Much forgetting occurs during extended time intervals; but rapid recovery, as a result of practice, is often noted.

An obvious weakness of retention studies that are conducted in school situations is the lack of the kind of controlled conditions an investigator should impose to derive valid and reliable results. Explanations of the results of these studies must of necessity be speculative, since in all cases the investigator could not describe or control the conditions under which the reported learning occurred and could not identify the nature or measure the amount of the subjects' activity following the time of initial measurement. Also, very little is reported about the teaching methods used or the kinds of learning cultivated during a study. The only constant factor found in the studies is the type of tests used. Some of the conditions affecting permanence of learning, with special reference to laboratory situations, will be discussed in the next chapter.

study questions

1. Under what conditions may there be retention if the learner can neither reproduce nor recognize materials?
2. What implications are suggested by the fact that detailed factual informa-

tion is forgotten quickly but that abilities to apply principles and interpret data are retained over long periods with slight loss?

3. What part may properly planned review play in checking the forgetting that occurs in most learning situations?
4. Discuss retention in relationship to (a) length of time during which courses are taken, (b) number of subjects taken at a given time, (c) frequency of testing during a course of instruction, and (d) the final comprehensive examination.
5. Criticize this statement: "J. does not remember much about what he learned in school." Under what conditions may this be true or untrue? In the light of your criticisms of this statement, discuss how conventional retention scores may be misleading?
6. For permanence of learning, how significant are a pupil's (a) general interests and (b) interest in a subject both during instruction and the years that follow?

conditions affecting permanence of learning

3

The typical retention curve shows a descending or negatively accelerated form, indicating that there are two stages to the forgetting process: (1) A large percentage of what is learned is forgotten quickly. (2) The knowledge that remains after this initial decline diminishes at a slower

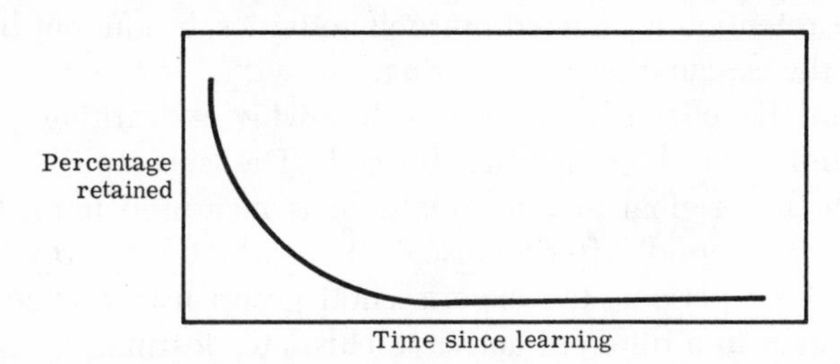

Figure 11. Amount retained in relation to the time interval, as measured by the relearning technique. From K. Lovell, *Educational Psychology and Children* (New York: Philosophical Library, 1958), p. 122.

and more stable rate. Figure 11 shows a curve based on meaningless laboratory material as measured by the relearning technique. The retention curve has the same general characteristics, whether the method of measurement is *relearning, reproduction,* or *recognition* or deals with meaningless or meaningful materials. The curve, however, may be influenced by many factors, including the kind of material, the method of measurement, the distribution of practice, and the degree of learning.

One of the first observations one makes of the retention curve is the apparent relationship between the amount retained and the length of the time interval that elapses between original learning and later recall. Within the limits established by investigations, the amount retained appears to be inversely proportional to the length of the interval. It is not the purpose here to suggest explanations for the shape of the curve; but rather the purpose is to consider the more general problem of the conditions that influence retention. Some conditions inhibit retention; others facilitate it.

inhibiting conditions

Because of this apparent relationship between the amount retained and the length of the time interval, a major approach taken to investigate the causes of forgetting is to study the effects on retention of activities that follow the original period of learning.

intervening activities

In studying this problem one should not assume that the learner is completely inactive at all times. He may, in fact, be very actively engaged in activities that either stimulate or inhibit his retention. Consequently, it is possible to vary the activities following original learning and measure the effects that the activities produce. If time is the important factor, retention may not be influenced by activities that follow learning. But if retention is affected by such activities, a different basis is established for the explanation of forgetting.

To determine the effects of activities following a learning period, experimental and control groups are formed. The accomplishment of both groups on the original learning material is measured immediately following a training period. After a lapse of time, which may vary from a few seconds to long periods, the experimental group learns some other material or engages in a different activity. This later learning is referred to as interpolated activity. Instead of engaging in interpolated activity, the control group rests for the same length of time. The rest period may consist of sleep, reading humorous magazines, or aimless visiting with classmates. The experimental and control groups are then remeasured for their retention of the original learning. The experimental design may be extended to include additional groups so that the effects of varying kinds and amounts of interpolated activity may be determined. The effects of interpolated activities have been tested in both laboratory and classroom situations.

kinds of interpolated activities

A widely held belief is that interference is more likely to occur if the interpolated activity and original learning are similar, especially when the activity deals with meaning. Another belief is that the greater the degree of similarity between original learning and interpolated activity the greater will be the inhibitory effect. These beliefs, however, are based mainly on the results of laboratory studies. Consequently, investigators have been testing the beliefs by using meaningful materials in classroom settings.

Hall[1] tested the hypothesis that interpolated activity similar to the original learning produces greater interference than dissimilar activity. The subjects consisted of *one* control and *two* experimental groups of college students enrolled in an introductory psychology course. The original learning material consisted of 30 sentences prepared for the experiment, the content being based on anthropological sources that described the customs of a hypothetical primitive tribe. Efficiency in learning was measured by use of a completion-type test given immediately after a predetermined amount of practice.

After the original learning period, the *control* group was administered the Minnesota Spatial Relations test and the Dubois-Bunch learning test. The reason these tests were given was to keep the control group busy while the two experimental groups were engaged in differing kinds of interpolated activity. One experimental group, Group I, studied prose material that described the characteristics of a *second* hypothetical primitive tribe. This material was kept as dissimilar from the original as possible. The interpolated material studied by the other experimental group, Group II, consisted of twenty sentences identical to questions studied by Group I and ten sentences identical to sentences used in the original material. The investigator thus had one group, the control group, whose interpolated activities were quite different from the original learning; and two experimental groups whose interpolated activities varied in degrees of similarity. To equalize the total amount of time spent on interpolated activities for all groups, the two experimental groups were also given the Minnesota Spatial Relations test and the Dubois-Bunch learning test. The study time allowed the two experimental groups, however, was less than that allowed the control group. The interpolated activities were scheduled immediately following original learning and consumed a forty-five minute period which was followed without intermission by a retest over the original material. The students were also retested on original material after a twenty-one-day interval. The findings showed that the interpolated activity, whether similar or dissimilar, had no effect on the ability to retain the original material after either an elapse of forty-five minutes or twenty-one days.

In a series of investigations, Ausubel[2] also measured the effect of different kinds of interpolated activity on retention of meaningful verbal

[1] John F. Hall, "Retroactive Inhibition in Meaningful Material," *Journal of Educational Psychology,* 46 (1955), 47–52.

[2] David P. Ausubel and others, "Retroactive Inhibition and Facilitation in the Learning of School Materials," *Journal of Educational Psychology,* 48 (1957), 334–343. See also David P. Ausubel and E. Blake, "Proactive Inhibition in the Forgetting of Meaningful School Material," *Journal of Educational Research,* 52 (1958), 145–149.

material. In one of his experiments, he used one experimental and three control groups made up of undergraduate college students. Each of these groups studied a 1,700-word passage on Buddhism. Their immediate learning was measured by a multiple-choice test. Twenty-four hours after taking this test the students studied certain materials according to a planned schedule. The experimental group studied a passage that compared Buddhism and Christianity. One control group restudied the passage on Buddhism; another control group studied a passage on Christianity; and the third group rested. The test used for measuring immediate learning was repeated eight days later. The purpose was to measure retention.

The amount of forgetting for each of the three control groups was similar. The degree of similarity between the interpolated activity and the original learning made little difference in retention. The inference was that activity preceding the original learning on Buddhism, rather than that which followed, was the factor that determined the degree of forgetting. Study of the passage, comparing Buddhism and Christianity, however, was an effective means of reducing loss in retention. Study of this passage had the effect of enhancing the discriminability[3] of Buddhism and served to differentiate it more clearly from Christianity.

In laboratory studies, original and interpolated materials are usually meaningless and are learned by rote methods over short periods of time. The original and interpolated materials also tend to be scheduled in rapid succession; thus the subjects are allowed only a limited opportunity to stabilize the effects of their practice. Under such conditions some interference is likely to occur regardless of the degree of similarity between learning tasks.

Studies based on meaningful materials represent a learning situation that is different from that found in laboratory experiments. Where investigators use meaningful materials and require logical rather than rote learning methods, the degree of similarity between original and interpolated materials would seem to be a negligible factor in forgetting. The interference caused by such materials seems to be influenced by their degree of discriminability. When materials possess individuality in their own right, they tend to be better retained. It is probable that in school situations certain subject matter cannot be clearly differentiated and learned until the individual has studied other related topics. This possibility exists in courses of instruction where units of material are sequentially organized and where interrelationships are stressed. Com-

[3] David P. Ausubel and Mohammed Youssef, "The Role of Discriminability in Meaningful Parallel Learning," *Journal of Educational Psychology,* 54 (1963), 311–336. See also David P. Ausubel and D. Fitzgerald, "The Role of Discriminability in Meaningful Verbal Learning and Retention," *Journal of Educational Psychology,* 52 (1961), 266–274.

parison and contrast are often used to develop characteristic similarities and differences between various concepts and principles. In such situations the discriminability of learning materials would be enhanced, thereby insulating the learner against interference in recall.

The degree of interference caused by activities interpolated in the interval between original learning and later recall is also influenced by other conditions. Two of the most important of these conditions are the time at which activities are interpolated and the degree to which the original and interpolated materials are learned.

timing interpolated activities

The student often observes that temporary interference occurs when his courses follow each other in immediate succession. In such a situation he may continue to think of the discussion and problems in class A after he has begun work in class B. The inhibiting effect may be even more pronounced when he takes two or more successive examinations without intermission.

When an activity is interpolated immediately following a learning period, retention tends to be more adversely affected than when a rest interval intervenes. In laboratory studies,[4] interpolated activity that is scheduled a few seconds after original learning tends to produce greater inhibitory effect than does interpolated activity that is scheduled several minutes later. Within limits, the further removed the interpolated activity is from the original learning period the less will be the inhibitory effect.

The effect that this timing of interpolated activities has on retention in laboratory situations has stimulated much discussion and has resulted in various explanations. One of these explanations suggests that an activity set in motion tends to persist after the stimulus evoking it has been removed. As a result of this tendency, the learner experiences a greater interference when he is asked to learn another task immediately than he does when he is asked to learn the same task some time later.

degree of learning

The greater the degree to which a student learns the original material the less will be his susceptibility to interference. At this point we are concerned with the degree of original learning in relationship to the interpolated activity that follows it. The effect of interpolated activity on original learning will be more adverse on partially[5] or superficially learned material than on material thoroughly mastered. If both the original

[4] B. J. Underwood, "Proactive Inhibition as a Function of Time and Degree of Prior Learning," *Journal of Experimental Psychology*, 39 (1949), 24–34.

[5] J. A. McGeoch, "Influence of Degree of Learning upon Retroactive Inhibition," *American Journal of Psychology*, 41 (1929), 252–262. See also B. J. Underwood (4).

and interpolated material are poorly learned, the inhibiting effect may be pronounced.

Partial or superficial learning produces interference even within the same task. Laboratory investigations show that errors committed during practice tend to cause interfering associations which in turn produce other errors. In some instances, the effect of interference from errors is general, causing various errors. In others it is specific, causing repetition of the same errors in repeated trials. This condition is often observed when pupils have made errors in subjects such as arithmetic, spelling, music, and grammar and are attempting to correct them. When the commission of errors leads to habitual ways of responding, interference may be marked.

In commenting on the implications of laboratory research on interference for school situations, Swenson[6] says:

> A mass of unorganized facts about an author's life and writings is a fertile field for retroaction. The integration of these facts into a broad understanding of what the author's writings stand for, the influences that made him write in a particular style, and the basic ideas represented in his work presents a different psychological situation. The meaningfulness of the learning becomes a preventive of the effects of interference from subsequent activities, and retention should consequently be higher.

As the learner achieves greater mastery of both original and interpolated material, susceptibility to interference diminishes. Poor learning of materials, the situation in which the learner fails to recognize certain sequences and interrelationships between one aspect of a topic and another, is a major source of inhibition.

other activities and conditions

As research workers continue their efforts to discover the causes of forgetting, they also discover that many other conditions interfere with learning. These conditions include those that exist prior to the original learning, those that exist during the original learning, as well as those that exist in the interval between original learning and later recall. Research has centered mainly on activities that follow original learning. Such activities cause interference in recall, but the extent of their influence as compared with those preceding and during original learning is difficult to determine. The conditions during and following original learning lend themselves more readily to experimentation. Many of those preceding the original learning are often beyond identification and control. Their influence must be inferred rather than empirically demonstrated.

Much controversy over the causes of forgetting has arisen from the

[6] Esther J. Swenson, *Retroactive Inhibition* (Minneapolis: University of Minnesota Press, 1941).

emphasis some laboratory investigators place on the short periods of interpolated activity following a training period. Certain experimenters contend that such interpolated activity is a major cause of forgetting. Others insist that what the individual previously learned in the laboratory and not what he learned during a given training period may be more influential. On the basis of his experiments, in which he used meaningful verbal materials, Ausubel[7] concludes that the determining factor in forgetting is the learning activity that precedes the original learning rather than the learning activity that follows. Underwood,[8] also interpreting laboratory research, concludes that forgetting is caused by interference from previously learned habits, from habits being currently learned, and from habits yet to be learned.

theories of forgetting

During practice, the learner develops varying degrees of efficiency as manifested through information, abilities, or skills. After practice ends, his efficiency usually declines. Primarily as a result of this observation, explanations of forgetting have often included such concepts as "disuse" and the "fading of neural impressions,"[9] using lapse of time following original learning as the constant factor. Such explanations are plausible but cannot be readily demonstrated empirically. Certainly, it cannot be assumed that time itself causes any loss of learned material. It simply affords opportunity for the operation of various conditions that affect retention. Theories of forgetting tend to center on such conditions. One of these is *interference;* another is *subsumption.*

interference theory

The theory on which there is the greatest amount of empirical evidence is that of interference. The learner forgets original materials because of newly acquired habits, particularly those that were learned in the interval between measurement of initial learning and remeasurement for retention. It is one thing to learn material and allow oneself no conscious or purposeful activity afterwards; it is another to learn material and then become actively engaged in learning something else. When individuals in a control group[10] sleep or otherwise relax or rest (not purposefully active), the extent of interference is reduced. Considerable forgetting is due to

[7] David P. Ausubel and others (3 and 4).

[8] B. J. Underwood, "Interference and Forgetting," *Psychological Review,* 54 (1957), 49–60. See also "Forgetting," *Scientific American* (March, 1964).

[9] B. R. Gomulicki, "The Development and Present Status of the Trace Theory of Memory," *British Journal of Psychology Monograph Supplement,* 20 (1953), 1–94.

[10] J. G. Jenkins and K. M. Dallenbach, "Obliviscence during Sleep and Waking," *American Journal of Psychology,* 35 (1924), 605–616. See also E. B. Van Ormer, "Retention after Intervals of Sleep and Waking," *Archives of Psychology,* 21, No. 137 (1932).

the inhibition of the old by the new. Application of the interference theory, however, is not limited to conditions that exist in the interval between original learning and later recall. It also applies to habits that were established previous to, as well as during, original learning. It now seems probable that what the individual learned previous to an original learning task may contribute more to his loss in retention than any other factor.

The interference theory was developed as a result of laboratory studies that employed meaningless materials and rote learning methods. And it is in such situations that the interference theory rationally explains the process of forgetting. The theory, however, does not explain the forgetting that takes place in learning situations that employ meaningful materials and logical learning methods. For such situations the *subsumption* theory has been proposed as an explanation for loss in retention.

subsumption theory

The subsumption theory proposed by Ausubel[11] grew out of experiments in which he used meaningful verbal materials. Ausubel's studies indicate that the degree of discriminability of meaningful verbal materials is a determining factor in forgetting. Where such materials are distinguishable and possess individuality, they may not adversely affect retention of original learning. In one of his investigations, for example, he found that the study of a passage on Christianity immediately before or after the study of a comparable passage on Buddhism did not significantly affect scores on Buddhism. This applied equally to tests of immediate learning and retention. Under such conditions the discriminability of the Buddhism materials and the clarity of the learner's knowledge of Christianity seemed to be the significant factors.

The discriminability of related materials, however, may be reduced by a process of compressing ideas and materials into fewer and more general categories—a process of subsumption. During this process information is blended into a broad comprehensive topic or problem. To reduce forgetting, it is necessary to enhance, up to a point, the discriminability between related materials. Ausubel believes that the subsumption theory takes into account the learner's existing organization of meaningful materials, his incorporation of new materials into that organization, and his tendency to reduce the new materials to a common denominator. In this sense, the subsumption process facilitates learning; but at the same time it inhibits recall.

Much learning, seemingly forgotten, is, in fact retained. It has merely

[11] David P. Ausubel, "A Subsumption Theory of Meaningful Learning and Retention," *Journal of General Psychology,* 62 (1962), 213–224. See also David P. Ausubel, *The Psychology of Meaningful Verbal Learning* (New York: Grune and Stratton, 1963).

been converted to a different form. In some instances a learner may reorganize items of information to such an extent that they no longer exist as originally learned. The sustained effects of training, however, may take a form that cannot be readily measured. Many of us, for example, have forgotten some of the devices we used to acquire skill in reading. We no longer limp through the pronunciation of words, supporting our steps on arbitrary values for vowels and consonants, but read by a different process. The detailed facts of many subjects, such as chemistry, English grammar, or algebra, are not needed in typical thinking. Most individuals recall facts only when they are needed. Useful detailed kinds of information do not long remain in our minds as isolated facts but are organized into practiced patterns of activity.

Theories of forgetting have not as yet been tested in typical school situations where materials are systematically organized within a course of instruction and where effort is made to recognize the progressive and cumulative nature of learning, situations where the individual actually advances within a field from elementary to more advanced subject matter. It is in these kinds of situations that the subsumption theory holds promise of wide applicability. Under conditions of careful organization of materials and thorough learning, interference in school situations would be held to a minimum.

facilitating conditions

The time interval between original learning and later recall may be a period during which certain facilitating conditions operate. One of these conditions is the possibility of mental practice following a learning period; another is reminiscence.

mental practice

In most retention studies, measurement reveals how well the individual is able to recall what he has initially learned. No effort is made to determine what he may have done with his material in the interval between initial measurement and remeasurement. It is not known whether he was able to derive important meaning from his learning, use it for a gainful purpose, assimilate it, or mentally practice it. Consequently, when it is shown that a high percentage of a learner's knowledge is forgotten within a certain time, all that can be concluded is that he is less proficient in satisfying comparable test requirements.

Abilities possessed at the time of measuring original material may be only one phase of an individual's learning. The interval following original learning may be a period during which the learner forms new associations, clarifies difficulties, applies principles, or mentally practices[12] the

[12] L. Verdella Clark, "Effect of Mental Practice on the Development of a Certain Motor Skill," *Research Quarterly*, 31 (1960), 60.

material. And even though he may have mastered the material to the point of recall, he may not thoroughly understand it.

reminiscence

Improvement would be expected to occur during the interval between original learning and later recall if the individual has mentally practiced his material following a training period. Also, he may improve in the interval between original learning and later recall even though he does not practice or intend to retain the material. Such improvement is referred to as the phenomenon of *reminiscence,* which is often defined as improvement in retention of *incompletely learned materials* that takes place without any effort by the learner. In a sense it is an unsolicited gift or "windfall." Some investigators make a distinction, however, between reminiscence and improvement. For them, improvement means a larger total score on the second testing than on the first, either for the individual or for the group. On the other hand, reminiscence refers to the specific items answered incorrectly on the first testing but answered correctly on the second. Reminiscence could occur without a measurable improvement, in the sense used here; but improvement could not occur without reminiscence.

In a study designed to test reminiscence, McGeoch[13] used 403 third- and fourth-grade pupils in the Columbia, Missouri, public schools. The learning material consisted of "The Spider and the Fly." A test was given immediately after the pupils had studied this material five minutes. The test was repeated 24 hours later to measure retention. After the children had completed the retention test, they were asked: (1) Had they ever learned or heard about the poem before? (2) If they had, had they learned any part of it? (3) Had they discussed the poem with anyone during the 24-hour interval? The results showed that improvement after this 24-hour period occurred independently of review or intention to retain.

Experimental data suggest that reminiscence is more likely to occur when the learning situation requires use of motor rather than verbal tasks. Fox and Lamb[14] sought to determine whether reminiscence would occur in softball skills and whether the results would vary with different periods of nonpractice. The subjects were 87 seventh-grade girls in the Oak High School, Burlington, Iowa. These girls studied a unit of softball during a four-week period. Tests to measure progress were given at the beginning and end of the unit. The tests were repeated after five- and

[13] Grace O. McGeoch, "The Conditions of Reminiscence," *American Journal of Psychology,* 46 (1935), 65–89.

[14] Margaret Fox and Ethel Lamb, "Improvement During Non-Practice Periods in a Selected Physical Education Activity, *Research Quarterly,* 33 (1962), 381–385.

seventeen-week periods of nonpractice. Their skills showed improvement for both the short and long nonpractice periods. The mean gains, however, were not significant for the first nonpractice period but were for the second.

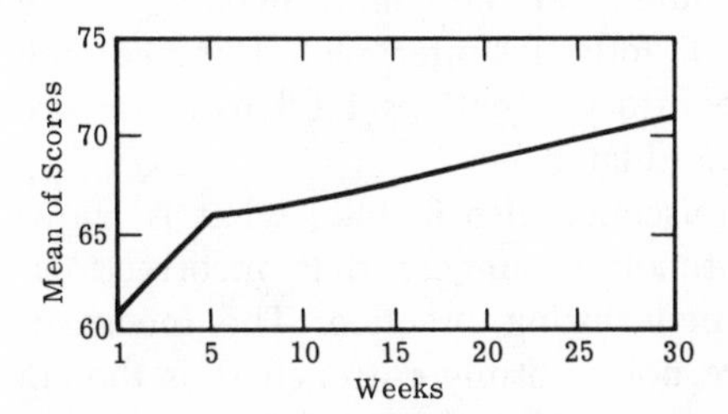

Figure 12. Learning curve for softball repeated throws. From Fox and Lamb (note 14).

In another study Fox and Young[15] analyzed the effect of reminiscence on learning badminton skills. Two comparable groups of women students enrolled in service classes at Parsons College, Iowa, were used as subjects. One group had six weeks of instruction; the other had nine weeks. The nonpractice periods were six weeks and twelve weeks. The wall volley and short serve tests were given at the beginning and end of the instructional program and repeated at the end of each nonpractice period. A major purpose was to determine the relationship between the degree of original learning (the amount of time spent on instruction) and the length of the nonpractice period. The results showed that, for the group having nine weeks of instruction, reminiscence on the wall volley skills occurred during the six-week period of nonpractice. For the group having six weeks of instruction, it occurred on the wall volley skills during the twelve-week nonpractice period. Reminiscence did not occur for either group on the short serve skills. The authors were unable to account for the difference in the results for the two kinds of tests. A possible explanation is that, although the short serve tests were probably appropriate for experienced players, they were too difficult for beginners.

Various explanations have been proposed to account for reminiscence, most of which have grown out of laboratory studies. Some writers, notably McGeoch and Irion,[16] suggest that an activity leaves a residue, which tends to prevent recurrence of previously learned skills. This interference-causing residue may be due to fatigue. A rest period would permit the learner to recover from the effects of fatigue, especially if his practice were massed.

[15] Margaret Fox and Vera P. Young, "Effect of Reminiscence on Learning Selected Badminton Skills," *Research Quarterly*, 33 (1962), 386–394.

[16] John A. McGeoch and Arthur L. Irion, *The Psychology of Human Learning* (New York: Longmans, Green and Co., 1952).

Some theories attempt to account for the inhibiting effects of interpolated activities. It is suggested, for example, that reminiscence may be caused by some form of activity that is persisted[17] in after the cessation of practice. Once neural activity has been set in motion, the activity may continue for some time after the stimuli evoking it have been removed. As already indicated, activities interpolated immediately following original learning in laboratory situations tend to cause greater interference than those interpolated later.

Theories of reminiscence also include what is known as "differential forgetting." Such theories suggest that incorrect as well as correct responses are learned during practice. The incorrect responses cause interference but are not so firmly entrenched as the correct ones. A rest period would permit the dying out of incorrect or partially learned responses and ensure the attainment of higher scores on retention tests.

Evidence for what is known as reminiscence is available, but explanations for its occurrence are largely speculative. Each of several groups of theories, recovery from fatigue, persisting neural activity, and differential forgetting, affords plausible explanations. In laboratory situations reminiscence tends to be most readily obtained following conditions of pronounced interference.[18] Its occurrence is also directly influenced by the length of the rest interval.

One of the major experimental difficulties in school situations is inadequate control of the learner's activities following original learning. It seems likely that, where meaningful tasks are used, mental practice following a period of learning activity could have the effect of consolidating and improving the individual's initial gains. Such practice does not come within the definition of reminiscence; but in school situations, it could be a significant factor in improvement, especially of highly motivated learners.[19] In some experimental situations, increased maturity and incidental learning would also account, in part, for the improvement that is noted. It seems possible that reminiscence would be enhanced in school by distributing course materials over relatively long periods and by following a plan of delayed testing to measure accomplishment.[20]

[17] E. R. Hilgard, *Introduction to Psychology* (New York: Harcourt, Brace and Co., 1957). See also G. S. Snoddy, "A Reply to Dore and Hilgard," *Journal of Experimental Psychology,* 23 (1938), 375–383.

[18] B. J. Underwood, "Ten Years of Massed Practice on Distributed Practice," *Psychological Review,* 68 (1961), 229–247.

[19] James G. Martin and Judy Davidson, "Recall of Completed and Interrupted Tasks by Achievers and Underachievers," *Journal of Educational Psychology,* 55 (1964), 314–316. These investigators found that high achievers recall more incompleted tasks than do low achievers.

[20] G. A. Kimble, "Performance and Reminiscence in Motor Learning as a Function of the Degree of Distribution of Practice," *Journal of Experimental Psychology,* 39 (1949), 500–510.

special programs for retention

The most effective basis on which to ensure retention is to provide conditions that favorably affect the learning process—a theme to be emphasized in Part Two. Nevertheless, there is some justification for special programs designed to recover or prevent losses in retention. One of these is relearning or review; another is continued learning of the same kind of subject matter.

relearning or review

An immediately practical method for overcoming the problem of forgetting is what is known as *relearning* in the psychological laboratory and *review* in the school.

Ebbinghaus,[21] one of the first to use the *relearning* method, believed that, after the susceptibility of recall had been weakened, the best means for measuring the strength of associations was by the number of repetitions required to relearn material to the same degree it was initially learned. His technique consisted of learning material to the point of one errorless reproduction and, after a lapsed time interval, relearning it to the extent it was initially mastered. The difference between the number of repetitions required for initial learning and that needed to relearn the material to its initial status represents the amount of saving. Laboratory investigations of the type described show that relearning takes place more readily than does initial learning, indicating considerable saving in time and effort. It seems probable that anything once learned is never completely forgotten and that it can be restored to its initial status with relatively small amounts of practice.

When the relearning technique is used in the schools, it is likely to be restricted to drill on items supposedly once known. More frequently, however, this technique, as applied in the schools, consists of review that goes beyond repetitive exercises. It may be review that assists the learner to organize his material into large units, to clarify and apply principles, to trace movements, to coordinate relationships of facts and ideas, and to solve problems. The review may also take the form of further reading, lectures, discussion, and tests. Used in this manner, review is a process of continued learning of the same topic or subject. It is a process that helps the learner to revise and extend his knowledge rather than to duplicate previous experiences.

Programs to prevent or recover losses in retention during summer vacation include reviews either at the beginning or end of a school term.

[21] H. Ebbinghaus, *Memory: A Contribution to Experimental Psychology* (New York: Teachers College, Columbia University, 1913).

Kirby[22] found that 75 minutes of drill on addition in the fall were required to bring his group to the same degree of proficiency it had attained by 30 minutes of drill the previous spring. Special reviews may be given at the beginning of a school year to check the background of pupils and prepare them for the new work. They may be given at the end of a school year to reduce loss in retention during summer. Morgan,[23] for example, studied the effectiveness of specific training in preventing loss during summer. His results showed that a group of sixth-grade children who received special training for a two-week period before the end of the school year made a much better showing at the beginning of the fall term than did a comparable group of sixth-grade children who did not receive such training. The advantage of planning review at the beginning of a school term is to be found in the opportunity it affords to correlate the learner's previous knowledge with new materials.

continued learning of similar subject matter

In using this plan, pupils do not relearn or review but continue to study the same kind of subject matter. Interest in this plan has centered mainly on the problem of forgetting in the elementary school during summer vacation.

A program designed to prevent loss during summer vacation was directed by Cook,[24] who conducted a study over a twelve-year period. The subjects chosen for study were arithmetic, reading, and writing. During this twelve-year period more than 400 pupils between the ages of seven and nine were enrolled. Both first- and second-grade children were included during the first two years of the study; the remaining years included second-grade children only.

The procedure consisted of three steps: (1) giving standardized tests in May, (2) subjecting pupils to varied kinds of reading experiences during summer vacation, and (3) giving a duplicate form of the same tests in September to measure changes that had taken place during summer.

Four types of program were used at one time or another during the twelve-year period. One of these consisted of materials, prepared at the end of the school year, which the pupils could take home and study fifteen or twenty minutes per day during vacation. The study period was

[22] T. J. Kirby, "Practice under School Conditions," *Teachers College Contribution to Education* (1915), 58.

[23] L. D. Morgan, "How Effective Is Specific Training in Preventing Loss Due to Summer Vacation," *Journal of Educational Psychology,* 20 (1929), 466–471.

[24] Ruth C. Cook, "A Dozen Summer Programs Designed to Promote Retention in Young Children," *Elementary School Journal,* 52 (1951–52), 412–417. See also Ruth C. Cook, "Vacation Retention of Fundamentals by Primary Grade Pupils," *Elementary School Journal,* 43 (1942), 214–219.

to be devoted mainly to guided reading. In another program, certain books were to be read, followed by completion exercises to be filled in by the pupils. In a third program, individualized work sheets were provided, 50 of these being supplied for each child. These work sheets were a means of checking on the child's reading. The purpose of the fourth program was to create interest on the part of both pupils and parents in reading books in the library. The work sheets were omitted in this program, however, and a public library reading plan was substituted.

Children who participated in any one of these four programs made more progress than did those who did not participate. Those who participated could be classified into three groups: (1) those who forgot about reading or who dropped it after the second or third week, (2) those who worked more or less consistently up to the first of July and then lost interest, and (3) those who worked on reading almost all summer.

Pupils who did not participate in one or more of the programs lost, as measured by standardized tests, an average of .4 of a school year during the summer. Only five of the 230 children who read at least two books and worked on the material six or more weeks showed a loss in reading when retested in the fall. On the other hand, only eight of the 170 children who neither read nor attempted any of the work made gains on standardized reading tests.

Decisive results were also obtained by Aasen,[25] who studied the effect of a voluntary summer reading program on fourth-grade children in the Minneapolis public schools. An experimental group that participated in the reading program gained approximately seven months in reading ability during the summer, as measured by the Stanford Achievement Reading Test. The control group neither gained nor lost. No explanation is given for this finding. The pupils in this control group apparently followed their own individual interests during the summer vacation.

Summer-study plans of the type described have apparently achieved their purpose—maintenance or improvement of abilities developed during the academic year. Retest results, however, would be influenced by a number of factors, one of which is the type of subject matter. Evidence that abilities had been maintained or improved is more readily obtained for elementary subjects that stress skills—reading, arithmetic, and spelling. It is more difficult to obtain accurate evidence in advanced subject matter that stresses principles, generalizations, and insights, especially when the tests emphasize recall. Under such conditions it is possible that continued learning within the same subject matter field could be a cause of reduced accuracy in recall, operating through the process of reorganization and expansion of existing ideas and concepts.

[25] Helen B. Aasen, "A Summer's Growth in Reading," *Elementary School Journal,* 60 (1959), 70–74.

Repeating the tests used for measuring original learning would not necessarily reveal the growth that occurred.

some practical problems

The retention curve (Figure 11) presented at the beginning of this chapter was based on laboratory material as measured by the relearning technique. It shows that one forgets at a very rapid rate soon after original learning and then forgets more slowly.

Retention curves based on school subject matter often are not unlike those derived from meaningless laboratory material. Where objective tests, stressing recall, are repeated at varying time intervals following original learning, the amount of forgetting closely parallels that measured in laboratory studies. It would be valuable to analyze retention scores based on tests that stress recall and note the trends for varying time intervals. What particular items seem to be retained after several retesting periods? For example, what items are retained after a two-week period? And what items are retained after a period of eight weeks, twelve weeks, or a year? The purpose would be to identify the kinds of items that represent the lasting effects of instruction.

The rapid decline in the retention curve, especially for recall of information, would seem to be accepted without explanation for its occurrence. Does it occur because school officials unintentionally induce forgetting by testing materials when they are fresh in the students' minds but are as yet unassimilated? Does delayed testing—testing that is scheduled sometime after completion of individual courses and subjects —cause the learner to reflect on materials that he has mastered to the point of recall but has not thoroughly understood? Is forgetting encouraged when test results are considered final and the student knows he will not be retested on the same material? What effect do the quarter, the semester, and tri-semester plans have on learning and retention?

The marked decline in the retention curve immediately following original learning seems to be regarded as inevitable, as judged by the admonition given teachers. They are advised that it is advantageous to distribute reviews so that they conform to the rate of forgetting. It is suggested that reviews spaced close together and given soon after an instructional period lessen the marked initial forgetting characteristic of the typical retention curve. After this initial decline, it is recommended that reviews be spaced further and further apart.

The rules for distributing reviews stimulate a number of questions. What should be the nature of such reviews? Are they applicable to learning situations other than those stressing recall? Should reviews differ with varying types of subject matter? What relationship should they have to the organization and length of a course of instruction? And when should reviews be discontinued, if ever?

There remain other more fundamental questions on the subject of permanence of learning. Do conventional measuring techniques, such as reproduction, recognition, and relearning, adequately measure the most important persisting effects of instruction? It seems likely that the learner would be able to demonstrate more mature kinds of learning several months or perhaps years after his original learning had been measured. These more mature kinds of learning are best measured by delayed tests that emphasize the functional aspects of knowledge. Available tests that measure such abilities are those which emphasize educational maturity.[26] Such tests measure knowledge of vocabulary, ability to understand and apply what is read in various subject matter fields, and ability to use sources of information. The information needed for applying knowledge is provided as a part of the testing situation, thus reduced emphasis is placed on recall as it is generally measured.

In considering the learner's net gain two questions should be asked: How much of his learning is ultimately transformed into functional abilities? And how much of it can be used in making other learning situations easier and more meaningful? This second question relates to the major problem of transference in learning, which will be discussed in the next chapter.

study questions

1. Discuss conditions that inhibit retention in the interval between measurement of initial learning and remeasurement for retention.
2. Discuss those conditions that facilitate retention during this interval.
3. How may reminiscence be fostered in school situations?
4. To what extent does the nature of an individual's activities following instruction affect long-term retention? Are any types of learning affected more than others? If so, suggest an explanation.
5. To what extent do you agree with the point of view that thorough learning results in high retention?
6. As a means of ensuring retention, how do you regard the plan of giving pupils a thorough review before the end of the school year as compared with that of providing a review at the beginning of the fall term?
7. How may a teacher's scholarship and interest in a given field affect the procedures he follows in producing long-term retention in his students?
8. You perhaps have been hopeful that your pupils may some day remember you as a teacher who "really taught them something they did not forget." Summarize the most important learning conditions that you must produce to deserve such praise.

[26] *Iowa Tests of Educational Development, Grades 9–13* (Chicago: Science Research Associates, 1958).

transference of learning

4

In a study of transfer one confronts problems similar to problems of retention. Possibilities for both facilitating and inhibiting conditions exist. When the training in one situation *assists* the individual in another learning situation, the transfer is positive. When the training in one situation *interferes* with learning in another situation, it is negative. The conditions under which facilitating and inhibiting conditions occur can be illustrated by experimental methods.

experimental methods

Experimental methods used in the study of transfer follow either one of two possible designs:[1] the *proactive* design and the *retroactive* design.

If the *proactive* design is followed, two comparable groups are used as subjects. One group learns Task A and then takes a test on Task B. To determine any effect that the learning of Task A has on Task B, it is necessary to use a control group. This control group does not learn Task A but usually rests. In its simplest form the design is as follows:

Experimental group:	Learns Task A	Test on Task B
Control group:	Rests	Test on Task B

If Task A affects efficiency on Task B, the two groups will differ in their performance on Task B. If Task A assists in learning Task B, there is *proactive facilitation* or positive transfer. If learning Task A hinders

[1] R. A. Mednick, *Learning* (Englewood Cliffs, N.J.: Prentice-Hall, 1964).

performance on Task B, there is *proactive inhibition* or negative transfer.

The *retroactive* design also requires use of two comparable groups. Both groups are measured on Task A; but only one group is given training in Task B. The change (either positive or negative) made by the experimental group is compared with that of the control group (which usually has conventional training) so that the effect of a certain kind of training may be determined. The simplest form of this design is as follows:

Experimental group:	Test on Task A	Train on Task B	Retest on A
Control group:	Test on Task A	Conventional Training	Retest on A

It will be noted that both groups take the test on Task A rather than learn it. This procedure is used in most school situations, because the learner already has had some training or experience in the tasks being considered. It is necessary, therefore, to determine the learner's present state of attainment. After this, the experimental group receives some form of special training. The two groups are then *remeasured* on Task A to determine any change that has occurred. It will also be noted that the control group does not *rest* but is subjected to conventional training. It is usually impracticable for any group to be deprived of some training while an experiment is in progress, especially if it extends over a considerable period of time. Consequently, when an investigator reports the results of a transfer experiment in school situations, the effectiveness of *special* training is likely to be compared with that achieved under conventional conditions.

The retroactive design is most applicable to school situations in which the learner may already have some training or experience in the tasks used to measure transfer efficiency. The proactive design, in contrast, is most likely to be used in laboratory situations where the artificial and meaningless nature of tasks would tend to preclude any previous background or experience. Both designs, however, may yield either positive or negative transfer.

Interest of the teacher in experimental study of transfer derives from his concern for conditions that will assist him to lead the students to attain certain goals of instruction. These goals differ with subject matter, age, and maturity of learners; but all his goals share certain common elements. In arithmetic, one of the important aims is to have the students acquire the ability to use arithmetic skills in the solution of problems; in English language, a principal objective is to acquire the ability to write and speak accurately and effectively; and in the sciences, a major aim is to acquire the ability to apply principles to new situations. Within each subject-matter area there is the objective of making the learner aware of potential applications of knowledge to theoretical or practical problems. In addition, there is the aim of developing the student's ability to perceive relationships between one branch of subject matter and others, thus extending his ability to apply knowledge beyond the areas in which it may have been cultivated initially.

experimental studies of transfer

Transfer of training has been a popular subject for investigation during the greater part of this century. As a result, numerous studies are available for review. A majority of these, however, are of a laboratory nature, which for the most part prevents one from applying their findings to school situations. Nevertheless, such studies are valuable in determining the nature of transfer and in defining the conditions under which transfer occurs. The purpose in this discussion is to emphasize studies that were conducted in classroom situations and to use laboratory investigations only to supplement the treatment.

The experiments to be reviewed have been selected because of their teaching implications and because each is representative of various areas of subject matter. These subject-matter areas are language arts, mathematics, and science.

language arts

To consider the varied aspects of the language arts requires much discussion. Those aspects most important for transfer deal mainly with the structure of reading and language.

Reading. Because of the universality of the reading process, transfer from one situation to another would not seem to pose problems. A difficulty does exist, however, because reading materials vary widely in content, terminology, length and balance of sentences, organization of paragraphs, and writing style.[2] There are also certain materials of a highly abstract and technical nature in which professional terminology and complex sentence structure retard both speed and comprehension in reading. It is just such situations that have prompted this observation: "Reading efficiency for one type of material may not be closely related to that of another."

Substantial transfer in reading efficiency may be expected, however, regardless of types of material. Schwartz[3] trained college students in reading nontechnical materials and then tested their efficiency in reading

[2] Wilbur R. Miller, "Readability versus Reading Ability," *Journal of Educational Research,* 56 (1962), 205–209.

[3] M. Schwartz, "Transfer of Reading Training from Nontechnical to Technical Material," *Journal of Educational Psychology,* 48 (1957), 498–505.

technical materials. These students showed more than 100 percent improvement in speed of reading after having been trained in nontechnical reading matter. Accompanying this improvement in reading speed was a decrement in comprehension of only five to seven percent. Any program that contributes to reading improvement also tends to facilitate general achievement. In a comprehensive investigation, Rudolf[4] determined the effect of incorporating reading instruction into an eighth-grade social studies curriculum. Experimental and control groups were formed. In the experimental groups, attention was directed to the understanding and interpreting of social studies material; the control groups were taught according to conventional practice. The experimental classes made significant gains over the control classes in knowledge, study skills, and reading comprehension as measured by the Cooperative Social Studies Test. One of the important outcomes of such programs is that the student's interest in improving his own reading skills is increased. He becomes aware of the relationships between reading efficiency and scholastic achievement.

Language structure. Correlation studies generally show a low relationship between knowledge of grammar and ability to write compositions. Using college freshmen as subjects, O'Donnell[5] conducted a study for the purpose of answering two questions: (1) What is the relationship between awareness of syntactic relationships of words and sentences and ability to write compositions? (2) What is the relationship between ability to verbalize knowledge of the rules of traditional grammar and ability to write compositions? The coefficients of correlation for each of these situations were low. Also, there was very little difference between the results for the two questions. In an analysis of standardized English tests, Groff[6] concluded there was very little, if any, relationship between knowledge of parts of speech and effective use of English. In these and other studies, such findings do not imply that knowledge of language structure is unnecessary in writing compositions; but rather the findings suggest that teachers ordinarily do not establish functional relationships between them. In typical situations a teacher tends to regard grammatical knowledge and written composition as two independent functions.

In experimental situations, however, it may be assumed that a different psychological situation exists. It may be supposed that the objectives and the designs of the experiments would have the effect of making the student aware of the relationship between language structure and

[4] Kathleen B. Rudolf, *The Effect of Reading Instruction on Achievement in Eighth Grade Social Studies* (New York: Teachers College, Columbia University, 1949).

[5] Roy C. O'Donnell, "The Correlation of Awareness of Structural Relationships in English and Ability in Written Compositions," *Journal of Educational Research*, 57 (1964), 464–467.

[6] Patrick J. Groff, "Parts of Speech in Standardized English Tests," *School Review*, 69 (1961), 457–460.

composition efficiency and that the experimental treatments would be chosen to increase the possibility of success. A number of experimenters have been interested in testing the effect on writing ability of certain teaching methods that emphasize the "new grammar" and "linguistic science." In essence these newer techniques emphasize the usage of language as contrasted with traditional methods that stress memorization of parts of speech, kinds of sentences, kinds of pronouns and adjectives, and the conjugation of verbs.

Schuster[7] designed a study to determine the effect of the new grammar on writing ability. For experimental groups, tenth-, eleventh-, and twelfth-grade students were used. A second twelfth-grade group was used as control. In the experimental classes, the structural method of teaching was employed; the control group used the traditional method. The average improvement for all groups was slight; but several large individual gains were noted for some students in the experimental groups. In Sugg's[8] study of the effect on writing ability of teaching the principles of linguistic science, the results were more conclusive. In her study, two eleventh-grade classes, one experimental and the other a control group, were formed. The experimental group studied structural linguistics; the control group studied traditional grammar. With the exception of differences in teaching methods, both groups pursued the same studies. In writing progress, there was a difference of ten points in favor of the experimental group.

The results of these studies demonstrate the possibility of bringing about a closer relationship between knowledge of language structure and its use in written compositions. The findings suggest that the new grammar and linguistic science afford greater transfer opportunities than do traditional subject matter and methods. If other investigations support these findings, the advantages are probably these: The new grammar and linguistic science provide a more realistic and practical approach to writing ability. And the students, for having learned by this method, are better able to perceive relationships between the elements of grammatical structure and their use in the writing of themes.

It is becoming increasingly evident that emphasis on theme writing is not only a means of improving written composition but is also a means of increasing proficiency in other aspects of English. In an extensive study, McQueen[9] and his associates compared the efficiency shown in college English classes by students who had had considerable writing experience

[7] Edgar H. Schuster, "How Good Is the New Grammar?" *English Journal,* 50 (1961), 392–397.

[8] Lena Reddick Suggs, "Structural Grammar versus Traditional Grammar in Influencing Writing," *English Journal,* 50 (1961), 173–178.

[9] Robert McQueen and others, "Relationships between Writing Required in High School and English Proficiency in College," *Journal of Experimental Education,* 31 (1963), 419–423.

in high school with the efficiency of another group who had had limited writing experience in high school. On almost all criteria, including scores attained on the English Placement Test and grades earned in English classes, the group that showed the superior performance in college English was the one that had had the greater writing experience in high school.

mathematics

Teaching aims in mathematics are similar to those in the language arts. Mathematics teachers are interested in establishing an active relationship between skills and their use in problem situations. Added to this is the aim of developing ability to generalize and apply mathematical principles to nonmathematical situations.

A direct approach to the problem of developing ability to generalize was made by Thiele,[10] who tested the effectiveness of two contrasting methods of teaching the addition facts. One group was taught the addition facts during a fifteen-week period by the "generalization" method, in which meanings and relationships were emphasized. The other group was taught the same material by the drill method for the same period. After being taught by these different methods, both groups were given two types of test. One of these measured the addition facts, the aim being to determine the rate and accuracy of computation, but little more. The other measured the ability to solve verbal arithmetic problems. The generalization method of teaching proved to be significantly superior to the drill method of teaching as demonstrated by the results of both the tests. The most significant result of this experiment was that pupils who were taught to generalize addition facts not only transferred their training to problem situations but demonstrated superior proficiency in computation exercises.

Schoaf[11] also determined the effectiveness of generalization training in mathematics. He was especially interested in knowing if it was possible to improve the generalization ability (mathematical and nonmathematical) of students in a ninth-grade algebra class. For experimental subjects he used ninth-grade algebra pupils in the Ohio State University School. As a basis of comparison he used comparable algebra classes in the Columbus, Ohio, public schools. The latter students were taught by conventional methods. The course materials used with the experimental group were chosen for their value in illustrating principles. They included numbers and operations, graphs and formulas, equations, problem solving, proportions, and certain indirect measures. An aptitude

[10] C. L. Thiele, "Contribution of Generalizations to the Learning of Addition Facts," *Teachers College Contribution to Education,* No. 763 (1938).

[11] Oscar Schoaf, "Student Discovery of Algebraic Principles as a Means of Developing Ability to Generalize," *The Mathematics Teacher,* 48 (1955), 324–327.

test and a generalization test were given to the experimental group at the beginning of the study. The generalization test was given a second time to the experimental group at the conclusion of the study. In addition, two achievement tests were given at the end of the study to both the experimental group and the public school classes. Pupils who were taught to generalize their training made marked improvement during the year. At the same time, their mastery of algebraic concepts, as shown by the achievement tests, was equal to or above that of the public school classes. Schoaf believes the experiment demonstrated that by purposeful effort algebra can be used as a means of developing generalizing ability not only in mathematics but in nonmathematical situations.

Capoferi[12] designed an instructional program to correlate the teaching of mathematics with science. Two groups of ninth-grade students in the Tappan Junior High School (Detroit, Michigan) were selected for the experiment, which continued for a semester. Each of the two groups was taught mathematics and science; one instructor taught mathematics to one group and science to the other; another instructor followed the opposite procedure. The two instructional programs were correlated to emphasize the scientific application of mathematical concepts and the explanation of science by mathematical principles. Although this study was planned mainly as a demonstration and not as a refined experiment, the results indicated that mathematics can be used to strengthen the science program. The approach also made the students interested in both mathematics and science.

These studies in mathematics are examples of efforts to achieve transfer by use of certain instructional materials, and they all emphasize generalization of training. In the study by Thiele, pupils transferred their training in addition facts to problem solving in arithmetic. In Schoaf's study, training in algebra was transferred to nonmathematical as well as mathematical situations. In Capoferi's study, mathematical principles were applied to science and science principles were also applied to mathematics.

science

Transfer studies in the sciences have been concerned mainly with the ability to recognize principles and the ability to apply principles in new situations. The first of these abilities is relatively easy to develop; the second is more difficult. In testing situations, the learner is generally expected to state what the effect of certain principles will be and to give reasons to support his decision.

Using tenth-grade biology and chemistry students, Owens[13] designed

[12] Alfred Capoferi, "How Can a Junior High School Mathematics Teacher Strengthen the Science Course?" *School Science and Mathematics,* 56 (1956), 233–236.

[13] J. Harold Owens, "The Ability to Recognize and Apply Scientific Principles in New Situations," *Science Education* 35 (1951), 207–213.

an experiment with two objectives: (1) to study the relationship between ability to recognize scientific principles and ability to apply them in problem situations and (2) to determine the effect of directed instruction on the ability to apply scientific principles to new situations. Ten principles were selected, an example being: "Matter and energy can be transformed, but they cannot be created." Students in the experimental classes were encouraged to identify principles in their readings and to discover situations in which the principles were applicable. All students demonstrated greater ability in recognizing principles than they did in applying them. Also, students who had been taught to apply principles made higher scores on an application test than did students who had not been taught to apply principles.

Babitz and Keys[14] were also interested in studying the effect of direct instruction on the ability to apply principles. They used for their subjects high school students who were enrolled in second-semester chemistry. In the experimental classes, the instruction consisted of exercises that required the student to give examples to illustrate principles. The control groups studied according to conventional practice, with only normal emphasis being placed on such principles as arose in the course. Although this experiment was limited to twelve class periods, the groups receiving special instruction in application of principles were uniformly superior to the control groups, as evidenced by the results of tests designed to measure application. The most obvious conclusion one can draw from this study as well as from the study by Owens is that efficiency in applying principles depends on special training.

Some evidence indicates, however, that students with considerable training in the sciences may have some advantage over students in certain other fields when it comes to applying knowledge. In a series of investigations, Mudge[15] determined, among other things, that a year of high school chemistry produces the ability to apply knowledge to the solution of everyday problems, especially problems of a chemical nature, and enables one to understand popular scientific writing. The experimental groups consisted of tenth-, eleventh-, and twelfth-grade students who were beginning their work in the regular chemistry course; the control groups consisted of comparable students who took no chemistry. The experimental groups, which received only conventional training in chemistry during the school year, developed a uniform superiority over the control classes in ability to understand popular scientific materials as well as in ability to apply knowledge to everyday problems based on chemistry. These abilities seemed to be due largely to chemistry instruction.

[14] M. Babitz and N. Keys, "Experiment in Teaching Pupils to Apply Scientific Principles," *Science Education*, 23 (1939), 367–370.

[15] Evelyn L. Mudge, "Transfer of Training in Chemistry" (unpublished Ed.D. thesis, Johns Hopkins University, 1935).

Smith and Glock's[16] study also indicated the spreading effect of science instruction. Their purpose was to determine the comparative efficiency of undergraduate college students, trained in biology and chemistry, in ability to apply psychological principles to subject matter other than their majors. These students were more efficient in applying psychological principles to sociological situations than were majors in certain other fields that emphasize comparable psychological knowledge.

The effectiveness of certain teaching methods in cultivating transfer ability in the sciences has also been tested. Boeck[17] compared the effectiveness of the inductive-deductive and deductive-descriptive methods of laboratory instruction in high school chemistry. The study was designed to determine the effectiveness of these two approaches as measured by four types of tests, one of which was the ability to apply principles to new situations. Two groups, selected at random from the University of Minnesota High School, were used in the experiment. To test the "generalizability" of the results, seven comparable groups of Minnesota high school students were taught by the same methods. Students who were encouraged to derive their own principles and generalizations during laboratory instruction, as implied by the inductive-deductive approach used by their teachers, made uniformly greater gains on the application-of-principles test than did students who used the deductive-descriptive method they had learned through the expository teaching they received. O'Connell[18] tested the effectiveness of inductive and deductive methods of laboratory instruction in high school chemistry. The author apparently did not devise a test specifically to measure transfer. The results, however, showed that classes taught by the inductive method were superior to those using the deductive approach, as measured by course examinations and by a test of ability to balance chemical equations.

Transfer studies in the sciences, like those in the other subject-matter fields, suggest that efficiency in applying knowledge to similar as well as dissimilar situations depends on direct, purposeful training. Some evidence indicates, however, that science students may be superior to those in certain fields in the ability to apply principles to nonscience situations. It would seem that teaching methods that require active involvement of the individual in his learning, as in laboratory exercises and experiments,

[16] Donald Smith and Marvin D. Glock, "Measuring Knowledge and Application: An Experimental Investigation," *Journal of Experimental Education,* 21 (1953), 327–331.

[17] Clarence Boeck, "The Inductive-Deductive Compared to the Deductive-Descriptive Approach to Laboratory Instruction in High School Chemistry," *Journal of Experimental Education,* 19 (1951), 247–253.

[18] Sister Ernestine Marie O'Connell, "The Comparison of Inductive and Deductive Methods of Teaching High School Chemistry" (Doctor's thesis, Boston University, 1958).

are effective means of ensuring transfer. Such activities undoubtedly bring into focus the application of principles to bodies of facts and skills. It is also relevant to note that high school physics students[19] rated laboratory experiments and demonstrations as having the highest interest and greatest value of any of their learning activities.

The transfer studies that have been reviewed differ somewhat from one subject-matter area to another; but all share common characteristics. The most evident conclusion one can draw is that experimental groups that have the benefit of special instruction make greater gains than do control groups that do not have special instruction. It would seem that almost any kind of relevant training tends to produce some transfer. Without special training, as in the control groups, transfer is usually positive but the amount may be slight. Negative transfer in classroom experiments is rarely found. Positive transfer in such experiments may be attributed in part to the tendency of special training to treat several different aspects of a subject or explore extensions of it. This situation does not exist in many laboratory studies in which inhibition as well as facilitation is observed.

conditions of transfer

One of the conditions that affects transfer is the obvious degree of similarity that exists between the tasks used for special training and the tasks employed to measure the effects of transfer. Another consists of the kinds of learning that are cultivated in the experimental groups as compared with those cultivated in the control groups. The thoroughness of learning, especially that of the experimental groups, is also a conditioning factor. Added to these is the nature of the tasks used to measure transfer and the time at which transfer is tested. What kinds of test are used to measure transfer? Is it measured immediately following a training period or is it delayed? And how do individuals differ in transfer ability? The extent to which these and other conditions are defined and controlled cannot be determined readily from the reports of transfer studies in school situations.

similarity of tasks

The greatest amount of transfer occurs when old learning and new problem situations have common or similar elements. Suppes[20] tested transfer efficiency in situations that had varying degrees of similarity.

[19] Rebecca E. Andrews, "Some Methods of Instruction in High School Physics and Some Goals and Psychological Factors Relating to Them," *Science Education,* 48 (1964), 146–156.

[20] Patrick Suppes, "Modern Learning Theory and the Elementary School Curriculum," *American Educational Research Journal,* 1 (1964), 79–94.

The experimental design provided for the classification of pairs or sets of members in four mutually exclusive ways as follows:

> The first possibility is that the two sets are identical in terms of their members and in terms of the order assigned to these members.
>
> The second possibility is that two sets are identical in the sense of having the same members, but the members are not given in the same order. For example, the set consisting of the numbers 1 and 2 is identical in this sense to the set consisting of 2 and 1.
>
> The third possibility is that the two sets are equivalent, but not identical; that is, they have the same number of elements, but the elements are different. For example, the set consisting of 1 and 2 is equivalent but not identical to the set consisting of 3 and 4.
>
> The fourth and final possibility is that the two sets are not equivalent; that is, they do not have the same number of elements.

These four possibilities were regarded as subconcepts when the learning of more general concepts was analyzed. In Suppes' experiments, one group of first-grade children was given 56 trials on identity of ordered sets and then was given 56 trials on identity of sets with no concern for ordering. Another comparable group of first-grade children was given 56 trials on identity of *unordered* sets. The progress of the children who began the experiment on *identity* of sets was compared with the progress of children who practiced *identity of sets* after identity of *ordered sets,* and the degree of positive or negative transfer was determined. When the different categorized pairs are *identical* but not in the same order, the results indicated that two different responses are required in passing from *identity of ordered sets* to identity of *unordered sets.* Under these conditions there was clear evidence of negative transfer. On the other hand, there was evidence of slight positive transfer when the remaining categories required identity of ordered sets, equivalence of sets, and nonequivalence of sets.

The findings of this experiment illustrate trends that are noted in laboratory studies.[21] A response transfers from one situation to another because of the similarity of the situations. When the same responses are required in two similar situations, transfer is positive. On the other hand, if the two situations are similar but require *different responses,* the transfer is negative. This situation is illustrated by Figure 13, which shows that as the present stimulus situation becomes less and less similar to the old situation, the amount of positive transfer declines.

Inhibition may also occur when the learner studies two closely related topics at or near the same time, especially if he is a beginner and knows very little about either topic. Entwisle and Huggins,[22] for example, obtained negative transfer, both proactive and retroactive effects, when

[21] S. A. Mednick (1).

[22] Doris Entwisle and W. H. Huggins, "Interference in Meaningful Material," *Journal of Educational Psychology,* 55 (1964), 75–78.

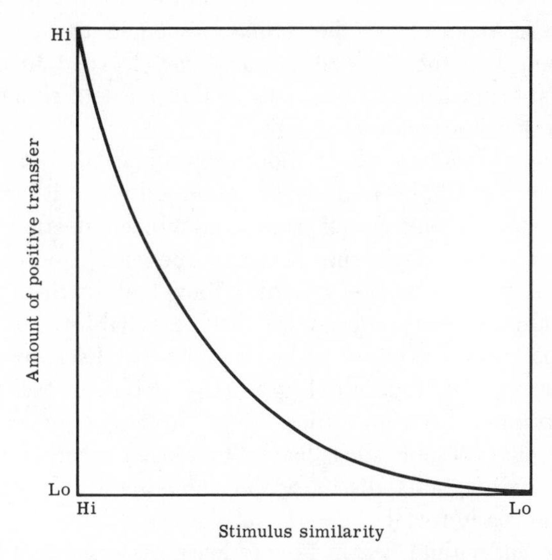

Figure 13. A typical stimulus generalization gradient. From Mednick.

they observed beginning engineering students who studied dual topics that covered the principal subject matter of circuit theory.

learning techniques

An important characteristic of learning is that it helps itself along. As a result of learning, the individual acquires techniques that assist him in learning new tasks. In developing such techniques, he "learns how to learn."

Studies based on animals and human beings demonstrate the effect modes of attack have on learning how to learn. Probably the best known of the studies that use animals as subjects are those conducted by Harlow.[23] In his experiments, monkeys were presented with a series of discrimination tasks, each using two blocks. The two blocks were in some way distinguishable from one another: either in quality (one being black, the other white), in shape (one cylindrical, the other conical), or in some other manner. On each trial in a series of learning activities, the monkeys were permitted to look under only one block. A reward, such as a raisin, was hidden under one of them. If during the first trial a monkey did not find a raisin after he had looked under the white block, he would have reacted intelligently if during the second trial he looked under the black one. During the initial stages of practice, the success of the monkeys could be accounted for by the laws of chance. But as they gained more experience with the test series, they became increasingly proficient and

[23] Harry F. Harlow, "Learning How to Learn from the Formation of Learning Sets," *Psychological Review,* 56 (1949), 51–65.

eventually attained more than 90 percent accuracy on the second trial. As a result of these experiences, the monkeys seemed to develop general habits in response to the total situations. They learned to differentiate between relevant and irrelevant aspects of the problem situations and to adjust their modes of attack accordingly.

Human beings obviously profit more from their learning experience than do animals; but similar findings are obtained with either as subjects. Ward[24] determined the number of trials that subjects needed before they were able to learn the relationship between one list of nonsense syllables and previous lists of nonsense syllables they had learned. His results showed that almost every succeeding list of syllables was learned in fewer trials than were required to learn preceding lists. In this type of learning situation, the individual gradually acquires techniques that facilitate his progress. Among other things, he becomes accustomed to the timing of the presentations, learns to associate the syllables with commonplace words, and discovers the advantage of some plan of organization for ready recall.

Although the individual "learns how to learn" as a result of his learning experience, instruction in study methods is needed. The learner's independent methods may be characterized by random effort and uneconomical procedures. Special how-to-study[25] courses are generally helpful but are not substitutes for the guidance that may be incorporated into particular courses of instruction. Study techniques that have wide applicability include a problem-solving attitude, an ability to identify the main points in an assignment, an ability to outline and organize learning materials, and an ability to locate and use sources of information. These are strengthened by continued use and provide an advantage in studying any subject matter.

kinds of learning

A student may develop a high degree of ability in mere recall without acquiring facility in application, even when he studies the same material. O'Donnell's[26] study showed a low relationship between knowledge of grammatical structure and its use in English compositions. Horrocks[27]

[24] L. B. Ward, *Psychological Monograph,* 49, No. 220 (1937).

[25] Louis T. DiLorenzo, "The Discriminating Effect of a College How-to-Study Course," *Journal of Educational Research,* 57 (1964), 472–473. See also Doris R. Entwisle, "Evaluations of Study Skills Courses: A Review," *Journal of Educational Research,* 53 (1960), 244–251. This review shows that study-skills courses are usually followed by improvement. Gains noted, however, are not necessarily related either to the content or to the duration of courses.

[26] Roy C. O'Donnell (5).

[27] J. E. Horrocks, "The Relationships between Knowledge of Human Development and the Use of Such Knowledge," *Journal of Applied Psychology,* 30 (1946), 501–507.

obtained low coefficients of correlation between knowledge of human growth and its application. Novak's[28] data suggest that problem-solving ability may be relatively distinct from the ability to recall facts or principles. It should be noted, however, that such studies are generally based on conventional teaching practice in which little effort may have been made to emphasize application of knowledge.

Bridging the gap between knowledge and its application depends upon the extent to which the individual generalizes and applies learning materials during his training. Lawrence[29] tested the effectiveness of understanding principles as compared with knowing mechanics. Two comparable groups made simulated radar sightings on a target. The members of one group were informed only of the correct mechanical responses on the various trials. Those of the other groups were asked to explain on a chart the reasons for their corrections on the target. The members of the latter group were also given instructions as to *why* they were asked to make the changes that were indicated. This group made significantly superior gains over the group whose instructions were limited to the mechanics of performing the task. Parker and Fleshman[30] also found that skill learning was facilitated when subjects were given detailed knowledge of what they were doing and *why*. Duncan[31] was interested in discovering the reasons why certain groups, in learning a motor task while using an apparatus, made greater improvement than did another group that did not use the apparatus. His results indicate that the factor having the greatest effect on performance in related but different tasks was a combination of "generalization of responses" and "learning how to learn."

The learner transfers when he reaches the point of generalizing information and making applications to specific situations. He transfers, for example, when he generalizes certain number combinations in arithmetic. When a child learns to add 2 and 3 plus 4 and gets 9 as the sum, it can be assumed he has mastered more than the single operation he has applied to these particular numbers. By performing similar exercises, he gradually recognizes numbers as means of generalizing about quantity. He also discovers that the arithmetical relationship between the numbers is equally applicable whether he is computing a sum of people or blocks of wood.

[28] Joseph D. Novak, "An Approach to the Interpretation and Measurement of Problem-Solving Ability," *Science Education*, 45 (1961), 122–131.

[29] Douglas Lawrence, "Evaluation of Training and Transfer Programs in Terms of Efficiency Measures," *Journal of Psychology*, 38 (1954), 367–382.

[30] J. F. Parker and E. A. Fleshman, "Use of Analytical Information Concerning Task Requirements to Increase the Effectiveness of Skill Training, *Journal of Applied Psychology*, 45 (1961), 295–302.

[31] Carl P. Duncan, "Transfer of Motor Learning as a Function of First-Task Learning and Intergroup Similarity," *Journal of Experimental Psychology*, 45 (1953), 1–11.

individual differences

Some individuals are capable of readily perceiving relationships and applications in learning materials; others can recognize only evident relationships and applications of knowledge. In general the greatest amount of transfer is concomitant with superior intelligence. In Owens[32] study, students in the upper ability levels made higher scores on tests of ability to recognize and apply principles than did students in the lower ability levels. Porter and Anderson[33] found that ability to understand and apply the scientific method in chemical situations was more closely related to intelligence *per se* than to any of the other abilities measured by their tests of chemistry attainment. Trow[34] believes that one of the most consistent conclusions to be drawn from investigations made over the years is that transfer is positively related to ability and that the results formerly attributed to the effects of formal discipline were due mainly to genetic factors.

conclusions and implications

Transfer is a process of acquiring ideas, information, attitudes, or skills in one situation and using the results of this training in other situations. Specifically, it is the application of one's learning in particular situations; generally, it is the application of education in the solution of life problems. Transfer is essentially a process of perceiving relationships and making applications. It may take place while one studies a particular unit of subject matter; or it may occur later when the learner attempts to generalize and apply his knowledge to other units of the same course, to subject matter of different courses or fields, or to life problems.

1. *All subjects possess transfer potentialities.* The need for applying knowledge and solving problems places a motivating force behind every subject and stresses the importance of transfer as a learning objective. This objective is achieved when time and effort are devoted to its attainment and is measured in tests of accomplishment. Each subject possesses intrinsic values which may be transferred to other subjects or to life situations. For this reason every subject contains within itself a means for the discovery of situations in which to apply its particular elements of knowledge. One basic subject differs very little from another in transfer possibilities; transfer is not determined by subject matter but by the method of instruction and the situation in which it is developed.

[32] J. Harold Owens (13).

[33] Marjorie Porter and Kenneth E. Anderson, "A Study of the Relationship of Specified Abilities in Chemistry and to Each Other," *Science Education,* 43 (1958), 12–19.

[34] W. C. Trow, "The Problem of Transfer Then and Now," *Phi Delta Kappan,* 40 (1958), 68–71.

2. *Transfer occurs at an advanced stage of learning.* Two common practices in teaching situations tend to retard transfer. One is the practice of stressing the *who, what, when,* and *where*—fundamental, though low levels of learning—that are most readily observed and measured in tests that emphasize recall. When these fundamentals are stressed, other kinds of learning, such as drawing generalizations, interpreting data, applying principles, and solving problems, may be only slightly recognized or overlooked entirely. The other, closely associated with the first, is the practice of covering large amounts of subject matter within a limited time, thus unintentionally emphasizing the memorization kinds of learning.

Rapid coverage of subject matter, with limited opportunity for comprehensive treatment of topics, and memorization methods are deterrents to transfer. At one stage in his learning, the individual may be able to recall given material but with little understanding. At another, he may assimilate this material and demonstrate understanding of it. This latter kind of learning is the minimum acceptable requirement for establishing a foundation in any subject; but it does not ensure transfer. Time and effort are needed to extend one's learning beyond the stage of understanding learning materials or of developing certain skills. Opportunity is needed to study the varied aspects of significant topics, to search for causes underlying principles, and to make applications[35] to problems. This activity of searching for relationships among materials and of applying principles is a necessary part of the comprehensive treatment of a topic by the teacher and is equally necessary to thorough learning by the student.

3. *Certain experimental courses of instruction may provide new clues to the transfer problem.* In certain experimental courses of instruction the tendency is to lead the student through the stages of thinking characteristic of mature scholars. This procedure is almost antithetical to the psychological approach in which effort is made first to present information with which the learner is familiar and second to advance from the known to the unknown.

An example is the Illinois Mathematics Program,[36] planned for high school students, that is designed to develop the students' understanding of the nature of mathematics. Theory forms the basis for the introduction

[35] Claude J. Bartlett and Royce R. Ronning, "A Study of Evaluation Techniques with Special Reference to Application of Knowledge," *Journal of Educational Psychology,* 51 (1960), 162–168. After experimenting with various types of test for measuring outcomes in educational psychology, these authors concluded that the case study is best. The case study establishes the situation definitely; it also provides information on which to base applications.

[36] L. J. Cronbach, "Psychological Issues Pertinent to Recent American Curriculum Reforms" in *Child and Education* (Proceedings of the XIV International Congress of Applied Psychology [Munksgaard, Copenhagen, Denmark, 1962]).

of topics, the emphasis being placed on the rationale of mathematics rather than on its techniques. Instead of requiring the student to define a parallelogram and indicate its properties, he is asked, for example, to consider what kinds of quadrilaterals have diagonals that bisect each other. The student studies a series of problems by his own methods and is encouraged to develop for himself an understanding of the principles and theories underlying solutions. Teachers of this program believe that the kinds of topics selected for study are of minor significance. Of greater importance is the insight the students gain into the nature of mathematical principles.

A similar program is a physics course sponsored by the Massachusetts Institute of Technology.[37] The student studies problems that confront the physicist and reviews significant research reports related to such problems. The problems are selected to illustrate theoretical explanations of the universe. Stress is placed on the tools of the field and not on its products. Teachers of this course, like teachers participating in the Illinois program, make a distinction between meaningfulness and usefulness. Meaningfulness is achieved when the student is able to perceive, for example, the relationship between a formula and its use in a system of thought.

A major purpose of these instructional programs obviously is to develop the ability to perceive relationships between a body of facts and skills and the theories in which they operate. Transfer is made within the theoretical system of the field, and no effort is made to apply principles to practical problems. These programs are conspicuous because of the absence of any conventional organization of learning materials by the teacher and because of the emphasis placed on independent discovery by the student. It should be noted, however, that students enrolled in these programs are intellectually superior and probably possess special aptitudes in mathematics and physics.

4. *Transfer possibilities present a continuing challenge.* The varying stages in development of the ability to perceive relationships and make applications are shown in Figure 14.

First, there is the ability to perceive relationships among the various units or topics within the same course or subject. Recognition of existing relationships can be assured if either the textbooks or the course outlines are carefully planned. They may not be recognized, however, if the learner is not stimulated to regard his material as a continuing body of related subject matter.

Second, there is the ability to recognize relationships between one subject and another within the same area. It can be assumed, for example, that the psychology student perceives relationships between a course in general psychology and other subjects within his field.

[37] L. J. Cronbach (36).

Third, there is the ability to discern relationships between one field and others within the area of related subjects or disciplines. The advanced psychology student is encouraged to perceive the relationship between his field and others within the broad area of behavioral sciences.

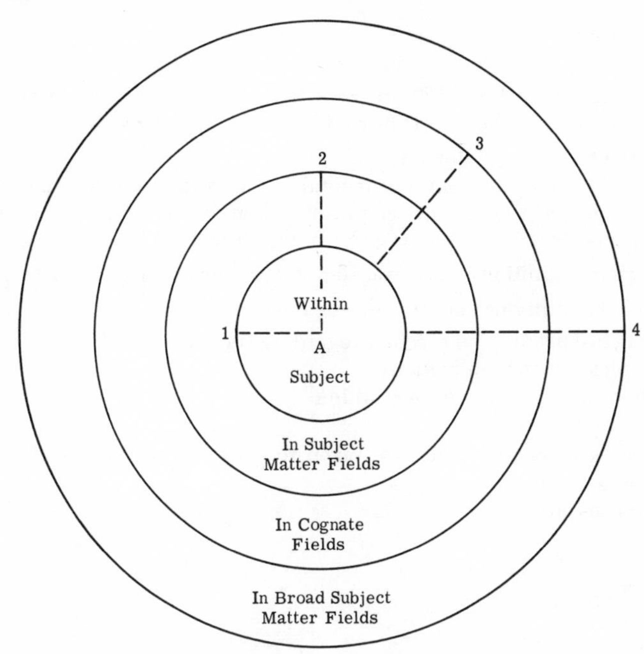

Figure 14. Expansion of ability to perceive relationships and apply knowledge.

Fourth, there is the ability to identify relationships among broad areas of subject matter such as the social sciences, biological sciences, and humanities. At this point, it is conceivable that one might organize major areas of knowledge into a unified whole and disregard subject-matter distinctions.

The first level of ability is relatively easy to achieve; the others are increasingly difficult and complex. The fourth level is so difficult that it can be achieved by only a few scholars who have devoted a lifetime of study in search for interrelationships of knowledge.

Plans for stimulating transfer on advanced educational levels sometimes include survey courses wherein effort is made to review and synthesize the contributions of various subjects or fields. These courses may be offered during the student's initial stages of concentration in an area of subject matter in order to provide an overview; or they may be scheduled toward the end of his program as a means of integrating his knowledge and preparing him for comprehensive examinations. Such plans, however, do not substitute for the ability to recognize relationships and make applications the student should possess at the time he takes his courses and studies subjects.

study questions

1. How are transfer of training and retention related? Could there be transfer without retention of the effects of training in the specific sense?
2. Explain the following statement:
   "The transfer effective from any mental function to any other mental function, or from one school subject to any other school subject, may be substantially modified by conscious effort in that direction."
3. Under what conditions may transfer occur during the learning process?
4. Under what conditions may transfer be delayed?
5. What conclusions may be reached regarding transference of:
   a. Principles and generalizations?
   b. Methods and techniques of learning?
   c. Attitudes and ideals?
6. What practical measures may be taken to prevent possible interference in:
   a. Learning situations?
   b. Testing situations?

part two

improvement of learning: search for favorable conditions

learning materials

5

The materials presented in Part One were concerned primarily with the descriptive aspects of learning, retention, and transfer. Little recognition was made of the conditions that affect their efficiency. What may be done to enhance these processes? What conditions contribute to efficient learning? To retention? And to transfer? Experimental work on this problem tends to emphasize the criteria of learning and retention; but transfer is equally important.

Through advanced preparation, some of the conditions for effective learning can be built into an instructional program. Other conditions must be provided during instruction. In either case, the greater the amount of deliberate planning the better will be the chance of success of a program.

organization of materials

Among the many advantages of organizing learning materials, two should be emphasized. One is that organization is inherent in the learning process itself; full understanding of learning materials cannot be achieved without organization. Learning materials also need to be organized so that there may be a continuing reference to the cultivation of abilities. Changes in the learner's abilities develop gradually and often slowly, sometimes requiring months or even years for a high state of attainment. Organization is the means by which the cumulative effect of learning activities is made possible.

When a course of instruction is organized effectively, it is possible for the learner to perceive relationships among the various units of subject matter. Also, as he advances from one unit to another, he can build a background that aids him in learning additional units. When materials are organized effectively, there is relationship among the units of work; they make sense and give evidence of some pattern.

Effective organization also enables the learner to view his materials both in prospect and retrospect and assures him a feeling of satisfaction upon completion of a course. Not only does it establish the main direction with appropriate signposts for guidance but it provides a basis for review and marks off the periods for measurement and evaluation.

some plans of organization

Plans of organization center on two divergent viewpoints. At one extreme is the logical emphasis; at the other, the psychological. Varying degrees between these extremes are observed in practice.

logical versus psychological emphasis

When the logical approach is used, systematic arrangement of learning material is established. Beginning with certain fundamental concepts and principles, materials are organized with increasing complexity and operational difficulty throughout a subject. Closely related information may be compressed into comprehensive units and organized according to a systematic plan that is based on order of difficulty, importance, natural consecutiveness, or chronological order. History organized as ancient, medieval, and modern is a classic example of this type of organization. The student who has devoted many years of study and research to history finds the logical approach meaningful.

In the psychological approach, effort is made to present information with which the individual is familiar first and then to advance from the known to the unknown. When new information is thus brought into relationship with the experience of the learner, he supplies it with meaning. The psychological plan of organization is designed to conform to his experience.

Organization of material from the standpoint of the learner may be characterized as "lifelike." On such a basis his activities begin with concrete experiences that are closely related to his needs. Visits to local manufacturing plants, observations of the operations of city government, or investigations of out-of-door life afford interesting experiences, extend his range of information, and stimulate his effort to acquire knowledge. He responds more readily to a program of "doing" than he does to a program of listening or reading.

During the early school years, the learner's range of experience is largely limited to concrete terms; his immediate present is more significant to him than is the past or future. As effort is made to establish contact with the child's world, the plan of organization becomes especially important. An effective plan provides a meaningful succession of topics and makes continual reference to the learner's experience and background. If it is necessary to pause during a logical unfolding of material to bring it within his comprehension, it should still be possible to return to the main highway without losing sight of the general direction.

A person organizing material for mature students may find it less necessary to digress among concrete experiences. For this group, however, a flexible plan is necessary so that topics at various points of a logical system can be reached by lateral branches that originate in the learner's background of experience and knowledge.

subject matter versus experience units

In planned courses of study and in textbooks, subject matter is frequently organized on the basis of units, homogeneous bodies of subject matter capable of standing alone meaningfully. Organization of material into units enables the learner to advance through a course by definite stages, to check progress at the completion of each unit, and to benefit by supplementary instruction suggested by evaluation of accomplishment.

By strict definition, a unit is a body of material with a beginning and ending point. It has come to mean more, however, than material organized comprehensively around topics. The unit approach often implies information to be collected, a problem to be solved, a decision to be reached, or a conclusion sought. Instead of passively absorbing the information of a social science unit, for example, students may engage in varied types of activity such as wide reading, discussion, library research, and visits to local museums. Their own experiences in home and community also make important contributions. Learning is active and purposeful.

Learning materials may be classified broadly into *subject-matter units* and *experience units.* In courses planned for high school and college students, a unit often means a major topic outlined in considerable detail. In United States history there may be a unit on the *Colonial Period;* in physics there may be a unit on electricity. Classification of material into comprehensive subject-matter units is characteristic of organization on advanced educational levels. Subject-matter units for mature students tend to stress abstract activities. Students may read extensively, discuss ideas in class, and study original sources. They frequently have a background of concrete experiences and do not need the realistic kinds of activity emphasized on lower educational levels.

Units frequently involve projects and group activities centered on a basic theme that represents some aspect of the learner's experience. For example, *The Transportation System* is a common experience associated with daily living. As the development of this topic proceeds, subtopics are proposed and studied. The outline of the experience unit is developed as learning proceeds.

Experience units may take various forms but have certain common provisions: (1) Effort is made to select significant topics within the experience of class members; (2) opportunity is afforded to work intensively on the various aspects of a subject; (3) emphasis is on doing, such as collecting information, working on problems, making reports in class, or participating in discussion; and (4) an attempt is made to reach a conclusion or to solve a problem. Pupils have the satisfaction of knowing they have accomplished their purpose.

Subject-matter units tend to stress outlines, books, and courses of study planned systematically in advance. Experience units, in contrast, tend to emphasize the reaction of students, their background, experiences and needs. The two major types of unit differ mainly in their emphasis. Those teaching at any educational level can make effective use of both organized subject matter and the learner's experience.

problems of organization

Preparation of learning materials requires consideration of a number of problems such as the amount of material to be used, the size of units, the degree of their organization, and the coordination between one unit and another.

large versus small amounts of material

The range and complexity of materials in most subject-matter fields suggest the importance of considering the advantage of selecting a few basic topics and exhausting their possibilities for learning instead of treating a large number less intensively. In courses with excessive materials, there is little time in which to vary responses sufficiently to ensure thorough learning. The learner cannot solve problems or think effectively without an adequate background of information. This information, however, must be interpreted if it is to contribute to orderly thinking. Coverage of large amounts of material without opportunity for their assimilation may easily result in the characteristic disadvantages of a crowded curriculum. Under such conditions, teaching effort, as well as learning effort, is thinly distributed. When we add to this situation the fact that the school organization may encourage rapid coverage of subject matter, there is the inevitable consequence of ineffective teaching and superficial learning.

small versus large units

Learning principles suggest that the large unit,[1] within limits, is superior to the small one. Where there are many small units, the learner tends to think of his material in parts rather than as wholes. In studying, he regards them as a series of unrelated and independent tasks and is likely to employ the memorization method. Where there are many small units, higher levels of learning are minimized.

A few large units, on the other hand, induce the learner to perceive relationships among the various elements of a topic or theme. He is stimulated to study his materials as wholes within which interrelationships are more readily evident. Large units encourage understanding and contribute to high retention.

materials organized in detail versus broad outline

The degree of organization may either aid or hinder learning. Here we are concerned with the problem of providing either too much or too little information in course outlines.

Where materials are organized in considerable detail, as may be done in a syllabus incorporating the various major and subordinate topics in subject-matter units, the learner tends to become engulfed by a mass of specific items. In studying, he may feel that each item of information is important and use the memorization method in the hope of meeting implied test requirements. Such detailed organization also reduces interest.

In contrast, where materials are organized in broad outline including only the major and significant topics in a course of instruction, the learner tends to become more actively involved. A broad outline encourages him to assist in supplying the relevant information. Such organization presents a challenge and heightens interest.

relationships between one unit and another

The organization of materials obviously requires provision for coordination among units. The materials of the first unit should provide a basis for the second, the first and second for the third, and so on throughout a course. Unless care is taken to ensure such relationship, the learner will experience difficulty in advancing from one unit to another; he may also regard units as a series of independent tasks.

[1] F. J. McGuigan, "Variations of Whole-Part Methods of Learning," *Journal of Educational Psychology*, 51 (1960), 213–216. McGuigan found that the larger the practice unit, the better the performance. This superiority is accounted for in part by the fact that it entails distributed practice.

Such continuing relationship should be recognized by planners of tests or other means of evaluation. Full understanding of the materials of a particular unit may not be possible until the learner has advanced to other related subject matter. Consequently, he may be expected to demonstrate varying degrees of proficiency as he progresses through a course of instruction; his performance may be at a low level of learning at one stage of his progress and at a high level at others. He could scarcely be expected to do more than acquire information when studying a new unit. As he continues study of other units, however, he gains additional insight and understanding, which result from further study of a subject.

Maintaining an active relationship between one unit and another is increasingly important as the learner nears the end of a course. Where the various units are coordinated, he is able to view his materials in retrospect and build up associations which aid him in understanding a course as a whole.

modes of presentation

Thorough mastery of learning material requires use of several modes of presentation. Textual modes include the kinds of words used and the length and balance of sentences. They also include devices such as generalizations at the beginning of paragraphs, followed by concrete illustrations, which in turn are followed by further generalizations. Other modes include charts, tables, graphs, and audio-visual materials. The need for varied media of presentation grows out of the limitation of words and abstractions to describe or explain.

Everyone would agree that learning is enhanced by direct experience. It would be valuable for the history student to visit historic landmarks, for the botany student to observe flora through field trips, for the mechanics student to assemble the parts of a motor, and for one in professional education to learn about schools and their management by actual experience. Such experiences, however, are not usually convenient or possible; substitutes are needed. Because of the extraordinary part played by seeing and hearing in the learning process, the discussion will be limited to the effectiveness of audio-visual materials.

The function of audio-visual materials is to make an appeal to those senses that can respond adequately. If the sound of a bird is to be presented, the most effective mode of presentation would be the bird itself while engaged in producing the sound. If this is not possible, some mechanical device may be used for its reproduction. It is difficult to describe color, smell, physical shape, sound, and motion by means of words. Few persons can resist the impulse to define a spiral by making motions with their hands. One can recognize the sound of a coyote upon hearing it and identify certain wild flowers by sight. These nonverbal evidences of knowledge suggest that seeing and hearing are more influential in forming initial impressions than is the printed page.

In appraising the effectiveness of audio-visual materials, investigators usually first measure their effect on immediate learning; the individual is given a test immediately following their presentation. The second step frequently consists of repeating the same test at a later date to measure the amount retained. Thus, the first testing is a measure of immediate learning; the second is a measure of retention.

An important problem in measuring *learning* and *retention* is the kind of test. The type most frequently employed consists of true-false or multiple-choice items stressing recall. Consequently, when an investigation shows the effects of a particular mode of presentation, the results are likely to be restricted to the amount of information. Does a particular aid assist the learner in understanding the material of a certain unit? Does it help him in making applications of the material? Does it affect his attitudes? Answers to such questions are needed before it is possible to evaluate the full effect of audio-visual materials on learning efficiency.

Educational and psychological journals are replete with research that is concerned with the different modes of presentation. The purpose of many studies is to compare the effectiveness of certain audio-visual materials with conventional methods. In some, effort is made to determine the effectiveness of one sense modality as compared with another. In still others, the reinforcing and combined effects of different modalities are tested.

audio-visual materials compared with conventional methods

The studies to be reviewed involve films, usually sound-motion pictures, and televised instruction.

films versus conventional methods

In research on films, the procedure may consist of determining their value in teaching certain topics or problems or an entire course of instruction. In either case, the results are generally compared with those achieved under conventional teaching conditions. A few typical studies will be reviewed.

Nelson[2] tested the effect of sound-motion pictures in teaching a unit on *sulphur* in high school chemistry. Two parallel groups were formed, one serving as the experimental group and the other as control. Two films,

[2] C. M. Nelson, "Effectiveness of Sound-Motion Pictures in Teaching a Unit on Sulphur in High School Chemistry," *School Science and Mathematics,* 52 (1952), 8–10.

shown twice each, were administered to the experimental group. The results were appraised by an achievement test given at the end of the course. This test was repeated unexpectedly five weeks later to measure retention. The film group made higher scores on the achievement tests given at the end of the course; but there was little difference between the film and non-film groups in retention. In Sakavitch's[3] study, films constituted the principal means of instruction for courses in chemistry and physics, a major purpose being to compare their retention value with conventional teaching methods. Standardized achievement tests were used in appraising the results. These tests were repeated seven and twelve months later to measure retention. For the seventh-month period, the conventional method was superior; for the twelve-month period, however, there was no difference in retention scores either for chemistry or physics.

In a study by Jenson and Romano,[4] the purpose was to determine whether pupils would learn and retain more science vocabulary when motion-picture films and projected still pictures were used than when taught by conventional methods. Subjects were 158 fifth-, sixth-, and seventh-grade science pupils, equated into experimental and control groups. The classes in each grade alternately became both experimental and control groups. For example, during the study of a particular unit, a class was shown films and projected still pictures; during the next unit, when it served as control, conventional methods were used. In both experimental and control groups, the teachers used the same outlines on science. Pupils using the motion pictures and projected still pictures made uniformly larger gains in vocabulary than did pupils who were used as control. Lower-ability pupils tended to profit more from the use of the materials than did pupils of higher ability. Retests after six months showed that pupils in every class in which films and projected pictures were used retained more than did pupils who did not use such aids. The decisive results of this experiment probably were due in some measure to the use of both projected still pictures and films in the experimental groups.

In a series of experiments, May and Lumsdaine[5] determined the effect of films when used under varying conditions. One group of experiments was concerned with the problem of determining the efficacy of films when attention of students was directed to their particular aspects. The techniques for directing attention included verbal instructions, pretest

[3] J. M. Sakavitch and others, "Retention Value of Filmed Science Courses," *Science Education*, 46 (1962), 22–27.

[4] P. J. Jenson and L. Romano, "Teaching with Films Increases Science Vocabulary," *The Nation's Schools*, 57 (1956), 98–102.

[5] Mark A. May and Arthur A. Lumsdaine, *Learning from Films* (New Haven, Connecticut: Yale University Press, 1958).

questions, and attention in relationship to a repeat-film showing. In one situation, the film consisted of a version of *David Copperfield—the Boy*. One group of high school students was told to concentrate attention on the characteristics of the principal characters of the story; another group was urged to give primary attention to the *plot* or sequence of events; and a third group was asked to give attention to the *setting*.

The results indicated that the amount learned can be appreciably increased by directing attention of students to various parts or aspects of a film prior to its showing. The means used for accomplishing this objective may be either oral or written instructions, pre-film test, or by attention to difficult questions before repeating the showing of a film.

In other experiments May and Lumsdaine used ninth- and tenth-grade classes in general biology, the topic for study being osmosis. The purpose was to determine the effect of films on learning by students who had had considerable instruction as compared with students who had had no formal instruction. The experimental group was thus composed of students who had had previous instruction on osmosis (the instructed group) and the control group was composed of students who had had no instruction (the uninstructed group).

The findings of this experiment are presented in Figure 15, which shows that the group that had had considerable instruction on osmosis learned considerably more from the films than did the inexperienced group in relationship to what each could have learned (i.e., relative to

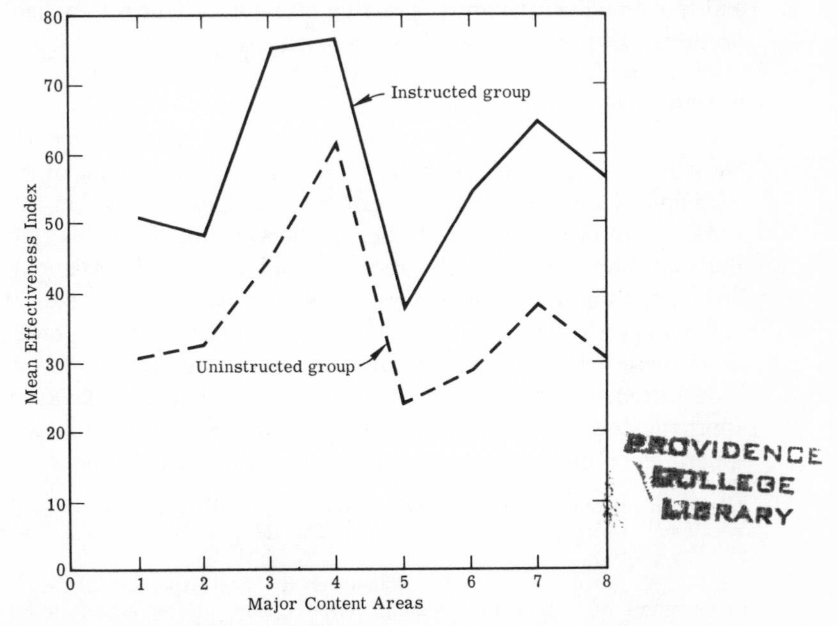

Figure 15. Results for instructed and uninstructed groups on eight content areas covered by film on Osmosis. Figure based on data obtained by May Lumsdaine (see note 5), p. 118.

the amount of material not initially known). And this finding is consistent for all of the eight subject-matter areas of osmosis. If other studies yield similar results, it would seem that students with limited backgrounds in given subjects are not likely to profit as much from films as will students who already possess considerable knowledge.

These studies do not afford a basis for definite conclusions; but they do indicate the kinds of results that may be expected when films and other aids are tested in typical school situations. Despite all of the variables that might influence the results, the studies demonstrate the effectiveness of audio-visual materials. Designing research on an either-or basis, however, where certain classes are subjected to one or another instructional medium, does not conform with typical classroom practice. In most teaching situations, audio-visual materials are used for certain purposes at various times—to supply significant information, to develop concepts, to illustrate skills, or to apply principles. They are used in conjunction with a variety of activities such as lectures, class reports, and demonstrations, thus becoming a part of a total learning situation.

Bentley's[6] experiments involving audio-visual aids in teaching vocational agriculture demonstrate the need for careful planning. His results showed that audio-visual materials were relatively ineffective in situations in which students used reference materials containing pictures and illustrations similar to those used in the special aids. On the other hand, audio-visual materials were effective in learning situations when they assisted students in acquiring related visual experiences they had not had or did not secure through reference materials.

television versus conventional methods

Educators have been especially interested in determining whether or not it is possible to achieve through television certain goals of instruction with no threat to the assumed merits of small class instruction.

As a part of a series of studies in the Cincinnati schools, Jacobs and Bollenbacher[7] compared the results of televised and classroom instruction in sixth-grade science classes. The learning material consisted of a unit on energy. The subjects were twelve classes of sixth-grade science, six of these being used as experimental groups and the others as control. These groups were used because they represented students who had approximately equal abilities and amounts of science knowledge. The experimental groups were taught by television three afternoons per week,

[6] Ralph R. Bentley, "Experimental Studies of the Use of Audio-Visual Aids in Vocational Agriculture," *Journal of Experimental Education,* 24 (1955–56), 211–220.

[7] James N. Jacobs and J. K. Bollenbacher, "An Experimental Study of the Effectiveness of Television Teaching versus Classroom Instruction in Sixth-Grade Science in the Cincinnati Public Schools," *Journal of Educational Research,* 52 (1959).

and instruction continued eight weeks from a local TV station. The achievement of pupils working under these differing conditions was measured by tests prepared by the research director in cooperation with sixth-grade science teachers not participating in the experiment.

The achievement tests indicated that the experimental and control classes were similar in terms of average gains. But when the results were analyzed, higher-ability pupils who had received instruction by television made significantly larger scores than did students taught by classroom methods. Pupils in the lower ability levels of the control groups achieved significantly more than did comparable students who were taught in the TV classes. For pupils in the middle ranges of ability, those taught by TV and those taught by classroom methods achieved approximately the same amount.

The investigations by Jacobs and Bollenbacher[8] included a comparison of televised instruction with conventional methods in teaching high school biology. A full-year course in biology was televised from a Cincinnati TV station. One teacher and four biology classes in each of three types of schools participated. In each school, two control classes were taught biology in the conventional manner, and two experimental classes alternated television and laboratory instruction during the same class period. A proctor was assigned to the viewing classes; the regular classroom teacher supervised the laboratory group. Appraisal of the television and non-television groups was made on the basis of standardized knowledge about science and scientists and various ratings by students. The results, like those for the sixth-grade science experiment, indicated that the televised instruction was more effective than was instruction by conventional methods for superior students. Such methods were not so effective for students of average and below average ability.

The Cincinnati studies also included provisions for checking retention of learning for certain groups that had been taught by television. Jacobs and Bollenbacher[9] were interested in determining if there would be significant differences in the amount of biology retained by students taught by television and students taught in the conventional manner. Tests repeated 22 months later showed that television instruction did not result in greater retention. Students taught by conventional methods, however, seemed to have had greater potential for applying knowledge than had students taught by television. Such students undoubtedly profited by opportunities for questions and discussion.

The effectiveness of televised instruction in Cincinnati seemed to be a

[8] James N. Jacobs and J. K. Bollenbacher, "An Experimental Study in Teaching High School Biology by Television in the Cincinnati Public Schools," *Science Education*, 43 (1959), 399–405.

[9] J. N. Jacobs and J. K. Bollenbacher, "Retention of Subject Matter in Televised Biology," *Audio-Visual Communications Review*, 8 (1960), 275–280.

function of the ability level at which instruction was adapted, the pace with which it was presented, and the amount of material that was taught.

In a large-scale investigation involving many different college classes and various types of subject matter, Siegel and Macomber[10] compared televised instruction with conventional teaching methods. The experimental groups were taught either as large classes—primarily lectures—or by means of closed-circuit television. The control groups were taught by conventional procedures. The results showed that the experimental and control classes were approximately equal in the amount of information they acquired. Student ratings of the instructors were not adversely affected by television. Their ratings of the courses, however, were less favorable in both TV and large lecture classes than they were in small sections used as control. Another extensive investigation[11] involved ninth-grade science students in the Albuquerque public schools. These students studied science either by television (the experimental group) or in the conventional manner (the control group). Standardized achievement tests were used to measure accomplishment. In this study, the experimental groups learned more than did the group used as control. The control groups, however, revealed consistently more favorable attitudes toward science, the method of instruction, and the teacher than did the experimental groups.

Televised instruction obviously would be more satisfying, as well as more effective, in studying certain types of subject matter. Moskowitz[12] determined the effectiveness of TV with respect to the attitudes of several groups of children who were studying foreign languages. The TV group consisted of fifth-grade children who studied French three times a week by TV together with a follow-up session with the classroom teacher. Two language groups within the same school were sixth graders who took French by TV and Spanish with a live teacher. A third nonlanguage group contained fifth- and sixth-grade classes in different schools in which no foreign language was studied. Questionnaires were administered to these groups to determine their attitudes toward foreign language. The responses indicated that in a foreign language, which requires verbal participation on the part of the pupil and interaction with the teacher, TV may not be as suitable as it is in certain other areas.

[10] Laurence Siegel and F. G. Macomber, "Comparative Effectiveness of Televised and Large Classes and of Small Sections," *Journal of Educational Psychology,* 48 (1957), 371–382.

[11] A. H. Rottman and G. L. Kapers, "The Effectiveness of Television Instruction in Science," *The New Mexico Society for Study of Educational Research Bulletin* (1963), 2–6.

[12] Gertrude Moskowitz, "Television versus Classroom Instruction in Foreign Language: A Study of Elementary School Children's Attitudes," *Journal of Experimental Education,* 33 (1964), 175–181.

In view of the extraordinary amount of research on television, it is pertinent to ask what general conclusions may be drawn about its actual and potential effectiveness. From the large amount of evidence available, there can be no doubt that television can teach. Failure to establish it as a definitely superior medium of instruction is due to many factors. Tanner[13] believes that insufficient attention has been given to the visual aspects of television, the tendency being to emphasize modes of presentation similar to those of conventional teaching methods. After reviewing the research conducted under the National Defense Act, Norberg[14] concludes that the real problem is to determine what types of teaching aids are most effective for learners at different ability levels and under what conditions they should be used, particularly with respect to the kinds of ability or outcomes to be produced, and to the relationships the aids have to other factors including the teacher.

effectiveness of different sense modalities

The effectiveness of different sense modalities in learning has long been a controversial subject, especially with respect to seeing as opposed to hearing. Interest has centered mainly on these two sense modalities when considered separately and together.

one sense modality versus another

Corey[15] tested the effectiveness of reading and lecture modes of presentation, using university students as subjects. One group heard a 2,500-word lecture; another group read the same material, achievement being measured by an objective test. The relationship was closer between scores on tests of material read and standardized test results for reading, vocabulary, and intelligence than for material heard in lecture. Students in the highest quarter on intelligence tests tended to do better on reading than they did on the lecture mode of presentation. Marr and Wakeley[16] performed a study to determine whether lectures or reading would make any difference in student achievement. The lecture and reading materials consisted of the same subject matter, and the students were not informed

[13] Daniel Tanner, "Television and Learning," *Teachers College Record,* 65 (1963), 243–249.

[14] Kenneth D. Norberg, *Research Abstracts and Analytic Review* (Washington: U.S. Office of Education, 1961). See also *Educational Television: The Next Ten Years* (Stanford, California: Stanford University, The Institute for Communications Research, 1962). This is a series of papers which attempts to evaluate the contributions of audio-visual materials and to indicate probable future developments.

[15] S. M. Corey, "Learning from Lecture versus Learning from Reading," *Journal of Educational Psychology,* 25 (1934) 459–470.

[16] P. Marr and W. Wakeley, "The Contribution of the Lecture to College Teaching," *Journal of Educational Research,* 51 (1960).

that an experiment was being performed. One group heard the lectures as given by the instructors while another group read the assignments only. The differences between the lecture and reading groups were statistically significant, the students in the lecture group receiving higher scores. Kreitlow[17] also compared the effectiveness of the lecture with a number of other media, such as bulletins and television, in presenting a series of research reports regarding school organization. The procedure consisted of presenting these reports by various media to groups of homemaking leaders, teachers, and college students and then measuring the results by an information check list. A comparison of the results on the information check list for all groups showed that the participants instructed by lectures gained more knowledge than did participants who received the research results by other ways. It seems likely in this study, as well as in the study by Marr and Wakeley, that the materials were presented more simply by lectures then by other media. Also, the students probably were better able to "spot" items regarded by instructors as important and thereby gain an advantage on the instruments used for appraisal.

Many studies indicate that reading comprehension is different from hearing comprehension. They also suggest that reading comprehension may be superior to hearing comprehension. This superiority, however, would be influenced by such factors as the learner's ability and the difficulty of the material. Students in the lower ability levels probably would do better when presented materials through lectures. Materials presented in lectures, regardless of the learner's ability, should be less difficult than those presented by the printed page if they are to be understood with equal effectiveness.

sense modalities used together or singly

The belief is widely held that more information is learned when auditory and visual modalities are used together than when one of these is employed alone. The assumption is that one modality supplements the other, thus ensuring more thorough learning and higher retention.

Craig[18] compared the effect of the silent and sound versions of the same film. In this study, two contrasting situations were presented. In one, both visual and auditory modes of presentation were used simultaneously; in the other, the presentation was limited to the visual mode of presentation. Two groups of first-year students in a modern secondary school (England) were used as subjects. The effectiveness of the two

[17] B. W. Kreitlow and others, "Effectiveness of Lecture, Bulletins, Films and Television in Adult Settings," *Adult Education,* 12 (1962), 142–152.

[18] Gordon Q. Craig, "A Comparison between Sound and Silent Films in Teaching," *British Journal of Educational Psychology,* 26 (1956), 202–206.

kinds of film presentation was measured by tests given immediately following a showing and four weeks later.

On tests given immediately, the differences in favor of the silent presentation were marked and statistically significant. On tests given four weeks later (delayed recall) similar differences were noted, these again being in favor of the silent presentation. In view of the unexpected results of this experiment, students participating as subjects were asked to suggest explanations. Typical comments were: "It was difficult to watch the film and listen to the sound at the same time." "The sound film was difficult to understand." "The silent film seemed to go more slowly."

In a study by Van Mondfrans,[19] nonsense syllables and words were presented either by the visual mode of presentation only, auditory mode only, or through both of these modalities. The task consisted of a serial learning situation and employed different speeds of presentation. The syllables and words were presented sequentially, and at the end of each presentation the subject was required to list all those he could recall. In general, the audio-visual modes showed no advantage over auditory or visual modes of presentation. When the rate of presentation was considered, however, the faster speed tended to become a deterrent to the efficiency of the audio-visual form of presentation, indicating that two modalities interfered with each other when used together. Travers and Jester[20] tested the hypothesis that if a student is given opportunity to both hear and see a passage of material, he will choose the sense modality more effective for him. The task consisted of reading test passages. They were presented at varying speeds through hearing alone, through seeing alone, and through both seeing and hearing. When the materials were presented at high speeds, many students attempted to block one mode of presentation by closing their eyes or covering their ears. They obviously inhibited the mode of presentation which was less efficient for them.

The results of these studies support the belief of some psychologists, notably Broadbent,[21] that the individual's perception process tends to operate "as a single-channel system having limited storage capacity," and is capable of responding efficiently through only one sense modality at a

[19] A. P. Van Mondfrans, "An Investigation of the Interaction between the Level of Meaningfulness and Redundancy in the Content of the Stimulus Material and the Mode of Presentation of the Stimulus Material" (unpublished master's thesis, University of Utah, 1963). See also P. Pimsleur and others, "Further Study of the Transfer of Verbal Materials across Sense Modalities," *Journal of Educational Psychology*, 55 (1964), 96–102.

[20] R. W. M. Travers, "Transmission of Information to Human Receivers," *Educational Psychology*, Vol. 2, No. 1 (1964).

[21] D. E. Broadbent, *Perception and Communication* (New York: Pergamon Press, 1958).

given time. The effect of two modalities, as in hearing and seeing, depends on the rate at which presentations are made. Where information is presented at a low rate of speed, it is possible for the individual to use different modalities. On the other hand, where the rate of presentation is high, the individual tends to switch from one modality to another. This switching process may easily interfere with the amount of information that may be learned. In one study,[22] the rate of loss in learning was found to be related directly to the frequency with which such switching occurred.

need for several modes of presentation

The need for several modes of presentation derives from the fact that different sense modalities produce different results. Many studies have shown that effects of different modes of presentation are not closely related. Harris and Buenger,[23] for example, found that scores on tests based on lectures and those on films covering the same material correlated .12, indicating that the amount of learning which occurs under one mode of presentation may be quite different from that which occurs under another.

In extensive studies, Johnson[24] tested the value of films and film strips in teaching geometry. The results showed that retention in particular was significantly improved by the use of three films combined with three film strips. Similar findings were obtained by Yorck and Erlandson,[25] who measured the effects of a laboratory demonstration and a movie in an exercise involving construction of dental plates. The group that observed the laboratory demonstration of this exercise did better than the group that saw the movie. The group that observed both the movie and the demonstration, however, did better than the group that saw the movie only. Collins[26] measured the effect of oral and silent reading on comprehension of prose material by college freshmen. The reading materials, consisting of stories, were chosen for their ascending difficulty levels as evaluated by the Flesch formula. For a majority of the stories, comprehension was better for oral than silent reading, especially in the case of the "fairly" difficult materials. The superiority of the oral method

[22] R. W. M. Travers (20).

[23] Chester W. Harris and Louise R. Buenger, "Relation between Learning by Film and Learning by Lecture," *Audio-Visual Communication Review,* 3 (1955), 29–34.

[24] D. A. Johnson, "Are Films and Filmstrips Effective in Teaching Geometry?" *School Science and Mathematics,* 50 (1950), 570–572.

[25] Douglas Yorck and Forrest L. Erlandson, "The Effectiveness of Visual Aids in Dental Teaching," *Journal of Educational Research,* 52 (1958), 12–15.

[26] Ray Collins, "The Comprehension of Prose Materials by College Freshmen When Read Silently and When Read Aloud," *Journal of Educational Research,* 55 (1961), 79–82.

was probably due in part to the use of several modes—visual, auditory, and motor.

It seems clear that no one sense modality is capable of ensuring thorough learning. The different modes of presentation tend to supplement and reinforce each other; several modes are often more effective than one. In a simple learning task such as spelling, best results may be expected when the child is asked to say and write the words he is spelling. The accuracy of his pronunciation would also contribute to his total spelling efficiency. Within limits, the greater the variety of sensory avenues brought to bear on a subject or problem the more thorough will be the learning and the higher will be the retention.

net effect of research

Numerous experimental studies designed to determine the effectiveness of the varied modes of presentation have been reported. Summaries of the results of this type of research are available, one being that by Allen,[27] who has generalized his findings as follows:

1. *Motion Pictures*
   a. *Knowledge of facts.* ". . . films can teach factual information effectively over a wide range of subject matter content, ages, abilities, and conditions of use. This factual learning, however, tends to be rather specific to the information communicated by the film."
   b. *Perceptual-motor skills.* "There is little doubt about the effectiveness of films in teaching perceptual motor skills."
   c. *Concepts.* "Although a frequent criticism of instructional films is that learning from them is "passive" and interferes with thinking and the development of concepts and inferences, there is no experimental research to support this negative supposition. On the contrary, the evidence is on the side of the film in developing concepts."
   d. *Motivation, interests, attitudes, and opinions.* ". . . films can modify motivations, interests, attitudes, and opinions if they are designed to stimulate or reinforce existing beliefs of the audience. There is, however, little evidence that films can make changes if they are contrary to the existing beliefs, personality structure, or social environment of the individual in the audience."

2. *Television.* "Teaching by television is effective at all levels of instruction from elementary school to military training. In very few cases has TV instruction been found to be inferior to conventional instruction, and in many cases TV was significantly more effective."

3. *Radio and Recordings.* " . . . relatively few basic studies have been made of the effectiveness of radio and recordings in teaching factual information and in changing attitudes and interests. In general, radio and recordings were found to be at least as effective as conventional teaching methods and to be liked by students."

[27] William H. Allen, "Audio-Visual Communications" in *Encyclopedia of Educational Research.* © 1960 by the Macmillan Company. Reprinted by permission.

4. *Film Strips and Slides.* " . . . the superiority of the motion picture probably resulted from the greater adaptability of movies for portraying interacting events, whereas the superiority of the filmstrip was probably due to the slower rate of development used in the actual presentation of the filmstrip to the audience."

Visual materials are especially valuable when the learner cannot visit or explore particular areas of the physical world. They make an important contribution by supplementing his limited experience and background. A visit to an art gallery, the leisurely contemplation of a collection of pictures, or the close examination of stereopticon views permits him to advance at his own pace and in accord with his own particular interests. Charts, diagrams, and tabulations in various forms make facts stand out. Film strips and slides are advantageous in arresting and freezing motion, permitting the learner to concentrate on specific items. They afford a convenient means of exhibiting charts, maps, pictures, or enlarged cross sections of material. Much information available for instruction can be converted to slide form.

Sound-motion pictures are particularly valuable in revitalizing important historic events. They enable the learner to view a situation as though he were present when it occurred. Dramatic force is applied to the learning process by the feeling of nearness and aliveness such presentations make possible. Many of the newer films are also valuable in showing steps in a process and in portraying various aspects of life.

The sound-motion picture, the phonograph, the radio, and television have vastly increased the flexibility with which ideas may be communicated. An advantage of the sound-motion picture is its ability to portray continuous action with fidelity. A major advantage of the phonograph is that recordings may be used whenever desired and repeated when they are needed. Radio is most effective when its programs can be synchronized with classroom schedules. Television is now vastly increasing the number of students to whom ideas may be communicated. Movies in color possess a strong appeal from the standpoint of their attractiveness and interest. In a study of animal and plant life, use of color also makes possible a completely life-like presentation.

Research findings leave little doubt concerning the contribution of audio-visual materials to learning efficiency. Questions regarding their value have arisen mainly in connection with their use and not with their net contribution. Each kind of presentation, whether it involves seeing, hearing, or motor responses, makes itself felt in learning.

proper conditions

The full effect of audio-visual materials cannot be realized unless certain conditions exist. When comparatively simple devices such as film strips and slide equipment are used, the instructional material for each presentation should be organized with reference to its maximum learning value. Some of these conditions will be outlined.

1. *Before deciding to use an instructional aid, a teacher should know its contents thoroughly.* He should preview it to determine its possibilities for teaching a particular topic.

2. *The learner should be prepared to watch for certain items in advance of their presentation and he should be held responsible for the information they provide.* Such preparation may consist of giving some "hints" or pointers on significant materials to be observed. This preliminary preparation may also include reference to items not particularly relevant to the discussion at hand. If it is desired to measure the effect of a particular aid, a pretest may be given. Such a test, when repeated after a showing, provides a basis for measuring the amount of learning that has occurred.

3. *After seeing an aid, the group should have a discussion to develop the main points.* This discussion should show the relationship the contents of the aid has to the topic under consideration and indicate any features that have a bearing on the effectiveness of the aid.

4. *Instructional aids should receive consideration when tests are prepared to measure accomplishment.* The effects of such aids may be measured immediately following their use, or they may be made a part of more comprehensive examinations to be given later. The point to be emphasized is that the learner should be held responsible for their content in the same manner that he is held responsible for any other material presented by textbook, teacher, or collateral reading.

study questions

1. To what extent do you think it is characteristic of the typical learner to develop his own system of organizing learning material?
2. Give your interpretation of the term *meaningful* as it is applied to subject matter.
3. Describe how full adherence to either logical or psychological plans of organization would affect the "teachability" of a subject in which you may be interested. In what modified forms would you accept these plans of organization?
4. Present arguments for and against the practice of preparing in advance the organization of learning materials.
5. Discuss the nature of the learning process as a guide for effective organization.
6. What learning principles are involved in organizing subject matter for a course of instruction?
7. Evaluate the use of large amounts of learning material from which only the most significant information is gleaned as compared with small amounts by means of which fundamental principles may be stressed intensively.

8. Compare large and small units of learning material with respect to the mental organization their use stimulates.
9. Suggest some of the possible effects upon learning of (a) reducing the length of the school year to six months or (b) extending it to twelve months.
10. Build a unit for a course that you are now teaching or intend to teach in accordance with learning principles.
11. Evaluate audio-visual materials as aids to learning from the standpoint of:
    a. Learning
    b. Retention
    c. Other criteria (These are important although not frequently investigated.)
12. Suggest certain conditions for securing the greatest possible value for learning when visual and auditory materials are used.

learning activities

6

Learning activities occupy a central position in a learning program because they are the principal means by which the student comes into possession of information and abilities that are expressed as objectives. Activities are the kinds of things the student does in studying a subject. Practice is the amount of time and effort he devotes to them.

In elementary school, the pupil may work on a list of words, compute exercises in arithmetic, recite with classmates, or listen to a story told by the teacher. He may also sing, dramatize a story, draw a picture, or create a desert scene in a sandpile. In high school, the learner's activities are more abstract. There he listens to explanations by his teacher, reads assignments, works on questions and exercises, views demonstrations and audio-visual materials, takes field trips, performs laboratory experiments, participates in class discussion, and solves problems. Other activities include the project, the case study, independent study, and group-study procedures. In college he continues similar kinds of activity but relies to a greater extent on lectures and readings.

activities and learning outcomes

Teachers have varied opinions on activities that contribute to learning efficiency. Some teachers believe the individual learns best when he uses a form of the problem approach. Others insist that he learns best when he listens to explanations and participates in discussion. Certain teachers employ a variety of activities but rarely give tests. Others use few activities but give tests frequently.

Many difficulties are encountered in the effort to evaluate the full effectiveness of different learning activities. One of the most obvious is that an activity is rarely employed exclusively, even in experimental situations, but rather in combination with others used in instruction. The success of an activity may also be closely associated with the personality and skill of the individual teacher. In addition, there is the problem of devising instruments with which to measure the kind of learning cultivated by different activities. Not the least of the difficulties in evaluating the results of activities is due to the nature of the learning process.

Instruction would be easy if the teacher could select and supervise particular activities with the assurance that certain results would be attained. The learning process is not that simple. The overlapping and spreading effects of activities must be recognized. In a social science course, for example, three learning objectives may be outlined: the ability to assimilate information about social science, the ability to interpret social science data, and the ability to solve social science problems. A direct route for developing ability to assimilate information would be through reading. If the learner is to develop ability to interpret social science data, his activities must include interpretation of such data. If he is to become proficient in solving social science problems, he must study learning situations that require solution of such problems.

The teacher selects activities believed to be effective in cultivating certain kinds of learning. Almost any kind of activity he may use, however, contributes in some measure to all abilities being cultivated. While the student is reading assignments in the social science course, for example, he is learning how to interpret social science data, and he is also gaining some understanding of the methods used in solving social problems. Similarly, the other activities in the social science course contribute to assimilation of information. The spreading effect of a single activity assists in attaining several objectives. The reinforcing effect of several activities contributes to thorough learning.

The purpose here is to discuss activities helpful in the attainment of objectives associated with information, effective thinking, attitudes, and appreciations. The activities to be considered relate mainly to the learning situations outlined in Chapter 1.

activities and information

Activities helpful in acquiring information include reading, viewing audio-visual materials, group discussion, field trips, and listening to lectures. The most effective of these, however, is probably reading.

Reading continues to pose problems not only in elementary and secondary school but in college. Many students read poorly—they know what an author says but not what he means. Black[1] asked college students to read prose selections and then take tests on the selections. The results showed that the most frequent type of error was failure to understand an author's purpose.

A standard criterion for measuring efficiency in reading is the amount understood based on a test of the material that has been read. Another means for measuring understanding of material is to require its application. Katona[2] used an application test to measure understanding of passages that had been read. This test consisted of questions, the answers to which had not been taught but could be found by applying the information to new situations. His results showed that the ability to apply information, particularly principles, is a valuable criterion for determining the degree of understanding.

One of the difficulties in acquiring information through reading often is the passive nature of assignments. The learner may be assigned a certain number of pages in a textbook or asked to study collateral references. A report may be required; but frequently the assignment simply requires familiarity with the information or points of view. There may be no questions to be answered, no facts to be interpreted, no viewpoints to be harmonized, and no conclusions to be drawn. Under such conditions, the learner's attitude and effort tend to be passive. He simply makes mental record of what he has read.

The mode of presenting information seems to have less significance than does the purpose[3] in acquiring it. If the student knows that he will be held responsible for a large number of items of information, he is likely to stress the memorization method. If he knows he will be required to discuss and explain the information, he will seek to understand the essential ideas. If, in addition, he knows he will be expected to make some application of it, he will try even harder to understand its intent and significance.

An effective means of acquiring information is the problem approach, which provides a common thread around which information can be organized to ensure purposeful effort. A series of experiments was devised by Cook[4] to test the effectiveness of certain activities in teaching

[1] E. L. Black, "The Difficulties of Training College Students in Understanding What They Read," *British Journal of Educational Psychology*, 24 (1954), 17–31.

[2] George Katona, "On Different Forms of Learning by Reading," *Journal of Educational Psychology*, 33 (1942), 335–355.

[3] Vernon Troxel, "The Effects of Purpose on the Reading of Expository Mathematical Materials in Grade Eight," *Journal of Educational Research*, 55 (1962), 221–227.

[4] Lloyd A. Cook, *College Programs in Intergroup Relations* (Washington: American Council on Education, 1950). See also Lloyd A. Cook and Rupert C. Koeninger, "Measuring Learning Outcomes in Introductory Sociology Courses," *Journal of Educational Sociology*, 13 (1939), 209–225.

introductory sociology courses. The studies were designed to measure the effect of different activities on the acquisition of *information* and ability to *solve problems.* In one of his studies, a class was taught by the usual lecture method, whereas another was organized into small groups. Each subgroup concentrated on a problem chosen by its members. For students in the second group, there were few lectures but many field trips. Certain specialists were also invited to share their ideas in group discussion. The instructor assisted in directing the activities but did little more.

In this experiment two contrasting learning situations were used. In one, the students attended lectures, took notes, and read assignments. In the other, the students assumed major responsibility for the class. They chose their own problems and collected the needed information, which was discussed in small groups. They were expected to discover solutions to problems with a minimum of direction.

The results of the experiment decidedly favored the group that assumed major responsibility for solving problems. The problem group made as much gain on the information test (22.5 points) as did the students who used the lecture-textbook system despite the fact that acquisition of information was subordinate to its main objective. On tests of problem-solving ability, the gain of the problem group was 12.1 compared with 3.5 for the lecture group. In a similar experiment, Dawson[5] found that lecture and problem-solving activities had an equal effect on recall of information. On tests measuring problem-solving efficiency, the problem procedure was significantly superior.

In using the problem approach, the student may study a significant topic, collect relevant information from various sources, organize his findings, and draw conclusions. In a particular instance, he may study a scientific problem, reviewing and then organizing the relevant research. His major purpose may be to determine the present state of knowledge on his problem, but during his study he acquires a mass of associated information. Much information is learned poorly and forgotten quickly because it is acquired apart from major problems, concepts, or theories. In the problem approach, numerous items of information (names, locations, and dates, as well as principles) are learned and retained as a part of a total situation.

activities and effective thinking

The activities to be considered are those selected to cultivate ability to think critically and to solve problems.

[5] Murray D. Dawson, "Lectures versus Problem Solving in Teaching Elementary Soil Science," *Science Education,* 40 (1956), 395–404.

critical thinking

In a comprehensive questionnaire study, Fox[6] sought to determine the difficulties experienced by high school teachers in teaching critical thinking in a Problems of Democracy course. He also sought to determine the reasons for the difficulties. The four most frequent difficulties encountered in developing skill in critical thinking, ranked according to the difficulty of their use, were: (1) teaching students to analyze, interpret, and evaluate information, (2) teaching them to evaluate sources of information, (3) teaching them to determine the most reasonable and logical conclusions, and (4) motivation. The four most frequent reasons given by these teachers for difficulties in teaching critical thinking were: (1) lack of student training or experiences in analyzing, interpreting, and evaluating information, (2) lack of interest, (3) the tendency to accept the printed word as gospel, and (4) general lethargy.

The first task of a teacher who is interested in improving the critical thinking of his students is to determine what particular critical thinking abilities are appropriate for his subject. After this, he may prepare special units in which critical-thinking abilities are cultivated directly, or he may develop such abilities as a part of normal classwork through the use of supplementary materials and exercises.

The direct approach was used by Hyram,[7] who tested in the St. Louis public schools the effectiveness of certain instructional procedures in training seventh-grade pupils to think logically and critically. An experimental and a control group were formed. The experimental group received instruction on seven concepts of logical reasoning for 250 minutes per week during a four-month period. The conventional group was taught in accordance with methods used in the St. Louis public schools. The tests used to evaluate accomplishment measured five areas under the two sets of conditions.

Pupils who were taught logical principles made significantly higher scores on reasoning tests than did students who were taught by conventional methods. The results indicated that a seventh-grade level of reading ability was the only prerequisite needed to profit from the instruction in logical reasoning. Hyram believes logical thinking depends on an understanding of the principles of logic and that seventh-grade pupils can be trained to think logically through instruction that emphasizes such principles. The practical value of such direct instruction in

[6] Raymond B. Fox, "Difficulties in Developing Skill in Critical Thinking," *Journal of Educational Research,* 55 (1962), 335–337.

[7] George H. Hyram, "An Experiment in Developing Critical Thinking in Children," *Journal of Experimental Education,* 26 (1957), 125–132.

logical thinking, however, would depend upon the extent to which pupils transfer their skills and abilities to school subjects. No effort was made to determine such transfer effect of the special training.

Another approach to critical thinking is to select a list of critical-thinking abilities that are appropriate for a particular subject and teach them as part of a course of instruction. Devine[8] shows how critical abilities can be developed in a ninth-grade English course. As part of their work in reading skills, he suggests that teachers prepare a series of exercises to provide practice in: (1) recognizing a writer's inferences, (2) distinguishing between printed statements of fact and opinion, and (3) recognizing a writer's bias. The materials for developing these abilities may be selected from magazines and newspapers duplicated for classroom use. He also believes that as a part of a unit on listening a variety of activities may be devised to encourage ability in: (1) recognizing a speaker's inferences, (2) distinguishing between oral statements of fact and opinion, and (3) recognizing a speaker's bias. Materials for cultivating these abilities may include taped reproductions of political speeches, television and radio commercials, and conversations recorded in and around the school. In a controlled experiment using current events as subject matter, Creutz and Gezi[9] provided special skill exercises as assignments to one group of high school students. The other group in the experiment followed conventional teaching methods. The special exercises of the experimental group included *interpretation, evaluation,* and *awareness of trends.* Marked gains (as compared with those of the control group) in these abilities were noted after ten weeks of training.

The ability to think critically can be developed in any subject if the student is stimulated to extend his learning beyond the point of assimilating information or developing simple skills. It may be stimulated wherever he is required to search for causes that may not be readily evident, to draw generalizations from bodies of uninterpreted information, to analyze the rationale of viewpoints, or to test his understanding of principles by identifying situations in which they may be applicable. Critical thinking is best characterized as a questioning attitude by which the learner satisfies himself as to the validity of interpretations, theories, or conclusions.

problem solving

Our interest in problem solving centers on two questions: What is the nature of the problem-solving process? And what activities are helpful in

[8] Thomas G. Devine, "Critical Thinking in the English Class," *Peabody Journal of Education,* 39 (1962), 359–365.

[9] Gloria Creutz and Kalil I. Gezi, "Developing Critical Thinking in the Current Events Class," *Journal of Educational Research,* 58 (1965), 366–367.

developing problem-solving efficiency? Implied in each of these questions is the nature of the guidance necessary to achieve successful results.

The problem-solving process. In confronting a problem situation, does the individual tend to rely on previous associations and experiences or does he react to the immediate situation without recourse to recall of familiar circumstances? Does he react to a problem principally by trial and error or are certain reasoning principles discovered and applied in the solution?

Buswell[10] observed more than 500 students while they worked on various kinds of mathematical problems. The students were observed as they attempted to discover and transfer generalizations and while they selected the procedures they wished to use. Wide individual differences were noted in the students' methods of attack, the tendency being to use trial and error rather than systematic approaches. Various patterns were evident; but in no case were there as many as twenty percent of a group that represented any one pattern of thinking. There was no evidence that the problem-solving process followed definite rules.

The problem-solving process has also been studied to determine differences in procedures used by successful and unsuccessful problem solvers. Bloom and Broder[11] made an analysis of differences between the two types of students in a problem-solving examination. Various kinds of descriptions were made of the procedures used by the two groups. These included ability to understand the nature of the problem, ability to understand the ideas involved in the problem, and attitudes toward problem solving. Differences between the unsuccessful and successful students were noted for all of these factors. The results indicated, however, that successful and unsuccessful students differed not so much in the information they possessed as in their application of information.

Similar results were obtained by McNemar,[12] who determined differences between students of high and low reasoning ability. These groups were compared on learning situations, including free and controlled association, induction and deduction, and a water-jar type of problem. The high and low groups did not differ noticeably on the free-association problems; but the differences in favor of the high group became evident as the associations were controlled. On the induction problem, the high group was better in both speed and accuracy; but on problems of deduction, the high group was superior in accuracy only. There were no

[10] G. T. Buswell and others, "Patterns of Thinking in Solving Problems," in *University of California Publications in Education,* 12 (1956), 63–148.

[11] B. S. Bloom and L. J. Broder, *Problem Solving Process of College Students* (Chicago: University of Chicago Press, 1950).

[12] O. W. McNemar, "An Attempt to Differentiate between Individuals with High and Low Reasoning Ability," *American Journal of Psychology,* 68 (1955), 20–36.

differences between high and low groups with respect to certain training exercises on the water-jar problem. The high group in this task, however, was superior on certain problems that had more than one solution.

Varying procedures were evident when the students were questioned about their manner of solving the problems. Students having high reasoning ability, however, uniformly demonstrated superior ability in differentiating between relevant and irrelevant aspects of past experience.

When confronted with a problem situation, the learner tends to rely at first upon his stock of previous experiences and familiar situations. If these do not readily advance his progress in solving a problem, he is likely to use trial and error methods until generalizations or principles are discovered. Good and poor problem solvers exhibit many of the same characteristics. Good problem solvers differ from the poor most in their abilities to use relevant past experience and to discover generalizations and principles that provide clues to solutions.

Problem-solving activities. Problem-solving activities in the schools have been directly influenced by formal steps in the complete act of thought. The tendency is to follow Dewey's sequence—begin with recognition of a problem and end with a solution or conclusion. Such steps afford a systematic approach to instruction and provide both teacher and student with a feeling of security.

One of the better studies that used the step-by-step procedure (despite its date) is the one made by Newcomb,[13] who performed an experiment with seventh- and eighth-grade classes to determine whether there might be some general principles applicable to all arithmetic problems. Experimental and control groups were formed. For the experimental groups, the learning materials consisted of twenty prepared problems arranged in order of their difficulty. These groups were required to solve one problem each day for six weeks according to the following plan:

1. Understand each word in the problem.
2. Read the problem intelligently.
3. Perform the operations with speed and accuracy.
4. Tell what is given and what is required.
5. Select the different processes to be used.
6. Plan the solution wisely and systematically and check readily.

As a further means of guidance, pupils of the experimental groups were provided with a separate solution sheet for each problem. This sheet had spaces for the following items:

1. Statement of the problem.

2. How to read the problem.

[13] R. S. Newcomb, "Teaching Pupils How to Solve Problems in Arithmetic," *Elementary School Journal*, 23 (1922), 183–189.

3. The data given.
4. The data required.
5. The processes necessary for the solution.
6. The approximate answer.
7. The solution proper.
8. Checking the results.

Teachers of the control groups taught their classes in the usual way and knew nothing of the plan used by the experimental groups. Both experimental and control groups were given the Stone Reasoning Test in arithmetic at the beginning and again at the end of the six-week period.

The experimental groups showed a superiority over the control groups by 14 percent in speed, 3 percent in accuracy, and 15 percent in speed and accuracy combined. Newcomb believes that many difficulties encountered in problem solving are due to faulty methods and that marked improvement may be expected as a result of special instruction. Herriott,[14] in an informal study, also found that pupils profit by instruction that follows the step-by-step procedure.

In laboratory situations, certain aspects of the problem-solving process are usually studied rather than any sequence of steps. Corman,[15] using twelfth-grade students, tested the effectiveness of varying amounts of information on the solution of a match type of problem. The information consisted of aid given the student in both method and principle. In one situation, *no* information was provided; in another, *some* was provided; and in a third, *much* information was provided. The problem-solving efficiency of students who were above average in intelligence increased in proportion to the increased amount of information given on method. For students in the lower intelligence levels, *some* guidance on method was more effective than *no* guidance. For students in the higher intelligence levels and for those in the lower levels, information on the principle was ineffective. For the simpler aspects of the *match* problem, however, the more intelligent students benefited most from a combination of definite information on the principle and indirect clues on the method.

In a series of investigations, Saugstad[16] and his associates measured the effect of supplying the learner with the experiences needed in the

[14] Robert E. Herriott, "An Aid in the Analysis of Verbal Problems," *Arithmetic Teacher,* 5 (1958), 143–145.

[15] Bernard R. Corman, "The Effect of Varying Amounts and Kinds of Information as Guidance in Problem Solving," *Psychological Monographs,* Whole No. 431 (1957).

[16] Per Saugstad and Kjell Raeheim, "Problem Solving, Past Experience and Availability of Functions," *British Journal of Psychology,* 51 (1960), 97–104.

solution of problems. In one of their experiments, the method consisted of demonstrating the functions regarded as critical in the solution of a "ball" problem. The subjects were seventeen-year-old boys.

The boys who had been given a demonstration of the critical functions in solving the ball problem obtained solutions quickly; those who were not given demonstrations of these functions made little progress. Nineteen of the twenty boys who were given demonstrations solved the problem within 30 minutes; of 45 boys who were not given demonstrations, only ten attained solutions. The authors believe that their results point to the need in many types of problem for supplying the learner with the necessary functions. They also feel that improvement in problem solving is enhanced by demonstrations and illustrations based on concrete objects.

One of the most obvious conclusions one can draw about the effect of special instruction on problem-solving efficiency is that most students need help and that almost any kind of guidance will result in improvement beyond what is normally expected. A first step toward improvement is to remove the psychological barrier many students experience when confronting a problem situation. This barrier can probably best be overcome by demonstrating that problem-solving procedures are extensions of the more familiar types of learning, such as memorizing and assimilating information. Also, activities requiring critical thinking (as defined in the preceding section) afford a means of bridging the gap between the simpler types of learning and the problem-solving process. After the student has reached the point of thinking critically, the teacher's major role in problem solving is to assist him in defining problems, to encourage him to make suggestions and formulate hypotheses, and to help him organize materials systematically.

Teaching problem solving is probably as much an art as it is a science. Certain teachers develop the ability to a high degree. Guidance of problem-solving activities is demonstrated by a teacher in one of the University of Chicago laboratory schools, her procedure being reported by the late Professor S. C. Parker.[17] A seventh-grade class was reviewing the geography of the United States, and attention had been directed to sugar production in this country. The question was: "Should the United States produce its own sugar?" Parker has described this teacher's activities in conducting the class as follows:

1. She created an intense problem frame of mind by disconcerting the pupils with a graphic representation of the contrast between our large consumption and relatively small production of sugar.

2. She had the problem for discussion clearly formulated and wrote it on the board.

[17] S. C. Parker, "Problem Solving or Practice in Thinking," *Elementary School Journal,* 21 (1920), 16–25.

3. She kept the problem clearly before the pupils by frequent reference to it as written.
4. She encouraged suggestions from the pupils not only in matters of fact and data, but also in the matters of procedure, i.e., in regard to such questions as "What shall we do next?" or "How can we find out about this?"
5. She encouraged careful evaluation and criticism by the pupils of the various suggestions.
6. She gave practice in the use of scientific treatises as the source of data and as a means of verification.
7. She encouraged the attitude of desiring verification of suggestions by reference to standard authorities.
8. She conducted the lesson at a deliberate pace so that the pupils were required to think before answering. As a special device in this connection, she occasionally said, "When you have your minds made up you may rise," and then waited until most pupils had risen.
9. She kept the discussion organized along definite lines by outlining on the blackboard the various important suggestions that were made and then holding to the order in which they had decided to pursue the discussion. In this way the main problem became analyzed into a number of subordinate problems, which were disposed of in an orderly manner.

activities and other outcomes

Learning activities also contribute to other outcomes, such as attitudes and appreciations,[18] which may or may not be included as objectives and considered as a part of evaluation.

attitudes

When one expresses an attitude, one makes little conscious effort to analyze the factors involved or to rationalize. One's attitude may be positive, negative, or neutral and may be one of liking, disliking, or neither. Four[19] recognized means of influencing attitudes are outlined as follows:

Assimilating viewpoints from the environment. An individual reflects the opinions and attitudes held by persons in a community. The customs of the people are influential in shaping one's point of view toward racial discrimination, capital and labor, or the rightness and wrongness of a behavior. In most instances the individual absorbs attitudes of people in

[18] D. R. Krathwohl, B. S. Bloom, and B. B. Masia, *The Affective Domain,* Vol. II of *Taxonomy of Educational Objectives* (New York: David McKay, 1964). In this work effort is made to quantify and measure interests, attitudes, appreciations, and values. See also Frederick J. McDonald, *Educational Psychology,* 2nd ed. (Belmont, Calif.: Wadsworth Publishing Company, Inc., 1965). McDonald discusses teaching methods for developing these learning outcomes.

[19] Ralph W. Tyler, *Basic Principles of Curriculum and Instruction* (Chicago: University of Chicago Press, 1950). See also McDonald (18).

a community without being aware of what is taking place. Local opinions and viewpoints tend to be accepted uncritically but strongly influence his behavior.

The emotional effect of certain experiences. Where experiences have been satisfying, they have the effect of creating favorable attitudes. Thus, the student forms attitudes of liking or satisfaction when he takes an interesting course or one in which he makes effort to apply the subject matter to personal or vocational problems. On the other hand, he develops attitudes of distaste when he takes a course that is not interesting or is one that does not contribute to his real need. All experiences have some effect in forming attitudes.

Experiences that have a strong emotional effect. A student may form an attitude as a result of some unpleasant experience he has had: failing a course because of a misunderstanding with a teacher or experiencing embarrassment from being humiliated in the presence of a group. A single distasteful experience associated with a situation tends to create a negative or even an antagonistic attitude. As a result, many satisfying experiences may be needed to offset its damaging effect.

Applying the reasoning process. In applying the reasoning process, one tries to obtain information, to consider both sides of an issue, and to form a judgment on the basis of reason, uncolored by emotional bias or prejudice. One may have strong prejudices against child-labor laws, employment practices, or political organizations without knowledge of the facts or conditions governing their operation. After one has had opportunity to consider both sides of an issue, to interpret facts objectively, attitudes may and do change frequently. Such changes can be measured by attitude scales given before and after students have taken certain courses.

Attitudes tend to be most directly affected by real experiences. Cleland and Chambers[20] performed an experiment to test the effect on modification of attitudes of students visiting an institution for the mentally defective. High school and college students who participated in a guided tour of an institution for the defective showed marked shifts in attitude, not all of which were positive. Hillson[21] also measured the effect of a field trip to a mental hospital. Two comparable groups were formed. Attitude scales were given to both groups before and after the experimental group had visited the hospital. Attitudes of the experimental group were significantly changed as a result of the visit.

Any real experiences, such as visits to playgrounds, coal mines,

[20] C. C. Cleland and W. H. Chambers, "Experimental Modification of Attitudes as a Function of an Institutional Tour," *American Journal of Mental Deficiency,* 64 (1959), 124–130.

[21] W. W. Hillson, "The Field Trip as a Supplement to Teaching: An Experimental Study," *Journal of Educational Research,* 53 (1959), 19–22.

observations of the activities of juvenile courts, or various kinds of work experience, tend to make strong impressions.

appreciation

Appreciation is usually associated with art, music, and literature but may be related to any subject. One of its distinctive characteristics is insight into the value of the thing appreciated. Etymologically, appreciation is associated with the notion of price or value. Whenever a student continues to read the writings of a particular author, he is demonstrating it. Obviously, such appreciation is not developed in a vacuum; it is closely associated with knowledge, background material, and a host of other intellectual factors. Consequently, it could scarcely be said that a person has a genuine appreciation for a certain type of literature unless he has considerable information about it.

The effects of three activities on appreciation of fiction by high school students were tested by Burton.[22] The learning material consisted of short stories. The activities were (1) analyzing a story for its techniques or craftsmanship, (2) studying a story to provide additional light on a central theme or topic, and (3) studying a short story in connection with the original writing by the students. Is the student's appreciation heightened by analyzing techniques? Is it influenced by reading stories as a source of ideas for a theme? Do his own efforts at imaginative writing increase his ability to evaluate the work of others?

Appraisal of these activities was based on three objective tests and by an analysis of the students' answers on essay examinations. The three activities were almost equally effective in heightening appreciation; each seemed to be effective in some way. The method of analyzing techniques of fiction showed no advantage over methods in which there was little consideration given to techniques. The *theme* method in which students studied stories for their illumination on a topic did not have the effect of sacrificing appreciation. There was no evidence that the students' original writing was of greater help in developing appreciation than other activities.

Brandon[23] also tested the effectiveness of certain approaches in developing art appreciation. The approaches he used were: (1) the lecture in combination with a practicum and visual aids, (2) the lecture in connection with visual aids, (3) the lecture in combination with a practicum, and (4) a conventional method. Four groups of high school students, formed on the basis of random sampling, were used as subjects.

[22] Dwight L. Burton, "An Experiment in Teaching Appreciation," *English Journal,* 42 (1953), 16–20.

[23] Charles M. Brandon, "The Relative Effectiveness of Four Different Approaches to Developing Art Appreciation" (unpublished Ed.D. thesis, George Peabody College for Teachers, 1960).

Tests were given at the beginning and end of a semester. No single approach was found to be superior to any other; all approaches tended to be equally effective when appraised by the Mier and Graves tests. The gains of the groups were also similar when measured by a standardized test of art knowledge.

Research findings seem to indicate that no single kind of learning activity has the merit of developing appreciation. Instead, it is likely to be affected by many activities, especially those that broaden the learner's knowledge of a subject and increase his insight into it. Any satisfying learning experience probably makes some contribution to appreciation.

need for several activities

A single activity may contribute directly to the development of a particular outcome; but several are often required to ensure thorough learning. Nelson[24] compared the effect of vocal and instrumental instruction on musical comprehension. His results strongly indicated that the integration of both vocal and instrumental instruction develops a broader base of musical comprehension than does vocal training alone. Dearden[25] tested the effectiveness of four types of activity in teaching a biology course to college freshmen and sophomores who did not intend to major in science. The activities were *individual* (conventional), *demonstration laboratory, workbook exercises,* and *a term paper.* The effectiveness of these activities was measured by tests of biological knowledge and scientific thinking. Each of the activities had the effect of increasing scores on the tests. Dearden believes that all of these activities could be used advantageously in a course, although stress should be placed on individual laboratory work. He also feels that their use in combination would increase the student's interest in biology.

The student learns better when he devotes part of his time to recall while studying than he does when he continues to reread material. He learns more thoroughly when he participates in laboratory experiments than he does when he limits his activity to lectures and demonstrations. Taking notes while studying aids learning because the individual does something with his material at the time. He gains more when he organizes and edits his notes than when he simply records the main points. The individual learns best when he responds in a variety of ways to the materials at hand.

Several activities are also needed to provide for student differences. In a series of experiments in teaching zoology, Tyler[26] shows that certain

[24] Carl B. Nelson, "An Experimental Evaluation of Two Methods of Teaching Music in the Fourth and Fifth Grades," *Journal of Experimental Education,* 23 (1954–55), 231–238.

[25] Douglas M. Dearden, "An Evaluation of the Laboratory in a College General Biology Course," *Journal of Experimental Education,* 28 (1960), 241–247.

[26] Ralph W. Tyler, "Prevailing Misconceptions," *Journal of Higher Education* (June 1933), p. 285.

students learn principles through laboratory exercises, some through demonstrations and problems, and still others through different kinds of activity. He believes that no single kind of activity is equally effective with all students. Loomer[27] reached a similar conclusion on the basis of the effects of several activities in teaching art. He found that some learn best through lectures and demonstrations where the emphasis is on verbal learning; others learn best in laboratory situations where the actual manipulation permits more motor coordination in the learning process.

practice

A potentially effective activity may be unsuccessful for lack of practice. A less effective one may be rewarding because of it. It is relatively easy to select an activity and measure the results following its use; it is more difficult to determine the nature and amount of the learner's practice of an activity.

In the classroom, the learner may be asked to study a list of words until he can spell them correctly or drill on a series of arithmetic exercises until he meets a criterion of efficiency. He may also be given a reading assignment for the purpose of assimilating and recalling its main points. The learner's practice should result in definable performance, such as ability to recall and discuss the main points, to make applications of his material to everyday situations, or to solve problems based on his information.

The most easily observed practice is concrete. It is easy to observe the learner trying to spell a list of words or to perform exercises in addition and multiplication. In such situations, he obviously is working to meet set requirements. The results of his efforts can be measured objectively. This kind of practice is observed readily. Practice is not limited, however, to the visible and easily observed types.[28] It may involve the assimilation and interpretation of learning material without apparent effort. The learner may ruminate or mentally practice material with which he is familiar and interpret it in the light of his experience. His practice may consist of applying principles to new situations or silently thinking about materials he has read. He may reflect upon some fact or theory mastered

[27] Clifford C. Loomer, "A Study of Certain Effects of Three Types of Learning Experiences in Art as Revealed in the Drawings by Participants," *Journal of Experimental Education,* 22 (1953), 65–102.

[28] J. B. Stroud and Max Freeburne, "Symbolical Practice," *Journal of Educational Psychology,* 33 (1942), 65–71. See also L. Verdella Clark, "Effect of Mental Practice on the Development of a Certain Motor Skill," *Research Quarterly,* 31 (1960), 60. In this study mental practice was almost as effective as physical practice for certain groups. All of the subjects introspectively reported growth in the ability to visualize and imagine the shooting techniques involving the one-hand foul shot.

from a recall standpoint but as yet not fully understood. This kind of practice is symbolic or mental in contrast to the concrete or visible type.

Practice should be distinguished from repetitive activity. One may repeat his performance many times without noticeably increasing his efficiency, even when he is far from errorless in his solution and still has opportunity to improve. For practice to be effective, other conditions (such as *purpose, meaning,* and *awareness* of error) must be associated with it. The significant fact is that practice provides the learner with opportunity to vary and refine his responses at each study period.[29] His practice is a means of revising rather than of repeating his behavior.

Repetitive activity, however, is a means of ensuring retention. In laboratory situations, the learner's efficiency in memorizing material is often developed to the extent of one errorless reproduction. Repetition beyond that point is considered "overlearning." For example, if it requires twenty repetitions to reproduce a list of nonsense syllables once without error, ten additional repetitions would mean 50 percent overlearning. Ebbinghaus observed that as the number of repetitions increased, there was a tendency for the material to become more thoroughly entrenched in the learner's mind. He believed the degree of learning bore a definite relationship to the amount retained. For material, he used nonsense syllables, which were learned to varying degrees of mastery. After a time interval, they were relearned to the extent of their original status. He was thus able to determine the resulting savings in work in relation to the number of repetitions required for exact reproduction after varying time intervals. He found that a certain number of repetitions beyond that required for one errorless reproduction had a beneficial effect on ability to relearn. Rock's[30] experiments, using nonsense syllables, yielded essentially the same results, indicating that repetition strengthens learning and makes retention more likely.

organization of practice

The organization of practice has a long history of experimental investigation, the principal purpose being to test the effectiveness of whole and part methods of learning. In the whole method, the learner is expected to practice his material as a unit, using as many repetitions as necessary for mastery. When memorizing a poem, he studies it in its entirety to comprehend its various parts in relationship to the whole; practice is on the entire poem. In learning history, he studies a major

[29] David P. Ausubel, "The Role of Frequency in Meaningful Verbal Material," *Psychology in the Schools,* 2 (1965), 203–209.

[30] I. Rock, "The Role of Repetition in Associative Learning," *American Journal of Psychology,* 70 (1957), 186–193. See also I. Rock, "Repetition and Learning," *Scientific American,* 109 (1958), 68–76.

topic as a whole instead of breaking it up into parts. In using the part method, he studies separately the several parts of a poem or the various topics or units in history. Different forms of the part method are sometimes employed. A method frequently used consists of learning a portion of material, then another, and then practicing these together before proceeding to the next part.

The results of laboratory studies suggest that when all factors are considered, the whole method is superior to the part method, especially when evaluated on the basis of retention. It ensures the formation of pertinent associations and comprehension of individual parts. It also benefits from distributed practice (to be discussed later) with which it is associated. A weakness of the part method lies in the formation of irrelevant associations; its advantage resides in the opportunity afforded for concentration on the individual parts of a task. The "mediating" method, which is a combination of part and whole methods, includes the advantages of both.

relating wholes to parts

In using conventional organization, an analysis of a situation is often presented before the whole is even partially grasped or understood. Pupils may be required to learn information in bits or encouraged to analyze certain portions of some particular subject matter. In English classes they may be asked to read short assignments from a textbook. The materials may then be discussed to clarify subtle allusions with little attention given to the central theme of the assignment. Pupils could work more effectively with such material if they first understood what the author intended.

In teaching a foreign language, the teacher should use the largest vocabulary the learner can understand. He may be required to read or even speak the language at the outset. He may begin with a complete sentence for which he is given the total meaning. Thus, he becomes familiar with the *whole* before he studies the *parts*. He could then be helped to identify the verbs and later learn other grammatical construction and techniques of vocabulary. After this, the learner may use his knowledge by translating into and from the foreign language.

Facts learned in isolation cannot yield full meaning until their roles as parts in a total picture are made clear, and yet only in parts may attention be focused upon them. In approaching divisions or units within a course, a teacher may plan additional previews and single out various areas for intensive treatment. Such previews establish a pattern and familiarize the learner with the landmarks of his task. After he has gained an understanding of his task, he may study separately its different parts even though he may still not understand how the parts relate to the larger whole. During his study, the learner should proceed from wholes to parts and then back again to wholes. He completes his learning by some kind of synthesis that suggests a return to the whole approach.

advance organizers

Advance organizers are presented in advance of studying a piece of material but are more abstract, general, and inclusive than previews. Such organizers provide guidance that takes into account both the particular substance of a piece of material and the concepts that are a part of the learner's background and experience. They draw upon his knowledge and increase his familiarity with the new material. A major aim is to direct attention to similarities as well as differences between new materials and those previously studied. Ausubel[31] recognizes two kinds of organizers, each of which serves a particular purpose. The "expository" type provides "ideational anchorage" in terms that are already familiar to the learner. The "comparative" organizer is used to integrate new concepts with similar ones as well as to increase discriminability of them.

The value of advance organizers depends upon the manner in which course materials are presented. Where units of material are arranged sequentially so that interrelationships are built into a course of instruction, some of their purposes are already realized. In most learning situations, however, advance organizers[32] facilitate both learning and retention and are more effective during the initial stages of studying a unit or topic than later. Summaries, especially when placed at the beginning of a passage of material, may also be beneficial. In a study of the effect of varying locations of the summary (at the beginning of a chapter, at the end, and at both beginning and end), Murphy[33] found that both immediate and delayed recall were favorably affected when it was placed at the beginning.

distribution of practice

Learning curves show improvement with practice; but they are usually derived under conditions of distributed effort. If the learner continues practice, even on an easy task, during a long period, a stage is reached when his efficiency diminishes rapidly. This is what happens when an individual continues to multiply four-place numbers by four-place numbers. His efficiency increases up to a certain point and then declines.

[31] David P. Ausubel, *The Psychology of Meaningful Verbal Learning* (New York: Grune and Stratton, 1963), p. 82.

[32] David P. Ausubel, "The Use of Advance Organizers in the Learning and Retention of Meaningful Verbal Material," *Journal of Educational Psychology*, 51 (1960), 267–272.

[33] Harold Murphy, "The Effect of Different Locations of Chapter Summary on Immediate and Delayed Recall" (Doctor's thesis, George Peabody College for Teachers, 1962).

The college student learns through experience that he is more likely to achieve better results in studying an assignment if he uses three one-hour periods rather than one three-hour session. He also learns that the more intense and rapid the work the more valuable it is to distribute his practice.

The principle of distributed practice in the elementary school is partially recognized by variation in activities so that a pupil does not work very long on any single subject. Teachers of these grades are interested in maintaining interest and they prevent fatigue by frequent change of activities. In the high school, practice is likely to be regulated by study of various courses and not by the frequency and length of class meetings. With the exception of an occasional study period, the high school student spends the greater part of a school day attending classes. There may be only slight recognition of distributed practice in scheduling courses.

In college and university, wide variation in the practice of scheduling classes is evident. An undergraduate class, for example, may meet 50 minutes on each of four consecutive days during a week; or it may meet 100 minutes twice each week throughout a quarter or semester. In the graduate school, a class may meet 200 minutes once a week with a brief rest period following the first 100-minute session. Class meetings in college and university vary widely in length and may be spaced close together or far apart. At this educational level there may be little concern for distributed practice either in scheduling class meetings or comprehensive examinations.

Experimental study of the effect of distributed practice requires consideration of the total amount of practice available, the time intervals between practice periods, and the length of time during which practice is continued. The amount of time available for study of a given piece of material, for example, may be 60 minutes. The learner may study this material continuously for this period, the same material 20 minutes each day for three days, or 10 minutes each day for six days. In the first situation, his practice would be massed; in the others it would be distributed.

massed versus distributed practice

The effect of massed as opposed to distributed practice is demonstrated by experiments in both laboratory and school situations. Figure 16 shows the time required for learning lists of nonsense syllables of varying lengths.

In the schools, the effects of massed and distributed practice are illustrated by studies on "cramming." Using high school and college students, Pease[34] conducted an experiment to determine the effect of

[34] G. R. Pease, "Should Teachers Give Warning of Tests and Examinations?" *Journal of Educational Psychology,* 21 (1930), 272–277.

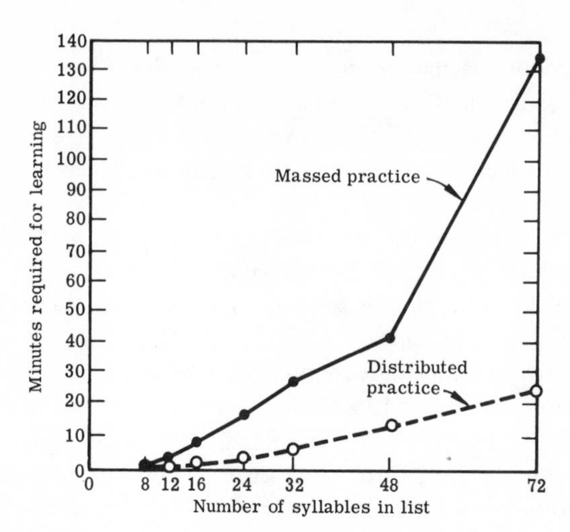

Figure 16. Mean number of minutes required for learning by massed and distributed practice with varying lengths of lists of nonsense syllables. Taken from Bernard Berelson and Gary A. Steiner, *Human Behavior* (New York: Harcourt, Brace and World, 1964).

cramming on achievement. Experimental and control groups were formed. The control group was given an objective test of 100 items without notice. The experimental group was dismissed and urged to devote at least an hour to "cramming" for the same test, which would be given at the next class meeting. The group that "crammed" gained 11.1 points more than did the control group. Six weeks later, however, when the same test was repeated on both groups, this gain was reduced to 6.3 points.

The experiment was repeated with two additional groups. One cramming group having average intelligence gained 8.2 points; but six weeks later this gain was reduced to 4.8 points. Another cramming group having superior intelligence gained 17.7 points; but six weeks later this gain was reduced to 2.7 points.

Cramming is characterized by intensive effort within limited time; consequently, there is limited opportunity to assimilate material. The learner is forced to concentrate attention on information that may be memorized to the point of immediate recall but sacrifices real understanding. Under such conditions, the learning that occurs has only temporary effect.

time intervals between practice periods

The effect of time intervals between practice periods on learning has been frequently investigated in laboratory situations. In reviewing investigations on this subject, Underwood[35] reported the effects of two

[35] B. J. Underwood, "Ten Years of Massed Practice on Distributed Practice," *Psychological Review*, 68 (1961), 229–247.

time intervals. In one situation, the learner was presented lists of verbal materials at intervals of two to eight seconds; in another, the lists were presented at intervals of fifteen seconds or more. The major purpose was to determine the conditions under which the short and long intervals differ in their effect on learning efficiency.

The net effect of laboratory studies involving memorization of verbal materials is that the longer intervals, as defined, facilitate learning only when interference occurs in the individual's responses. During practice, the learner develops error tendencies as well as correct responses. The assumption is that the long intervals allow for the elimination of such tendencies more effectively than do the short ones. If interference is pronounced and the interval is relatively long, forgetting occurs because of the weak associative strength of the correct responses and the error tendencies tend to block them. In determining whether or not learning efficiency will be facilitated, one needs to consider response interference and the length of the interval.

The results of laboratory studies also show that the effects of time intervals between practice periods vary with different kinds of tasks and their degree of meaningfulness.[36] For example, the longer time interval has a pronounced favorable effect on learning a motor task such as the pursuit-rotor; but in the typical verbal task, the effect is not so marked. The results also tend to differ for meaningless and meaningful materials. The lower the meaningfulness of the materials, the greater the likelihood that the longer intervals between practice periods will facilitate learning.

Laboratory studies provide principles governing the effect of varying time intervals between practice periods under highly specific conditions —that is, where relatively meaningless materials are used and where rote-memorization methods are required. Such principles cannot be readily applied in school situations, where meaningful learning materials are sequentially organized and different learning methods are employed. The obvious need in school situations is for studies that relate to the frequency and spacing of class periods in high school and college and the length and distribution of study periods in the elementary grades.

Raubenheimer and Davidson[37] tested the effect of spacing practice in introductory typing by high school students. These students were given fifteen-minute speed tests, the practice periods being spaced at two-, three-, six-, and fourteen-day intervals. Students whose practice was spaced at two-day intervals showed marked gains; those who had practice periods spaced longer than two days were retarded in both typing speed and accuracy. It would seem that in this type of learning

[36] B. J. Underwood (35).

[37] A. S. Raubenheimer and S. H. Davidson, "The Effects of Rest Periods in Learning Typewriting," *Education,* 53 (1933), 421–423.

situation, intervals between practice should not be of long duration. The effectiveness of varying time intervals for each of two kinds of review—rereading and taking a multiple-choice test—was tested by Stroud[38] and his associates. These two kinds of review were scheduled at intervals from one to seventeen days following initial learning. The learning material consisted of an article on the history of paper and paper making. The subjects were seventh-grade pupils. The reading type of review was not significantly influenced by the time at which it was given; it made little difference whether it was scheduled immediately after learning or several days later. The testing kind of review, when placed on the first and third days after learning, was more effective than rereading. Review is probably most valuable when it occurs before masses of detail become unwieldy and when materials are fresh but as yet unassimilated.

The optimum interval for spacing practice in school situations would vary with subject matter, interest, and the learner's maturity. It is evident, however, that extreme intervals between practice periods should be avoided. They should not follow each other in such close succession as to limit the learner's opportunity to "digest" material. They should not be spaced so far apart as to permit loss of continuity and interest to occur.

practice spread over an extended period of time

Intensive study of a subject within a short period is primarily useful in learning large amounts of information and in developing simple skills. Such acquisitional activity is only one phase of the learning process. A more productive phase emerges as a result of the learner's effort to evaluate his material and reflect upon its significance. A student may come into possession of large amounts of information within a short period, but he needs time in which to reflect upon their meaning. One working under conditions of intensive study may do well on tests stressing immediate recall of detailed kinds of information but poorly on those measuring reasoning and problem solving. Success on such tests is dependent upon the learner's ability to evaluate a wide range of learning experience over an extended period of time.

The longer the time allotted for studying a subject, within limits, the greater the opportunity for thorough learning. The semester plan is better than the quarter system for this purpose. A period of greater length than the semester probably is even more favorable for learning.

There should be fewer courses, more should be done with them, and

[38] A. M. Sones and J. B. Stroud, "Review with Special Reference to Temporal Positions," *Journal of Educational Psychology,* 31 (1940), 665–676. See also J. B. Stroud and E. Johnson, "Temporal Position of Review," *Journal of Educational Research,* 35 (1942), 618–622.

they should extend over longer periods. Intensive practice within short periods may be justified only under certain conditions and with particular types of subject matter. Concentrated practice may be appropriate when the aim is to acquire habits and skills that will be used immediately following their acquisition. Certain motor skills, for example, may be practiced intensively if they are to be used on a job. Similarly, concentrated study of foreign-language skills, when put to immediate use in speaking and writing, may be effective on the same basis. But in such cases, the assumption is that skills and habits developed during massed practice will be applied immediately to situations for which training has prepared the learner.

The principle of distributed practice applies to planning sequences of courses in subject-matter fields from grade to grade. If the high school student could take all his history requirements within the period of a single year, it would not be wise. Courses should be planned so they follow in sequential order. They should also extend over a sufficiently long period to permit opportunity for the results of learning effort to emerge.

explanatory principles

Several theories have been proposed to explain the greater effectiveness of distributed as compared with massed practice. One explanation is that during long practice periods the learner tends to get into a rut, and rest intervals permit him to return to his work with a new mental set and attack it in a different way. Explanations are also sometimes made in terms of a physiological process, because individuals make more improvement when their work is interspersed with sleep than when awake. The explanation on which there is reasonably general agreement is that distributed practice affords the individual an opportunity to recall and evaluate learning materials, to practice them mentally, and to reflect upon their meaning and significance.

guidance

Guidance is primarily a process of limiting trial and error behavior by preventing errors and focusing attention on responses that assure success. Depending on the time of its administration, it may either prevent or correct errors. Guidance may be administered by *physical means* or by *demonstration, explanation,* or *criticism.*

Guidance by *physical means* may consist of what is sometimes termed "putting the individual through the act." In teaching young children to write, for example, the instructor may direct the hand of the child through the motions of forming letters. In the finger maze (used in the psychological laboratory), the experimenter may take the hand of the individual and lead it through the proper pathways. When teaching certain steps of a drill, the instructor may turn the foot in a certain direction or place it in the correct position.

Guidance by *demonstration* consists of performing an act in the presence of the learner and requiring him to repeat it as given. Given a goal, the easiest way to attain it is to follow the example of one who has reached it. A teacher places a copy on the blackboard for a class in handwriting. Each child uses the pattern, yet none succeeds in making an exact duplication of it. Each individual shows characteristics that differentiate his work from every other member of the class. In guidance by demonstration, the learner interprets movements in the pattern in terms of his own perception and then tries them out. Demonstration is effective in teaching laboratory work in home economics and the sciences; it is also valuable in athletics, handwriting, and singing.

Explanation is the most common form of guidance used in the schools. The teacher tells the student what to do and how to do it. If written instructions are given, they should be explicit and complete, with nothing left to chance. Oral instruction is more flexible because the instructor has an opportunity to judge from personal contact the amount of direction and explanation that may be required and to repeat or elaborate as the occasion demands. Because of its adaptability and opportunity for explanations, oral instruction is the most useful form of guidance.

Criticism consists of indicating successful responses and suggesting methods for eliminating errors by substitution. Depending on the time of its administration, criticism may either prevent or correct errors.

In most cases, demonstration, explanation, and criticism should follow each other in the order named. The first two ordinarily should precede the learner's attempt, whereas criticism should parallel it with such repetition of the others as needed.

the guidance controversy

The effectiveness of guidance is well established by experimentation and experience (see Figure 17). The issue is not whether guidance is valuable in learning but rather whether a particular manner of guidance is valuable. The value of guidance, however, has been resolved into a number of controversial issues, such as direct instruction versus guided discovery, or expository teaching versus individually derived principles. In testing the effectiveness of guidance, the experimenter may compare one of its extreme forms with another; or he may design his procedure so that variations between such extremes may be evaluated.

Using sixth-grade pupils, Kittell[39] measured the effect of different

[39] J. E. Kittell, "An Experimental Study of the Effect of External Direction During Learning on Transfer and Retention of Principles," *Journal of Educational Psychology*, 48 (1957), 391–405.

amounts of guidance in solving a problem consisting of multiple-choice items. The purpose was to determine the effect of three amounts of guidance while the pupils were trying to discover principles that were needed in the solution of the problem. The group that received an intermediate amount of guidance was superior in immediate learning, retention, and transfer to groups that received either more or less

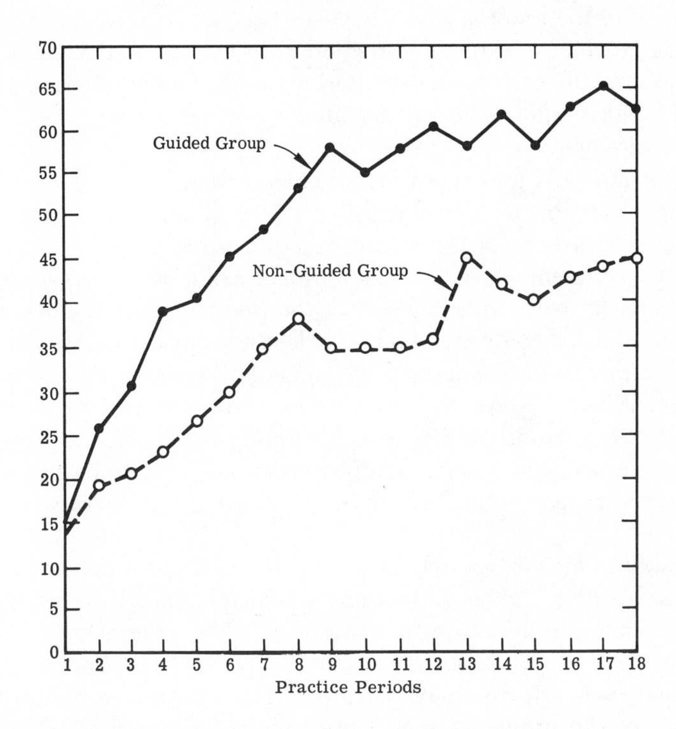

Figure 17. Daily average percentage scores for the two archery groups. From D. R. Davies, The Effect of Tuition upon the process of learning a complex motor skill, *Journal of Educational Psychology*, 1945, 36:352–365.

assistance. Craig[40] also provided college students with different amounts of guidance, in the form of clues, to correct responses in the solution of multiple-choice test situations. Three of his groups were provided with clues to discovery; one was not. Students who were provided with a statement of a principle common to a group of items were able to avoid many errors and greatly increase their efficiency. Kersh,[41] using high

[40] Robert C. Craig, *The Transfer Value of Guided Learning* (New York: Bureau of Publications, Teachers College, Columbia University, 1953).

[41] Bert V. Kersh, "The Motivating Effect of Learning by Directed Discovery," *Journal of Educational Psychology*, 53 (1962), 65–71. See also Jerome Moss, "The Relative Effectiveness of the Direct-Detailed and Direct-Discovery Methods of Teaching Letter Press Imposition," *Journal of Educational Research*, 58 (1964), 50–55.

school geometry students, tested the effectiveness of three degrees of guidance. One group learned by *rote* methods (representing virtually no guidance); another learned by direct instruction; and a third group was assisted in discovering its own methods of solution. Performance under these different experimental treatments was evaluated by immediate learning, retention, and transfer. The unexpected result of this experiment was that the rote learning group was consistently superior to the others on all of the criteria. Kersh believes that the self-discovery method is superior to that of external direction only insofar as it increases the student's desire to perform a task. Once the student is successful, as a result of his own efforts, he is motivated to extend his learning beyond formal requirements.

Different amounts and types of guidance have also been tested with particular reference to transfer. In a study of college students, the learning task consisted of translating a common four-sentence statement into twenty different codes.[42] These students who served as their own control were given the rule for half of the problems; for the other half, they were expected to derive the rule solely from example. The students did significantly better, as judged by immediate learning, when the rule was given. When they were given a transfer test a week later, however, the results were strikingly different. The findings on this test indicated that principles derived independently were more likely to be transferred than were principles that had been provided as authoritative statements.

In a study of elementary-school pupils, Hendrix[43] also determined the extent to which the manner of learning a principle affects the probability of recognizing an opportunity to use it. Two contrasting learning situations were used. In one situation the pupils were encouraged to derive their own principles; in the other they were given authoritative statements of the principles they were expected to apply. The greatest amount of transfer was achieved by pupils who had been encouraged to derive principles by their own efforts and the least by those who had been provided with principles at the beginning.

The variable and apparently conflicting results of the studies that have been reviewed are due to many conditions. These include differences in the manner in which guidance is administered, the time at which it is given, as well as the amount given. Other conditions include differences in types of task, maturity of learners, and the criteria used in appraising the results. Perhaps the most important factor contributing to controversy is the tendency to regard the problem of guidance as representing one

[42] G. M. Haselrud and Shirley Myers, "The Transfer Value of Given and Individually Derived Principles," *Journal of Educational Psychology*, 49 (1958), 293–298.

[43] Gertrude Hendrix, "A New Clue to Transfer of Training," *Elementary School Journal*, 48 (1947–48), 197–208.

extreme form as opposed to another. It is interesting to note, however, that Bruner and Ausubel, who have been most active in the guidance controversy, do not themselves advocate such extreme positions.

Bruner[44] contends that learning by directed discovery (not independent) increases the individual's ability to learn related materials, creates an interest in the task itself rather than in the external rewards that may be associated with it, develops initiative in attacking different kinds of tasks, tends to contribute to higher retention, and ensures greater probability of transfer. Ausubel[45] believes that the most effective kind of guidance is that which assists the learner in making his own discovery. He also feels that this type is a variant of expository teaching. It requires active involvement of the learner in a task in which he is encouraged to derive his own generalizations and synthesize knowledge in response to leading questions posed by the teacher. Ray's[46] conclusion centers on one of the significant points in the guidance controversy. He feels that the directed-discovery method can be used most effectively with low-ability pupils. He also believes that various types and amounts of guidance should be adapted to specific teaching situations, regardless of pupil ability. Much of the effectiveness of guidance depends on the manner in which error is controlled.

control of error

Two problems associated with the responsibility for controlling error are the need to help the learner off to a good start and the need to maintain a balance between too much and too little guidance. In each instance the interest is in assisting the learner to grow in responsibility and become able to work at his task with a minimum of help.

getting off to a good start

Guidance may be given in advance of a student's attempt at a learning task, at any time during his initial attempts, or at any other time while learning. He may be told, for example, what to look for in his next geometry assignment and perhaps helped to work one or two problems for illustration. He may also be assisted with his geometry after he has made several unsuccessful attempts to solve a problem. In general, guidance is most effective during the initial stages of learning so that errors committed may be corrected before they become habitual.

If the learner gets off to a good start and acquires the proper methods of attacking a problem, there will be no need for him to go through the

[44] J. S. Bruner, "The Act of Discovery," *Harvard Educational Review,* 31 (1961), 21–32.

[45] David P. Ausubel (31).

[46] Willis E. Ray, "Pupil Discovery and Direct Instruction," *Journal of Experimental Education,* 29 (1961), 271–280.

wasteful effort of unlearning. The relevant and significant aspects of a task should be pointed out. The pitfalls in a learning situation should not be brought to the attention of the learner at first. If the indication of errors likely to occur in a situation is believed necessary, this should take place after the main ideas have been grasped. A statement by Hovland[47] is applicable to many situations:

> The instructor must therefore see to it that the relevant phases of the work are attended to and the irrelevant ones disregarded. The reason it is so difficult to stop slicing in golf is that the difference between the correct drive and the slicing is not sufficiently obvious from the learner's point of view. What the professional has to do is to show the learner the specific respects in which the right and wrong methods differ.

During the initial stages of learning guidance is most helpful when it assists the learner in doing something rather than analyzing something. He should be encouraged to make a complete response even though his efforts may be characterized by omission and error. By doing something, he is able to familiarize himself with the total task and thereby form a basis for understanding the details of form and structure he will normally learn later. Response to a total task is the only way in which he can react intelligently to a new situation.

The learner should first respond to total situations and later learn details and techniques as a means of correcting error and perfecting form. His work in English, for example, should provide for use of language in oral and written composition and not await his complete mastery of rules of grammar and techniques of expression. In music, he should learn to sing and interpret rhythm before studying the techniques of notes and scales. In English literature, he should read the works of authors and get some notion of their meaning and significance before he analyzes them for style or imperfections.

too much versus too little help

Guidance may be given so minutely that even the slowest learner will perform without error. It may also be provided so inadequately that only a few of the abler individuals will report an errorless solution. Between such extremes, it is best to assume that a certain amount of error will occur and accept it as an indication that the task may require supplementary instruction.

The desire to ensure errorless responses may result in excessive guidance. During the initial stages of learning a task, there is usually a certain amount of confusion and error. Many of the learner's uncertainties arise before he has taken the time to determine the extent to which he can proceed without guidance. The teacher, however, zealous to be of assistance, may be tempted to take up the learner's problems at a point

[47] Carl I. Hovland, "Basic Principles of Learning and Their Application in Training," *American Association Personnel Series,* 47 (1941), 3–14.

where he experiences difficulty and continue to a point not far from the solution.

In a series of investigations, Torrance tested the effectiveness of varying degrees of overdirection and guidance in indoctrination situations. In one of his investigations[48] he determined the effect of varying degrees of pressure exerted by instructors in indoctrinating aircrewmen about an emergency ration. Promising results were obtained from the "low pressure" techniques in which the subjects relied mainly on objective information and straightforward instruction. In contrast, negative effects were obtained from conditions that emphasized personal persuasiveness. In another study,[49] involving indoctrination, similar results were obtained. Pressure up to a point was accompanied by increased acceptability; but beyond that point the influence was negative. Torrance[50] believes that much failure in school is due to overdirection and domination by teachers.

Evidence of insufficient guidance may be apparent in vague directions for assignments. When a learner is instructed to read a certain section of a biology textbook, to study six pages of advanced reading in his history book, to master the rules presented on a certain page of a textbook in English usage, frequently he is left in doubt about the demands to be made of him later. He may not know whether he should memorize the material to the point of verbatim reproduction, be able to discuss it with some degree of understanding, be prepared to listen to its further explanation with some comprehension, or make himself ready to apply certain facts in the material to situations that will be presented later. Assignments should be definite.

The time for giving guidance is necessarily associated with the amount. In every learning situation a stage is reached when the amount of guidance diminishes rapidly in effectiveness. Between the extreme of providing too little or too much help, there is a middle course. When it is clear the learner understands the significant principles in his task and is prepared to proceed with a fair degree of assurance that he will be successful, aid should be withdrawn.

learning principles at work

Almost every teacher has thought at one time or another of how he might use learning principles as a means of improving his instruction.

[48] E. P. Torrance, "Instructor Effort to Influence: An Experimental Evaluation of Six Approaches," *Journal of Educational Psychology,* 49 (1958), 211–216.

[49] E. P. Torrance, "An Experimental Evaluation of 'No Pressure' Influence," *Journal of Applied Psychology,* 43 (1959), 109–113.

[50] E. P. Torrance, "The Phenomenon of Resistance in Learning," *Journal of Abnormal and Social Psychology,* 45 (1950), 592–597.

Werf[51] became interested in this problem while directing amateur play productions. He first compiled a list of learning principles and then applied them in his day-to-day work. The principles that he selected and their applications to play production are as follows:

1. Meaning is a fundamental condition of rate and amount of learning and retention.

The first rehearsal should consist of a complete reading of the play with stress on its meaning. At this point, it is necessary for the actor to get a clear conception of the dominant purpose of the play. The setting, the characters, the acts, and scenes should be placed in logical relationship to the theme or mood.

2. Distributed practice by the repetitive-part method ensures equal learning of all parts.

During the first four weeks, for example, the rehearsals are scheduled as follows:

Monday, Act I
Tuesday, Act I once and Act II
Wednesday, Act II once and Act III
Thursday, Acts I and II
Friday, Act III

3. Practice as the material is used.

All rehearsals except the first should be on the stage in a setting closely resembling the finished product. After three weeks of practice, the scenery should be in place and all details having significance for the play should be in order.

4. A certain amount of overlearning up to the proper psychological limit is wholesome.

At least fifty hours should be devoted to group rehearsals. Much practice is required to build the actor's confidence and make skills habitual. The learner's performance should become second nature.

5. Troublesome parts should be practiced as units, then replaced in their sequence.

6. Stage business should proceed from major to minor, large to small, mass to detail.

Werf believes these principles may be used by any teacher who directs play production.

study questions

1. What activities are effective in developing certain kinds of learning?
2. How does the effectiveness of one activity compare with that of another?
3. Select a subject you are taking and analyze your activities in studying it. What activities tend to "pay off" best?

[51] Lester Vander Werf, "Learning Theory Applied to Amateur Play Production," *School Review*, 58 (1950), 97–99.

4. Give your reaction to the statement that "we learn what we do."
5. List several kinds of activity that influence attitudes or beliefs.
6. How are appreciations formed?
7. Activities usually serve the same purpose as tests in the elementary school. In the secondary school and college, however, tests afford the principal means of appraising students. Is there anything wrong with these practices?
8. Suggest principles of whole and part organization that may be applied to ensure learning in a subject-matter field with which you are familiar.
9. Discuss broad and narrow interpretations of drill, evaluating various types of repetitive activity as aids to learning. Of what significance for learning is variety in (a) responses sought and (b) the media used to present learning materials?
10. To what extent may prevention of error be regarded as an aim in the guidance of learning? Is error (a) a fault of the learner for which he should necessarily receive censure or (b) evidence that the learning process is functioning improperly? As a teacher, how would you deal with errors?
11. Discuss the part played by review with respect to:
    a. Getting the learner ready for tests.
    b. Reviewing examination results.
    c. Scheduling reviews frequently, soon after studying a topic, and distributing them farther and farther apart later.
12. Give your interpretation of "economy of learning." To what extent is the effectiveness of practice affected by (a) frequency and (b) the length of practice periods? Discuss the significance for economy of (a) incidental versus guided learning, (b) amount of material and effort required to learn, and (c) recall and recitation.
13. Summarize some of the unfavorable learning conditions that may be attributed to the necessity of teaching large classes. Suggest procedures for minimizing the effect of certain of these conditions.
14. Evaluate "cramming" as a study device for:
    a. Examinations stressing many detailed facts.
    b. Examinations requiring exercise of higher mental processes such as reasoning and reflective thinking.
15. Summarize various conditions that encourage "cramming" for tests. Differentiate between "cramming" and a type of review that may be recommended. Name several teaching procedures for minimizing "cramming."
16. Formulate your views on the proper balance between excessive and insufficient guidance.

motivation: interests

7

Learning programs may be carefully prepared and supervised and yet not stimulate the student to learn. Creating a desire to learn is the most difficult achievement in a teacher's work; it is also the most rewarding. One approach to the motivation problem,[1] which will be the theme of this chapter, is through interests. Another is through incentives, which will be emphasized in the next chapter.

Interests reveal the nature of many types of ability and various aspects of personality as manifested in social relationships. They are also indicative of the learner's stage of development and his degree of identification with his surroundings. One seeks to recognize interests in order to make instruction a meaningful experience for the learner. One also seeks it, because activities associated with interests liberate energy.

The different methods[2] of measuring interests reflect the varying degrees of strength and validity in which interest manifests itself. Accurate identification of these degrees is important in interpreting the results of studies. One of these is defined as *expressed* interests, as illustrated by asking the individual to indicate specifically what he would like to do in a given situation. Another is *manifest* interests, or those

[1] Jack Frymier, "Study of Students' Motivation to Do Good Work in School," *Journal of Educational Research,* 57 (1964), 239–244. Frymier found a definite shift in responsibility from student to teacher as higher educational levels were reached. Younger students gave evidence of greater personal initiative and inherent motivation, whereas older ones apparently assumed it was the teacher's duty to make them learn.

[2] See Louise M. Smith and K. Wientge, "The Vocational Interests of Gifted Adolescents in an Intensive Summer Academic Experience," *Personnel and Guidance Journal,* 42 (1963–64), 15–20.

activities in which the individual has participated. A third is *inventoried* interests, or those revealed by such instruments as the Kuder Preference Record or the Strong Vocational Interest Blank. A fourth is *tested* interests, in which effort is made to determine the retention, for example, of knowledge in an interest area such as occupational information. Informal methods include observing individuals at work or play and noting the frequency with which certain books are requested in a library.

In investigations on groups of children, interests usually are classified by age and grade. These studies have resulted in classifications such as (1) play interests, (2) reading interests, (3) vocational and academic interests,[3] (4) radio, movie, and TV interests, and (5) various hobbies. When these classifications are analyzed, changes are noted for age and grade groups, thus trends are indicated as the individual advances from one maturity level to another. The range and extent of activities preferred by the various age and grade groups are *common* interests. They are the activities preferred by many children, particularly those of the same age or grade. Interests are also *individual* as differentiated from those that are common. Individual interests may reveal much about one's personality. One person may find it interesting to collect zoological specimens during his spare hours; another may enjoy tinkering with a radio set in his basement. Still another may find satisfaction in reading the works of a particular author. The interests of certain age and grade groups provide a basis for planning; but it is more important to know those of a particular individual.

Some interests reflect a desire for vicarious experience and wish fulfillment. Individuals are constantly seeking experiences that afford them satisfaction. The experiences through which satisfaction is sought may be obtained through active interests or passive interests. Playing tennis or building a boat may be considered active interests. Reading a book or watching a tennis match is a passive interest in which the emotional effect is felt through mental participation.

The extent to which one identifies himself with characters in a movie or story and experiences vicarious satisfaction depends largely upon the individual. Some individuals are moved to tears by scenes of suffering or sorrow in a movie; others may regard the performance as over-sentimental or ridiculous. Through reading, one person may become emotionally identified with the characters or enjoy experiences of traveling in foreign countries. Another may experience thrills of danger by identifying

[3] See Ann Jungerblut and John H. Coleman, "Reading Content that Interests Seventh-, Eighth-, and Ninth-grade Students," *Journal of Educational Research,* 58 (1965), 393–401. See also James Inskeep and Monroe Rowland, "An Analysis of School Subject Preferences of Elementary School Children of the Middle Grades: Another Look," *Journal of Educational Research,* 58 (1965), 225–228.

himself with a character in a movie or story whose daring deeds he might be reluctant to imitate in real life.

Individuals attend movies and read books for various reasons. They may participate in such activities simply to relieve boredom or to experience the pleasure of witnessing favorite actors or reading works of certain authors. Successful painters, artists, writers, and musicians arouse in others the emotions they themselves experience. Movies in particular are interesting to many persons because of the completeness of detail with which they may enjoy a type of life different from their own. As a rule, the environment depicted in a movie is on a higher plane. The tendency of movies to glorify the most lowly activities possesses democratic appeal. Scrubwomen, newsboys, and domestic servants are kindly treated and their personalities are highly respected. Identification with hero or heroine may be close and their roles may stimulate emotions attached to success. Some individuals may discover a means of escape from their own drab surroundings and annoyances by imagining that they themselves are performing the activities they are witnessing.

The learner may be expected to be more interested in activities that provide opportunities for doing something than reading or thinking about something. He is also more likely to be interested in activities in which he has had some previous experience. Activities that are pleasurable are more interesting than are activities that are not. Successfully completed activities are more interesting than are unsuccessfully completed ones.

environmental influence

Children are not born with propensities toward certain interests. They select their sources of satisfaction from available opportunities, each child in accord with his own manner of regarding his particular environment. The continuity of play interests from one generation to another is assured as a reflection of the customs and mores of society. Certain types of game, such as hide and seek, are traditional. Games at which children dance and sing stem from ancient social rites and incantations. Young children learn them from older children and from those adults who regard certain types of play for children as their social inheritance. Sex differences in play often receive encouragement; girls, for example, are provided with dolls, and boys with mechanical devices. Proximity to lakes and rivers encourages swimming, boating, and fishing. Physical surroundings likewise limit types of play; ice skating and skiing are possible only in certain parts of the country. Opportunities for play interests in country and city differ. Types of hobbies in which children become interested are influenced by availability of material and equipment as well as by popularity. They become interested in making model airplanes when the necessary material may be purchased in local stores and when others are engaged in this activity.

The home is the most important single influence on reading interests. The early interests of children are stimulated by stories read or told to them in the home. They are also influenced in standards of taste by materials read and discussed by members of their families. Homes of superior social class are usually provided with a quantity of reading material that is of high quality. Skelton[4] made an intensive study of the reading interests of sixth-grade children in relationship to the background of their parents. Home background and favorable influences in the schools were reflected throughout their reports on reading activities. Smith[5] found that the interests as well as attainments of ten-year-old children differed with varying geographical environments—rural, urban, and "fringe" areas. Teahan's[6] findings suggest that interest in scholarship is directly related to the quality of relationships the child has with his parents and to the parents' attitudes toward learning.

Students whose parents attended college prefer occupations that rank high for accepted cultural status. Vocations requiring college education tend to be preferred by students whose parents attended college. The greater the number of books in the home, the greater the tendency for such students to choose vocations that represent accepted cultural status. Steimel and Suizedelis'[7] study indicated that parental influence as perceived by students had an empirically demonstrated effect on the direction of interests as measured by the Strong Vocational Interest Blank. Vocational ambitions also reflect the social traditions of countries. Wilson's[8] study showed that English secondary-school students were vocationally ambitious but not excessively so. The results of her study suggested that such students tended to aim at the highest vocational levels available to the group to which they belonged. In another English study, Kahl[9] found that family status was useful in predicting the

[4] Dorothy Skelton, "Pupils' Interests in Reading," *Elementary English,* 38 (1961).

[5] A. N. Smith, "A Survey of the Attainments and Interests of Ten-year-old Children from Different Geographical Environments within a Country," *British Journal of Educational Psychology,* 33 (1963), 325–326.

[6] John E. Teahan, "Parental Attitudes and College Success," *Journal of Educational Psychology,* 54 (1963), 104–109.

[7] Raymond J. Steimel and Antanas Suizedelis, "Perceived Parental Influence and Inventoried Interests," *Journal of Consulting Psychology,* 10 (1963), 289–295.

[8] Mary D. Wilson, "The Vocational Preferences of Secondary Modern School Children," *British Journal of Educational Psychology,* 23 (1953), 97–113.

[9] Joseph Kahl, "Educational and Occupational Aspirations of 'Common' Boys," *Harvard Educational Review,* 23 (1953), 196–203. See also Robert G. Brown, "A Comparison of the Vocational Aspirations of Paired Sixth-Grade White and Negro Children Who Attend Segregated Schools," *Journal of Educational Research,* 58 (1965), 402–404.

educational and vocational ambitions of "common" high school boys. Half of the boys who were interviewed did not desire college education and looked forward to "common" man occupations. Discontented parents, however, tended to train their sons from the earliest years to regard school work seriously and to use their education as a means of climbing into the middle class.

Many vocational choices are inspired by opportunities for entering occupations in the immediate vicinity. Patterns of vocational interest are based on concepts of occupations in which persons are engaged. Vocational choice is essentially a selection made from various possibilities in the environment.[10] Occupations such as those developing from investigations in the field of electronics and atomic energy are especially alluring to youth. Environment is the source of stimulation that encourages the development of interests. The more stimulating the individual's surroundings, the more likely he is to discover that his interests have educational and vocational possibilities.

stability of interests

During his early years, the individual is attracted by various activities in his local environment. Changes in interests as he advances from one age or maturity level to another are usual. But as he reaches the adolescent period, he begins to think of school subjects and vocations as having a direct relation to his purposes and goals in life. It is no accident, therefore, that the bulk of research related to the stability or permanence of interests has been concerned with subject and occupational choices, with the greater emphasis being placed on the latter.

Bledsoe and Brown[11] administered an interest inventory to fourth-, sixth-, and eighth-grade groups in 1961 and readministered the same inventory to these groups in 1963. The findings indicated a decrease in activities at higher grade levels, a trend interpreted as evidence of maturity and crystallization of interests rather than as a decrease in the interests themselves. The Kuder Preference Record was given to 129 ninth-grade students in the public schools of Tarentum, Pennsylvania.[12] Two years later a duplicate form of the inventory was given to the same group. The correlation between scores on the two administrations of the

[10] G. Frederic Kuder, "A Rationale for Evaluating Interests," *Educational and Psychological Measurement,* 23 (1963), 3–12.

[11] Joseph Bledsoe and Iva D. Brown, "The Interests of Preadolescents: A Longitudinal Study," *Journal of Experimental Education,* 34 (1965), 337–344.

[12] John A. Stoops, "Stability of Measured Interests of High School Pupils between Grades Nine and Eleven," *Education Outlook,* 27 (1953), 116–118.

inventory was regarded as the coefficient of stability. Coefficients of correlation were calculated for the nine areas of interest as measured by the inventory. The results showed that some areas were much more stable than were others but did not indicate high stability for the entire pattern of interests. Mallison and Crumrine,[13] also using the Kuder Preference Record, compared the interests of students when they were in the ninth grade with their interests when they were in the twelfth grade. The highest area of interest remained the highest for 52 percent of the students; the second highest area remained the second highest for 34 percent; and the third highest remained the third highest for 28 percent. When similar comparisons were made for the lowest three areas of interest at the ninth and twelfth grades, the lowest remained the lowest for 43 percent of the students; the second lowest remained the second lowest for 35 percent; and the third lowest remained the third lowest for 22 percent. When considering the group as a whole, 80 percent of the students in the highest area of interest in the ninth grade remained the highest in the twelfth grade.

As students advance to higher educational levels, vocational interests tend to become more stable. Reid[14] gave the Kuder Preference Record to an entering group of college freshmen at the beginning of the fall term and repeated it fifteen months later. Coefficients of correlation between the scores on the two administrations of the inventory were used as the criteria of stability. These coefficients ranged from .72 for computational interests to .89 for persuasive interests. The median coefficient for all areas of interest was .77, indicating that interests of these young adults tended to be relatively stable. In a follow-up study of the career choices of university freshmen, Selvin[15] two years later found a fair degree of stability but certain kinds of occupations had been influenced by the combination of father's education and type of residence groups.

Five years after administering the Geist Picture Interest Inventory, Geist[16] conducted a follow-up study to determine changes in vocational interests of college and trade-school students and of students in grades eight to twelve. The results indicated that in the mechanical, scientific, and outdoor types of interest, almost all of the students initially tested did not engage in any work outside their respective areas. The results

[13] George H. Mallison and William M. Crumrine, "An Investigation of the Stability of Interests of High School Students," *Journal of Educational Research,* 45 (1953), 369–383.

[14] J. W. Reid, "Stability of Measures of Kuder Interests in Young Adults," *Journal of Educational Research,* 45 (1951), 307–312.

[15] H. C. Selvin, "The Impact of University Experiences on Occupational Plans," *School Review,* 71 (1963), 317–329.

[16] H. Geist, "Five-Year Follow-Up of the Geist Picture Interest Inventory," *California Journal of Educational Research,* 13 (1962), 195–208.

also showed a close correspondence between inventory scores and their current work with respect to major in college, clerical, scientific, computational, and artistic areas of interest.

Occupational choices of college students indicate increased realism in evaluating certain factors that contribute to sound vocational selection. The social prestige of an occupation induces boys to consider fields such as medicine, law, banking, or government service. College students select occupations for such reasons as (1) contribution to social prestige, (2) contribution to social well being, and (3) probable economic return. As higher educational levels are reached, individuals consider occupational choices more realistically; but prestige and economic gain frequently outweigh personal interest and ability.

interests and ability

Bright children differ from the dull both in the number and kinds of interests they manifest. This difference is demonstrated by children of varying intelligence levels when their reading interests and their subject and vocational preferences are compared.

Bright children read far more than do average children. Their reading covers a wider range; it also includes material of higher quality. They are less attracted by fanciful material than to material that requires thinking and meditation. The gifted seek reading matter that challenges their understanding, and they approach it with eagerness. They enjoy material that concerns character development or the gradual unfolding of a dramatic background. Such children frequently reach the height of the reading craze between the ages of eight and ten years. Pupil differences, however, are marked among this group. Many gifted children of a given age read relatively little; others of the same age are avid readers, devouring almost anything readable. Cappa and Schubert[17] surveyed the home reading environment of fourth-, fifth-, and sixth-grade children having I.Q.s ranging from 130 to 185 (with an average of 138). Under the supervision of their teachers, the children supplied information about the availability of reading matter in their homes. The results showed that these children have fairly large personal libraries, an average of 41 books owned per child with a number owning 50 or more books. Approximately half of the children received magazines just for themselves, and more than half devoted an hour or more daily to reading at home.

Children in the lower intelligence levels tend to be satisfied with fanciful stories that provide entertainment. They are not generally interested in informational material or appreciative of many types of

[17] Dan Cappa and D. G. Schubert, "Do Parents Help Gifted Children to Read?" *Journal of Educational Research,* 56 (1962), 33–36.

humor. They tend to favor fiction rather than science, history, poetry, or drama. Children on these levels prefer materials that display action, sports, and familiar circumstances.

Bright and dull children also differ widely in their formal subject matter interests. Rice[18] compared random samples of fourth- through sixth-grade pupils from exceptional and normal groups with respect to their patterns of academic interests. The more highly gifted pupils displayed significantly more interest in academic areas, especially reading, science, and arithmetic. Subjects having the least interest for both normal and gifted pupils were social studies and writing. In the secondary school, students in the lower intelligence levels generally prefer trades and industries; bright students are more likely to select mathematics and science. Greater interest is usually shown in abstract subjects by gifted students and less in practical ones.

The occupational ambitions of gifted children tend to conform to the vocational activities of their fathers and show preference for public service or professions, especially in the case of boys. Unselected children also tend to favor occupations of their fathers. Among their choices are found not only the professions, but occupations involving mechanical, athletic, and clerical activities. Students who hesitate to make choices are frequently not studious, show superior physical development, and make low scores on intelligence tests.

The superior perception of the bright child enables him to derive meaning from many activities that might not command the attention of the dull. General intellectual ability is a necessary element in making possible the attraction of the individual to activities. Special aptitudes correlate even more closely with interests than they do with general ability, especially with interests in particular school subjects and vocations. A person, for example, who is genuinely interested in music is expected to possess some aptitude in it. Some evidence[19] suggests that where there are marked discrepancies between aptitudes and interests, personality maladjustments may result.

Two factors are important in determining the manner in which interests will be developed. One of these is the native ability of the learner. The other includes the skills, attitudes, and information that are acquired through learning. Without the necessary ability, activities and

[18] J. P. Rice, "Comparative Study of Academic Interest Patterns among Selected Groups of Exceptional and Normal Intermediate Children," *California Journal of Educational Research,* 14 (1963), 131–134. See also Wayne L. Herman, "How Intermediate Children Rank the Subjects," *Journal of Educational Research,* 56 (1963), 435–436. This study shows social science material to be lowest in popularity.

[19] Frank A. Nugent, "The Relationship of Discrepancies between Interests and Aptitude Scores to Their Related Personality Variables," *The Personnel and Guidance Journal,* 39 (1961), 388–394.

materials would be neither meaningful nor satisfying. Without opportunity for training and education, the individual could not discover activities commensurate with his abilities.

interests and achievement

A guiding assumption in studying relationship between interests and achievement is that students should do better in subjects they like than in those they dislike. In a study by Dean,[20] interests of fifth-grade children were measured by a questionnaire in which they listed the subjects they liked best. Standardized achievement tests were used to measure attainment in reading, arithmetic, language, and spelling. Pupils in the highest quarter in achievement were compared with those in the lowest quarter. Comparisons were also made of the average achievement of the preference groups with the nonpreference groups for the same school subjects. The results did not reveal significant differences in all cases, but there were definite trends in favor of the preference groups.

Nemoitin[21] asked 150 students who were completing the last half of their fourth year in high school to indicate in a specially prepared questionnaire the subjects they liked best and least. The questionnaire was prepared on the basis of the courses the students had had opportunity to take. They were instructed not to be influenced by their attitudes toward the teachers or by any other factors that could be involved in their ratings. The grades received by these students during their three and one-half years were obtained from the official records. Nemoitin thus had two sets of data for each student: the expressed interests for certain subjects (what they liked best and least) and the grades they had made in their subjects. The results indicated a close relationship between interest and achievement. In 80 percent of the cases, the average grade in the courses liked best was higher than the grades attained in all other courses; 59 percent showed higher average grades in courses liked second best than in all other courses; 83 percent showed lower average grades in courses disliked most; and 66 percent showed lower average grades in courses disliked still less in degree. Witty[22] also found that the subjects liked best among ninth- and tenth-grade students were usually those in which they won their best marks.

Several studies involve various measures and detailed statistical

[20] Stuart E. Dean, "Relation of Children's Subject Preferences to Their Achievement," *Elementary School Journal,* 51 (1950–51), 89–92.

[21] Bernard O. Nemoitin, "Relation between Interest and Achievement," *Journal of Applied Psychology,* 16 (1932), 59–73.

[22] Paul Witty, "A Study of Pupils' Interest in Grades 9, 10, 11, and 12," *Education,* 82 (1961–62), 169–174.

analyses. Jones[23] administered a battery of instruments to beginning high school students who were enrolled in a science institute during summer. These instruments included measures of ability, achievement, and interests. Correlation analyses indicated that when the student's *expressed* interest was combined with some measure of ability, it was possible to predict his *tested* interest. The data also indicated that it is possible to estimate science interest by means of an information test. Barilleaux[24] found that within the I.Q. range of 86–139 there was a high and very significant relationship between intensity of science interest and the probability of success in high school science. For students having I.Q.s below 86 the relationship was still positive but low. In a study designed to predict grades of college students in their major fields, French[25] used sixteen short "pure" tests of aptitude factors, and fourteen measures of interest. The aptitude tests contributed most to absolute prediction of academic success; whereas the interest measures contributed most to differential prediction. The results of both measures, however, were sufficiently definite to justify the development of expectancy tables for use by counselors and students.

Coefficients of correlation between interests (irrespective of the different measures) and achievement would probably range from .30 to .70. Frandsen[26] computed the relationship between interests, as measured by the Kuder Preference Record, and scores attained on the USAFI General Educational Tests and credits earned in courses. A coefficient of .50 was obtained between science interest and long-range achievement in the natural sciences. A coefficient of this size probably is typical. A student who achieves superior rating in a subject-matter area such as science is doubtlessly interested in it. One who demonstrates on an inventory a strong preference for science probably possesses considerable scientific knowledge. Interest leads to the acquisition of knowledge, which in turn often leads to increased interest.

interests: opportunity and responsibility

Not only do interests reflect the individual's cultural heritage; but they may be symptomatic of his inner cravings and motives. They are the

[23] K. J. Jones, "Interest, Motivation, and Achievement in Science," *Journal of Experimental Education,* 33 (1964), 41–53.

[24] L. E. Barilleaux, "High School Science Achievement as Related to Interest and I.Q.," *Educational and Psychological Measurement,* 21 (1961), 929–936.

[25] John W. French, "Comparative Prediction of College Major Field Grades by Pure-Factor Aptitude, Interest, and Personality Measures," *Educational and Psychological Measurement,* 23 (1961), 767–774.

[26] Arden Frandsen, "Interests and General Educational Development," *Journal of Applied Psychology,* 31 (1947), 57–66.

outward expressions of the individual's attitudes and ideals and are driving forces in his attainment. Recognition of interests is a means of motivating work in various subjects, which at the time may seem remote from the learner's present needs and ultimate aims.

Interests provide at once an opportunity and a responsibility. The opportunity is to use any interests already present; the responsibility is to stimulate development of new ones.

using present interests

Students reveal much about their interests while enrolled in a class. Their questions, themes, and written work provide clues. Much more may be gained, however, where effort is made at the beginning of a course to discover the learner's interests directly. The information needed can be obtained informally and requires little effort. Examples of informal techniques include making note of what students voluntarily do in and out of class, requesting them to list activities in which they normally engage, and asking them to indicate their preference for school subjects.

In considering reading interests, the teacher should find out how much time students spend in voluntary reading, what books and magazines they recently read, and what topics they prefer. The teacher may obtain more exact information by asking students to keep diaries for recording their voluntary reading. He may obtain details of hobbies by providing opportunities for students to describe them orally and in written composition. In some situations, students may demonstrate their hobbies to a class or display samples of collected items. For convenience in reviewing the interests that are discovered, students may record significant facts and make additional entries from time to time. A teacher who collects such information shows that he is interested in making his course something more than a systematic treatment of a subject. Students respond favorably to a teacher's awareness of their personal aims and preferences. And all courses afford opportunity for such recognition.

providing for special interests

One of the many ways of using interests is to encourage students to work on problems in which they have an expressed preference. It is realized that they may know more about their interests than any one else at a given time. Their preference for topics to be developed as themes, library research reports, or projects should be respected. Such activities increase meaningfulness and interest of required work. The work itself may be used as an additional basis for appraising accomplishment.

Many special abilities as well as interests are revealed through projects that permit the learner to express himself. A history student may develop a project on some aspect of local history. One enrolled in physics may select a special project such as work on a radio in his home. A home economics student may make a study of certain recipes. One studying biology may wish to report on specimens he has collected and classified. Some students may keep notebooks of interesting items they have read or observed. These may be reviewed at intervals.

Other means of using special interests include recognizing, during class discussion, students whose experiences qualify them to contribute to an otherwise abstract treatment of a topic. These experiences may include travel in foreign countries or activities such as camp education and scout programs. Unique experiences may also be recognized when students are organized into small groups for special reports or assignments.

associating old and new experiences

A teacher may arouse interest in a new subject by showing how it is related to previous materials or experiences. A course in civics is more interesting when the learner realizes that the topics discussed are similar to problems he sees in everyday life and when he is asked to relate them. A course in physics becomes more meaningful when applications are made to radio or TV sets in the home or school. Arithmetic is more attractive when applications are made to purchases in stores, insurance, or budgets. Pupils are more likely to be interested in activities in which they have had some previous experience, especially when they pertain to daily living.

importance of activity

The importance of activity in learning has already been discussed. The individual learns better when he is doing than he does when he is listening to explanations by his teacher or is reading from his textbook. Interest is heightened when students begin to engage in concrete types of activity. In home economics, interest is increased when students begin their laboratory work, in foreign language when they begin to speak and write the language, and in chemistry when they participate in experiments or demonstrations. After the learner has engaged in some concrete activity, he begins to ask questions, to search for reasons underlying principles, and to seek applications to daily life.

stimulating and evaluating interests

The extraordinary effect of environmental influences in shaping and developing interests provides a clue to their redirection and improvement. Pupils become interested in good reading material if it is made available and if taste for it is cultivated. Development of discriminating reading habits and tastes depends upon the accessibility and abundance of desirable books and magazines and upon the standards set by teachers. Of all the types of interest, reading is one which can be most directly controlled and redirected by the school. As a result of improved reading tastes and habits, the individual may be expected to use the knowledge gained as a means of extending and developing his other interests.

The results of efforts to stimulate interests should be evaluated from time to time. In doing so, one may use two kinds of information: (1) a record of the learner's major activities during a given period and (2) his responses to inventories or questionnaires that show the extent to which he "likes," "dislikes," or is "indifferent" to a variety of activities.

The principal concern is whether interests are in harmony with reasonable expectations of an individual at a given stage of his development. Certain criteria follow:

stability

During the individual's early years, his interests change as he advances from one stage of maturity to another. So long as he is learning, they reflect his stage of development. As he advances toward adulthood, his interests should become more stable.

harmony with other aspects of development

Interests should be in harmony with, and reinforce, other aspects of an individual's development. If they show little relationship to ability or if various activities are in conflict, superficiality may be suspected. Children are sometimes led to believe that they are interested in a given subject and, for example, may think of mathematics[27] as a field of specialization. It may be discovered that the attraction of mathematics, without the personal influence of others, is low. It is desirable to determine whether a given interest supports other facts related to the individual's development.

expansion and concentration

As the individual advances from one maturity level to another, interests are likely to expand in various directions. The child explores and enjoys many activities. By the time he has reached the adolescent period he may have already become interested in various types of sport, drama, movies, dancing, and a host of other activities that make his life meaningful. Such expansion is especially desirable as the adolescent begins the role of a young adult and is confronted with social responsibilities. During the expansion of interests, however, he needs to concentrate on educational and vocational goals. He needs to abandon interests that are in conflict or inconsistent.

[27] Thomas Poffenberger and Donald Norton, "Factors in the Formation of Attitudes toward Mathematics," *Journal of Educational Research,* 52 (1959), 171–176.

effect of instruction

Dora Smith's comment on reading may be applied to all interests: "The reading interests with which pupils come to school are our opportunity, but the reading interests with which they leave school are our responsibility." It is important to know whether instruction is having the effect of modifying present interests, of creating new ones, or of assisting the learner in understanding his potentialities.

study questions

1. Examine voracious reading or intense interest in movies or television as possible psychological mechanisms whereby the individual seeks (a) escape from reality and/or (b) enjoyment of vicarious experiences. Why might lack of guidance in such interests be more serious during childhood or youth than during adulthood?
2. Suggest apparent relationships of range, quality, and maturity of a child's interests with his intelligence level.
3. To what extent is it possible to predict interests on the basis of aptitudes? Aptitudes on the basis of interests?
4. Discuss in relation to possible vocational choices: (a) reading interests, (b) opportunities to attend movies, and (c) participation in music and dramatics.
5. Discuss the hazards incurred in attempting to provide opportunities for highly specialized vocational training in advance of the college level, at least for reasons associated with (a) stability of interests, (b) occupational opportunities, and (c) adequate appraisal of aptitude.
6. Summarize the (a) emotional, (b) social, and (c) intellectual effects that stimulating and broadening interest have on a child's scholastic progress.
7. Suggest a practicable method for using interests in educational and vocational guidance.
8. From the standpoint of social demands and the individual's ultimate welfare, formulate your point of view concerning the extent to which a child's interests should determine the nature of his school activities. How would you approach the problem of teaching a subject in which some pupils might profess complete lack of interest?
9. In what ways may a teacher be unwise in emphasizing certain of his own interests? Formulate criteria for evaluating the appropriateness of a given interest for a child.
10. Outline a basis upon which the development of a pupil's interests may be defended as an important outcome throughout all educational levels.

motivation: incentives

8

Interests afford an effective means of stimulating the learning process, but they cannot carry the burden of motivation alone. Incentives are needed. When using interests, the motivation tends to be intrinsic; when using incentives, it tends to be extrinsic. Incentives, however, also possess certain spontaneous characteristics because of their dependence upon motives.

incentives as appeals to motives

Motives are associated with an individual's concern for himself and his status with others. A majority of his concerns are associated with such considerations as need for achievement, social approval, prestige, and status among members of his group. The desire to be active and satisfy curiosity are also basic urges; others include concern for personal safety and need for food and shelter.

Individuals seldom reveal their true hopes and ambitions in learning situations. The results of one's performance may have intrinsic worth and constitute ends in themselves. A pupil, as a result of his success in arithmetic, for example, may derive personal satisfaction in the skills he has developed, or he may find no satisfaction in completing an arithmetic assignment except to avoid the necessity of remaining after school. He may also work harder on his arithmetic to obtain a mark that symbolizes approval than he will to gain satisfaction from solutions to arithmetic problems. Another pupil may apply himself to his learning task because it provides him with something to do. Still another may believe the information of a subject will help him in the pursuit of a hobby. Each individual may react differently to a teacher's effort to stimulate his learning.

Incentives are spurs to an individual to satisfy his motives. A pupil may be made conscious of an incentive when a direct appeal to a motive may be ineffective. Thus, he may work to obtain a satisfactory mark even though his basic motive is to maintain status in his group. Incentives are more effective when their influence is closely felt while learning. The distant prospect of becoming a mechanical engineer is less effective as an inducement to apply himself diligently to arithmetic than is some form of immediate recognition.

types of incentives

One type of incentive reveals the learner's accomplishment objectively, providing him with knowledge of results. Another employs encouragement or discouragement, praise or reproof. When these are used, a learner may not be informed objectively of his success or failure but rather be influenced by expressions of approval or disapproval for his performance. A third type consists of rewards and punishments, the tangible expressions of praise and reproof. A fourth includes devices designed to influence the performance of a learner when he is working in a group situation. He may compete or cooperate as a member of a group, with another group, or with individual members of his own group. He may also compete with his own record. Each of these types of incentive is used at one time or another to motivate the learning process. In addition to these there are certain group situations that have a stimulating effect.

knowledge of progress

The learner usually knows something about his progress, especially in self-checking subjects such as arithmetic, spelling, or a foreign language. In these, the results of one's efforts may be evaluated during study as well as in more formal situations. But in subjects that require extensive reading and where tests are given infrequently, the learner may not know the extent to which he is achieving the goals of a course. His study may be characterized by misconceptions, vague ideas, and false generalizations.

The most significant contribution of programmed instruction and automated teaching is the technique of providing the learner with knowledge of results as he proceeds from one item or problem to another. This is commonly referred to as *feedback*. In all learning situations the learner needs to know wherein his responses are correct or incorrect as objectively determined or whether they conform with expected answers. Knowledge of progress provides him with a basis for self-appraisal and gives direction and purpose to his efforts; without it he cannot maintain interest indefinitely in a subject or exert maximum effort to master it.

In experimental studies, a common procedure is to compare the effectiveness of one group that is working with knowledge of results with another group that is working without knowledge of results. The patterns of experimentation are frequently extended to show the relative effectiveness of groups that have *full knowledge, partial knowledge,* or *no knowledge.* The techniques may also be varied to determine whether or not efficiency is increased when knowledge of results, initially withheld, is added or decreased and whether knowledge of results produces more efficiency when given immediately or when the knowledge is delayed.

In an Air Force study, Stone[1] found that returning multiple-choice tests to his subjects improved their performance on retests. His subjects were also told why their incorrect responses were wrong and why the keyed choices were correct. This method proved superior to those techniques that provided partial knowledge of results. In a similar experiment, Alexander[2] provided knowledge of results to two experimental groups and withheld the knowledge from those used as control. The gains of the experimental groups were superior to those of the control groups. The learner also tends to profit most when given knowledge of results immediately. Angell[3] found that freshman chemistry students who were informed of correct answers immediately[4] after taking quizzes did significantly better on a final examination than did comparable groups whose quiz results were reported at the next class meetings.

The results of learning are continually evident to teachers in the elementary grades where the character of a pupil's work is revealed by daily activity without the use of formal tests. This close supervision in the elementary grades affords a basis for consistent appraisal of performance. Such supervision, however, is not practicable in the high school and college where much of a class period may be devoted to lectures, discussion, and assignments. Because most study and practice take place

[1] Raymond G. Stone, *The Training Function of Examinations: Retest Performance as a Function of the Amount and Kind of Critique Information* (USAF Personnel Training Research Center, Lackland Air Force Base, Texas, 1955).

[2] L. T. Alexander and others, "The Effectiveness of Knowledge of Results in a Military System Training Program," *Journal of Applied Psychology,* 46 (1962), 202–211.

[3] George W. Angell, "The Effect of Immediate Knowledge of Quiz Results on Final Examination Scores in Freshman Chemistry," *Journal of Educational Research,* 42 (1949), 391–394.

[4] K. E. Renner, "Delay of Reinforcement: A Historical Review, *Psychological Bulletin,* 61 (1964), 341–362. In certain situations, delayed knowledge may be more effective than immediate. Some delay in providing results may afford the learner opportunity to re-evaluate his responses.

outside class, there is no way of knowing the manner in which the student studies or uses certain mental processes in meeting requirements. The only practical means for meeting this situation is to give tests frequently enough to enable the learner to evaluate his achievement and to inform the teacher of his progress.

Equally important, tests energize the student to learn. Knowing that tests will be given, students who otherwise react to their work indifferently intensify their efforts to meet test requirements. If tests increase the learner's effort, they should perhaps be given frequently. The effectiveness of frequent, as opposed to infrequent, testing has been the subject of a number of investigations. Keys[5] tested the influence of weekly, as opposed to monthly, quizzes in an educational psychology course. Two classes studied the same material and took the same examinations. In one class, the tests were given as short weekly exercises; in the other class, the tests were longer and were given every fourth week. The group that took the tests as weekly exercises was superior to the control group as measured by scheduled tests. It was also superior to the control group on comprehensive examinations given without notice. In Scott's[6] study, an experimental group that took tests frequently during an extended period of instruction did significantly better on a final comprehensive examination than did a control group with which it was compared. Chansky[7] determined the reaction of students who had participated in an experiment involving several systems of guided learning. These students favored the system of continuous information, which provided a basis for corrective guidance and awareness of improvement.

Frequent testing is especially effective in courses in which lectures are emphasized and extensive amounts of reading are required. An experiment based on two large classes in government was conducted by Fitch[8] and her associates at Purdue University. The group used as control consisted of students who took the monthly quizzes only. The experimental group was composed of those who took the weekly quizzes in addition to the regular monthly examinations. The experiment was designed to determine the effect on achievement when short quizzes were given to one group over the weekly assignments and when voluntary discussion groups were provided for both classes. To stimulate learning, discussion groups were formed so that students interested in improvement could voluntarily receive additional help. The group that took frequent quizzes

[5] N. Keys, "The Influence on Learning and Retention of Weekly as Opposed to Monthly Tests," *Journal of Educational Psychology,* 25 (1934), 427–436.

[6] Ira O. Scott, "The Use of the Examination to Stimulate Learning," *California Journal of Secondary Education,* 13 (1938), 223–225.

[7] Norman M. Chansky, "Reactions to Systems of Guiding Learning," *American Educational Research Journal,* 1 (1964), 95–100.

[8] Mildred L. Fitch and others, "Frequent Testing as a Motivating Factor in Large Lecture Classes," *Journal of Educational Psychology,* 42 (1951), 1–20.

made consistently higher scores than did the group that took the monthly quizzes only. This superiority is accounted for in part by voluntary attendance at discussion groups. Frequent testing also appeared to motivate the students to read more extensively from supplementary sources and extend their preparation beyond routine requirements. Standlee and Popham[9] also found that frequent quizzes had the effect of increasing achievement in a lecture course, especially during its early parts. They attributed the effectiveness of the frequent quizzes to the combined influence of enforced activity, organization of materials, and knowledge of results. Their lessened effectiveness toward the end of the course may have been due to the overbalancing influence of these factors. A similar study by Selankovich[10] showed that quizzes were favored by students as a means of "keeping them on their toes."

Experimental evidence indicates that when tests are given frequently, lower-ability groups in particular are benefited. They need the energizing effect of tests to a greater extent than do higher-ability groups. They also require more help in analyzing their progress, which frequent testing provides. Higher-ability groups need less stimulation to learn and are better able to appraise their own progress.

The stimulating effect of tests depends partially upon the learner's possibility for success. For a learner capable of making a good record, testing may have a challenging effect; for one incapable of competing successfully in tests, testing may have a discouraging effect. The stimulating value of testing is also influenced by the learner's level of aspiration, whether he aspires to high, average, or passing accomplishment.

praise and reproof

Information about progress is a different device from the use of praise and reproof—although the devices may produce similar reactions. In using praise and reproof, the teacher assumes the role of evaluator and expresses some judgment about a learner's work. Consequently, the teacher's prestige and attitude are determining factors when this device is employed.

experimental results

In experimental study of praise and reproof, the procedure is similar to the one followed in investigating the effectiveness of knowledge of results. In one case, a group is approved and in the other reproved. Also,

[9] Lloyd S. Standlee and W. J. Popham, "Quizzes' Contribution to Learning," *Journal of Educational Psychology*, 51 (1960), 322–325.

[10] Dan Selankovich, "An Experiment Attempting to Determine Effectiveness of Frequent Testing as an Aid to Learning in Beginning Courses in American Government," *Journal of Educational Research*, 55 (1962), 178–180.

there may be a third group that is neither praised nor reproved and is frequently identified as the "neutral" group. The results achieved under these differing conditions of stimulation are then compared.

Dollins[11] determined the effect of teachers' praise on test performance of fourth-grade pupils. These pupils from twelve schools were classified on the basis of adjustment as measured by the California Test of Personality. Two experimental groups and one control group, drawn from the low adjustment group, were used in the experiment. Pupils were assigned tasks in addition and subtraction, three minutes a day being allotted for this work. In one of the experimental groups, they were given praise two out of every three school days; in the other, they were given praise one out of every three days, the children being praised for the work they did the day before. The control group received no praise. Pupils receiving praise showed the largest average gain, and the control group showed the least. Fleischman,[12] after giving subjects preliminary training on a rudder-control test, classified them into two comparable groups; one group was given a variety of motive-incentive instructions, and the other group received no instructions or encouragement. The gains of the motivated groups were significantly better than were those of the control group.

Seventy-four randomly selected teachers and 2,139 secondary-school students participated in an experiment conducted by Page.[13] The teachers administered to all students objective tests that were customarily given during a course of instruction. After scoring the tests in the usual manner and matching the students on the basis of performance, teachers assigned the papers randomly to one of three treatment groups. The *no-comment* group received no marks other than those for grading; the *free-comment* group received any comments the teacher regarded as appropriate for a particular student; and the *specified-comment* group received certain uniform comments that were predetermined for all similar letter grades and believed to be encouraging. The teachers returned the test papers to the students in the usual manner. They then reported scores earned on the next objective tests, which became the basis for comparison.

Students who received *free-comment* treatment achieved higher scores than did those who received *specified comments;* and those who received

[11] Joseph Dollins and others, "With Words of Praise," *Elementary School Journal,* 60 (1960), 416–450.

[12] E. A. Fleischman, "Relationship between Incentive-Motivation and Ability Level in Psycho-motor Performance," *Journal of Experimental Psychology,* 56 (1958), 78–81.

[13] Allis Batten Page, "Teacher Comments and Student Performance: A Seventy-four Classroom Experiment in School Motivation," *Journal of Educational Psychology,* 49 (1958), 173–181.

specified comments did better than did those who received *no comment.* The results showed that any comments of an encouraging nature have a favorable effect on a student's subsequent achievement.

Pupils are also influenced by encouragement from their parents. In a series of British studies, Wall and Miller[14] show that interest of parents in the success of their children has a measurable effect on their accomplishment. Children (ages eight to eleven), particularly boys, do much better when their parents are interested in their success. Pupils whose parents are rated as "very interested" tend to improve their test scores; those whose parents are rated as "uninterested" show a decline in scores. The results, however, vary with pupils of different ability levels. Intellectually

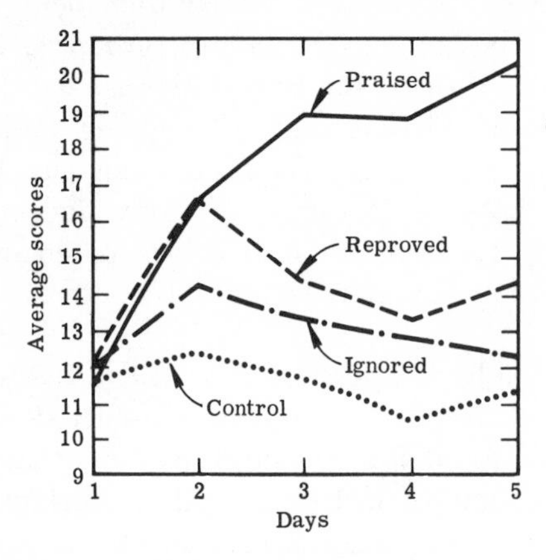

Figure 18. Effects of different incentives on average scores on arithmetic tests. From A. N. Frandsen, *How Children Learn* (New York: McGraw-Hill, 1957). After Hurlock.

superior children tend to secure grammar school status whether their parents are interested or not; but those only a little above average are more likely to achieve such status when their parents are interested in their progress.

A consistent research finding is that both praise and reproof stimulate learning. Each spurs the learner to greater effort. Ordinarily, praise may be expected to result in an individual's desire to continue the effort that brought him praise; reproof may be expected to result in a change in his mode of response, as shown in Figure 18.

The results are also affected when some form of approval or disapproval accompanies the learner's efforts. Either praise or reproof may disturb his equilibrium and cause him to exert effort to regain his balance. A positive incentive such as praise or encouragement, however, is more dependable in its effect than is a negative one such as censure or

[14] W. D. Wall and K. M. Miller, "Motivation and Counter-Motivation" in Proceedings of the XIV International Congress of Applied Psychology (Munksgaard, Copenhagen, Denmark, 1962).

discouragement. A positive incentive is interpreted by the learner as an attitude of helpfulness and interest. Reproof is more likely to produce a desired result when it is tempered with commendation about some aspect of achievement.

Pupils in the early grades in particular are affected by the teacher's reactions. They learn of their success through the teacher's attitude as expressed in commendation or encouragement rather than through objective results. Teachers of these grades must create positive attitudes if they are to be successful. In general, girls respond more favorably to praise; boys respond more favorably to reproof.[15] Intellectually superior pupils respond more favorably to reproof; those of low intelligence respond more favorably to praise. The effectiveness of praise and reproof also varies with personality characteristics. Thompson and Hunicutt[16] point out that the results of their study "indicate that praise as well as blame can be used unwisely if [the teacher] does not fully appreciate and understand the different personalities in his classroom."

precautions and implications

In experimental studies there is a tendency to regard praise and reproof on an either-or basis in which one extreme or another of the incentive situation is stressed. In the classroom, however, there may be gradations of intensity in the use of incentives. One may react unfavorably to lack of neatness in a pupil's work but favorably to the correctness of his responses. A learner may be praised for completing a large number of exercises but reproved for frequent errors. A teacher who is held in high esteem by his pupils and who is interested in them and their problems can use praise and reproof in varying degrees. It is more effective in most situations, however, to use them sparingly; this practice inspires trust and assures the learner a feeling of security. It is the teacher's attitude toward the learner's work and his possibilities for improvement that are most effective.

Since effectiveness of the teacher's reaction varies with individuals, one should know which pupils are likely to be most sensitive to praise and reproof. It is unwise to reprimand pupils for inferior work when they are working up to capacity; to belittle their effort is to frustrate their striving for even low accomplishment. Bright pupils, on the other hand, are better able to recover from reproof. Because they are capable of improving their

[15] W. J. Meyer and George G. Thompson, "Sex Differences in the Distribution of Teacher Approval and Disapproval among Sixth-Grade Children," *Journal of Educational Psychology*, 47 (1956), 385–395. These authors found that boys receive more disapproval from teachers than do girls. Also, both boys and girls nominated more boys for disapproval than girls.

[16] G. G. Thompson and C. W. Hunicutt, "Effect of Repeated Praise or Blame on the Work Achievement of Introverts and Extroverts," *Journal of Educational Psychology*, 35 (1944), 257–266.

status, it is easier to show them the value of higher standards of accomplishment.

reward and punishment

One type of reward is the offer of recognition for superior achievement —gold stars, places on the honor roll, prizes, and certificates. To receive such esteem and social approval the student must successfully complete certain tasks. Another type is associated with the satisfaction of doing a job well. Successful learning is its own reward; it reduces tension and builds up confidence in attacking other and more difficult tasks. Success reduces the learner's immediate drive but also builds his ambition to greater heights. When using the first type, the individual supposedly is motivated to perform a task in the hope of gaining prestige associated with superior work. In the second, he is expected to derive satisfaction from the work itself.

The threat of punishment may be emphasized for lack of effort. The learner's motive may be to escape punishment as well as to gain a reward. Withdrawal of privileges is an effective form of punishment, because it may be an incentive for their reinstatement.

The extrinsic types of reward, such as prizes and honor rolls, must be planned in advance with greater care and be administered more objectively than is the case in the use of praise and reproof. Certain types of punishment, such as loss of privileges, must also be planned in advance but with less objectivity than is necessary when using prizes and honors. Greater impersonality is possible when administering rewards and punishments than is possible when giving praise and reproof.

experimental results

Experimental studies of reward and punishment, like studies of praise and reproof, suggest a duality that rarely exists in school or life. Reward, the extreme positive aspect of the incentive situation, is compared with punishment, the extreme negative aspect. It is recognized, however, that the two incentives do not operate independently but tend to be complementary aspects of the same process. With reward, there is a change from a state of suspense to release when a goal has been reached. With punishment, there is a change from annoyance to relief. Both reward and punishment may exist within the same situation.

Forlano[17] determined the effect of money rewards on rate and amount of learning for pupils in grades four through eight. Promise of money was more effective as a means of securing achievement on the average than was an incentive that did not include a promise of money. Miller and

[17] G. Forlano, "An Experiment in Which the Delayed and Immediate Knowledge of Results with Monetary Reward Is Compared with Delayed and Immediate Knowledge of Results," *Teachers College Contributions to Education* (1936).

Estes[18] compared the effectiveness of monetary rewards with knowledge of results in a discrimination learning situation. Comparable groups of boys worked under three conditions of reward for each correct choice as follows: one cent, 50 cents, and knowledge of results. There was no difference in the efficiency of boys who received the 50-cent reward and those who received one cent. It was also found that boys whose incentive was limited to knowledge of results were most efficient of all. Holmes,[19] using students in one high school as subjects, tested the effect of honor rolls on achievement. The honor rolls consisted of students with grades 90 or better, those with grades 85–89, and those with grades 80–84. The results indicated that morale as well as scholarship was significantly increased under these conditions. Using second- and fifth-grade pupils, Otto and Melby[20] measured the effect of threat of failure on achievement on a standardized test. Pupils in the experimental groups were told there would be no failures regardless of their performance. Those in the control groups were warned of failure if they did not do well. The differences between the groups under these conditions were insignificant.

Experimental studies concerned with the effectiveness of reward and punishment in school situations are limited; but the results indicate that both incentive situations have a stimulating effect on learning. Brackbill and O'Hara's[21] study showed that learning was faster for children whose correct responses were rewarded and incorrect responses punished than it was for those who were reinforced only after correct responses. Most studies with children, however, show that reward provides stronger motivation than does punishment. Reward, like praise and encouragement, tends to produce attitudes favorable for further learning. It is also more stable[22] than punishment. Punishment may produce tension in the learner, causing him to be more alert; but it may also have a disruptive effect, resulting in divided attention. This situation may occur especially if the motive to avoid punishment is stronger than is the drive to attain the goal of a task. When this occurs, the two motives are in conflict.

Two types of reward will be described. The first possesses many

[18] L. B. Miller and W. B. Estes, "Monetary Reward and Motivation in Discrimination Learning," *Journal of Experimental Psychology*, 61 (1961), 501–504.

[19] Chester W. Holmes, "Honor Rolls as an Aid to Scholarship," *School Review*, 36 (1928), 465–468.

[20] Henry J. Otto and E. O. Melby, "An Attempt to Evaluate the Threat of Failure as a Factor in Achievement," *Elementary School Journal*, 35 (1935), 588–596.

[21] Y. Brackbill and J. O'Hara, "The Relative Effectiveness of Reward and Punishment for Discrimination Learning in Children," *Journal of Comparative Psychology*, 51 (1958), 747–751.

[22] Richard L. Solomon, "Punishment," *American Psychologist*, 19 (1964), 239–253. Solomon identifies various conditions that influence the effectiveness of punishment under laboratory conditions.

characteristics of a desirable incentive situation; it challenges the learner to do his best. The second, although motivational in purpose, is questionable in its effect.

A desirable type of reward. Schlesser[23] measured gains in scholastic aptitude under highly motivated conditions. Scholastic aptitude was measured by the American Council on Education Tests (ACE), and the motivation took place during the Navy Midshipmen Refresher program at Colgate University. The purpose was to provide enlisted men, who had an average of three years of college education, with the opportunity to complete midshipmen training on the same basis as candidates who had completed college. These men had been recommended as candidates for the program by their commanding officers. Each man wished to become an officer and knew that by completing this course and by passing sixteen weeks of training in the midshipman school he would become one. There was a definite objective to be attained and the steps taken to reach it were outlined in advance. Also, each student believed he possessed the ability to meet the challenge. Above all, there was the *reward* of becoming an officer if he were successful.

The significant effects of motivation are shown by the pretest and posttest scores on the ACE test. These students were retested after a period of twelve weeks. Retest results showed an average gain of 22 percentile points. Schlesser points out that approximately half of this gain may be attributed to practice effect, regression, and maturation; but a significant average of eleven percentile points remained. This gain is due to the effects of the training and the highly motivating conditions under which the students worked.

A questionable type of reward. Exemption from the final examination is sometimes offered as a reward for superior achievement. This inducement is offered students who maintain their test grades at a specified level or who achieve a stipulated average mark. The practice is supposed to encourage consistent performance and prevent last-minute cramming.

White[24] classified psychology students into experimental and control groups. The experimental group was told that its final examination would comprise material covered on weekly quizzes and that the term grade would reflect the average of quiz marks and the results on the final examination. The control group was told its term grade would be the average of quiz marks. All weekly quizzes were scored and returned. Immediately preceding the final examination, the control group was told to take the test and to do its best although, according to an agreement,

[23] George E. Schlesser, "Gains in Scholastic Aptitude under Highly Motivated Conditions," *Journal of Educational Psychology,* 41 (1950), 237–242.

[24] H. B. White, "Testing as an Aid to Learning," *Education Administration and Supervision,* 18 (1932), 184–194.

the results would not count toward a term grade. The average scores obtained by both groups on weekly quizzes were not significantly different even though the quiz results were the sole basis for the final grades of the control group. The experimental group, whose achievement on the final examination was to count toward its term grade, however, showed superior achievement in the final. There was evidence that this group made use of the results of weekly quizzes and also made special effort to prepare for the examination. Schutte[25] and Johnson[26] also found that expectation of a final examination improved achievement of college students.

Offering exemption may cultivate inconsistent attitudes toward testing. Implicit in this practice is the belief that students may fear the examination and be anxious to avoid it. On the other hand, it is desirable to encourage those who must take the examination to face it confidently and without anxiety.

Exemption also tends to ignore student differences. Slow-learning students are unable to meet exemption requirements, the reward for high achievement being set beyond their reach; rapid learners qualify readily. Exemption thus favors those most capable of doing well on the final examination and suggests punishment for those incapable of meeting the standards.

The final examination serves as an incentive for learning throughout a course. The need to organize and retain knowledge, step by step as it is learned, demands emphasis on an ultimate goal. Its motivating value lies in the opportunity it provides for demonstrating superior achievement. A final examination that makes fair demands of the learner is a legitimate incentive for thorough learning.

using reward and punishment wisely

The discussion has suggested that reward and punishment should be used cautiously. Some precautionary measures will be outlined.

The individual's characteristics should be known well. The effectiveness of reward and punishment is influenced by the relationship of the learner to his teacher, his classmates, the standards set by the school, as well as to his background and motives. Because of such variable factors, teacher attitudes toward reward and punishment may not conform with pupil opinions. Many pupils, especially slow learners, are not stimulated by the possibility of having a place on an honor roll or even of attaining "average" scholastic rating. This may also be the reaction of some of the abler ones whose levels of aspiration are not high. Moreover, some pupils

[25] T. H. Schutte, "Is There Value in the Final Examination?" *Journal of Educational Research*, 12 (1925), 204–213.

[26] Bess E. Johnson, "The Effect of Written Examination on Learning and on Retention of Learning," *Journal of Experimental Education*, 7 (1938), 55–62.

are not stimulated to modify their behavior as a result of loss of privileges, probation, or other measures intended as punishment. Only by knowing the individual can a teacher determine the incentive situations that produce the desired effect.

Learning itself is satisfying but may be reinforced by some form of recognition. It is frequently argued that external incentives, such as prizes, medals, or honor rolls, cause the learner to perform tasks superficially. In working for scholastic honors, for example, he may devote a disproportionate amount of time to memorization, which makes the results of his efforts impressive. In "working for grades" he may not develop insight associated with genuine interest and mastery of a subject. He should "get something" out of his work and not regard the attainment of marks as the principal objective. The fallacy of this argument is that there need not be any conflict between achieving satisfaction associated with doing a job well and receiving a reward in recognition of it. It is doubtful whether the learner is ever motivated solely by either alone.[27]

Punishment should follow as a consequence of one's behavior. The unpleasantness of punishment, however, may readily become associated with a learning task. As a result, the learner may develop a negative attitude toward his work, when otherwise he may have liked it. When punishment is administered on a personal and subjective basis, it is easy for the learner to claim the possibility of unfair treatment. On the other hand, when he knows he has violated an impersonal set of rules or standards or through lack of effort has failed to achieve the results expected, he is likely to be cooperative. Under such conditions he assumes the attitude that he deserves what he receives. When punishment serves to call attention to deficiencies or errors and suggests means for improvement, it may be converted into a reward. It is then that the learner may realize it is a method for improving his subsequent performance.

competition and cooperation

Children soon learn to compare their strength and skill with those of similar ages and thereby gain or lose prestige depending upon their abilities. If they are unable to compete in one activity, they may try others in which they have greater possibilities for success. A boy who is limited in physical strength may choose to gain status through intellectual activities.

Competition is fostered by various kinds of pressure. In school, prizes, awards, and the marking system serve to make one aware of his

[27] D. L. Thistlewaite, "Effects of Social Recognition upon the Educational Motivation of Talented Youth," *Journal of Educational Psychology,* 50 (1959), 111–116. See also John McDavid, "Some Relationships between Social Reinforcement and Scholastic Achievement," *Journal of Consulting Psychology,* 23 (1959), 151–154.

competitive role. In the home, there may be pressure by parents to seek to realize their own ambitions through the lives of their children. They may be anxious that their children achieve superior scholastic rating as compensation for their own limitations. They may also regard the social skills and athletic prowess of their children as a means of enhancing their own prestige.

In competition and cooperation are found impelling incentives similar to those operating within the social order. One must compete with others to achieve desired status in a group. One must also work as a member of a group in which each may contribute within the limits of his ability. Both competition and cooperation afford effective channels for achieving satisfaction. They frequently operate simultaneously. In a sense, competition and cooperation compete and cooperate with each other.

Personal gain is the ultimate consideration whether one competes or cooperates. A football player cannot engage in a football game alone; he must cooperate in the interdependent activities of team members. He cooperates to share in the experience of winning victory for his school. The team must cooperate with other teams so that its activity may have meaning. The player must compete with his teammates if he is to be selected for the position he desires. In all instances, it is the player who stands to gain or lose. Collective enjoyment is possible only when enjoyment is experienced individually by each person.

Classroom activities are cooperative in the sense that pupils are occupied with related materials and work toward common goals. When social influences impel them to seek individual or group superiority, the learning situation is competitive. Competition and cooperation in the classroom are genuine life situations.

types of competitive situations

Varying degrees of competition are evident in every group situation even though no effort may be made to create them. Experimental studies have been concerned with at least four motivating situations: (1) group versus group rivalry, (2) individual versus individual rivalry, (3) individual versus group rivalry, and (4) self-rivalry.

Group versus group rivalry. In "group versus group rivalry" a member of a group competes for the success of his group against another group. In experimental situations, two comparable groups are usually formed. One receives special stimulation; the other works under usual conditions. Various means are used to initiate rivalry. The members of one group may be directed to do as much work as possible but told not to try to think of rivalry with another group. The other group may be told to do as much work as possible and excel its rivals. The experimenter is aware that rivalry exists under any condition; he wishes to emphasize it in some situations and not in others. Through his directions, he wishes to make sure the individual is conscious of his competitive role in one situation and is not too much concerned about it in others.

Ryan[28] tested the effects of four types of incentive conditions on strength of grip. Four comparable groups of male subjects were used in the experiment. Group I was simply told to do as well as possible on the retest; Group II was urged to improve; Group III was shown the results of the previous test and permitted to observe the dynamometer dial on the retest; and Group IV was threatened with electric shock for failure to improve. The groups that were either simply told to do as well as possible or urged to improve made as much gain as did those that

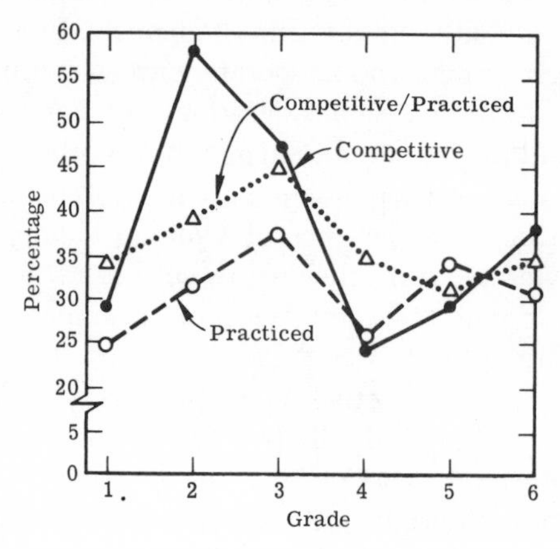

Figure 19. Percent of original responses in a "product-improvement task." From Torrance (note 29).

received other forms of incentive. Experiments conducted under school conditions also show that an attitude of rivalry causes groups to do more work. In a series of studies, Torrance[29] determined the effect of competition in creative learning situations. In the competitive situations, elementary-school children were required to think of as many ideas as possible for improving certain tasks. After the children were given a general orientation to the tasks, they went immediately to the testing situation.

The effectiveness of competition as compared with other experimental conditions is shown in Figure 19. In general, children who work under competitive conditions tend to make greater progress.

Individual versus individual rivalry. Attitudes of individual rivalry are always present in classroom situations. Pupils continually measure themselves against other pupils. Those who take pride in high scholastic

[28] E. Dean Ryan, "Effect of Different Motive-Incentive Conditions on Physical Performance," *Research Quarterly*, 32 (1961), 83–87.

[29] E. Paul Torrance, *Rewarding Creative Behavior* (Englewood Cliffs, New Jersey: Prentice-Hall, 1965).

achievement seek to equal or excel the records of others having similar ambitions. In doing so they compare themselves with standards set by others whose approval they most desire.

Competition between individuals is more spontaneous and requires less encouragement than does rivalry of one group against another. Within group-against-group competition are frequently found individual rivalries when the activity discloses the achievement of certain persons and permits comparisons. One may expect individual rivalry, for example, to a greater extent in a spelling match than in competition between two classes. In a spelling match, it is not only a question of the rival group to be eliminated but of the individual rivals who survive longest during the contest.

Individual versus group rivalry. In a study of individual versus group rivalry, Sims[30] used three comparable groups: a control group, a group-motivation group, and an individual-motivation group. In the group-motivation situation two groups of students were urged to compete against each other. In the individual-motivation group, the students were paired and each kept his own record as well as that of his partner. Substitution and reading tests were used for measuring progress. The group used as control improved 102 percent in substitution, the group-motivation group 109 percent, and the individual-motivation group 157 percent. The reading test showed similar results. The force of personal appeal is also felt more strongly when a prize is offered an individual than when it is offered a group. In one case, a pupil as a member of a group works for a prize that he or some other individual may win. In the other, the pupil as a member of a group works for a prize that his group may win. In Maller's[31] experiment the average child in the elementary grades worked 32.4 more arithmetic examples in a twelve-minute period when working for *self* than during the same amount of time when working for his *group*. The curves of those working for self (individual prize) rose with continued practice. On the other hand, the progress curves of pupils working for the group of which they were members consistently declined. Stendler,[32] also using elementary-school children, tested the effects of working for group and individual rewards. The activity consisted of painting murals. In one situation pupils were told that if everyone painted well and the paintings were of high quality, everyone would receive a prize. In the other, prizes would be awarded to

[30] V. M. Sims, "The Relative Influence of Two Types of Motivation on Improvement," *Journal of Educational Psychology,* 19 (1928), 480–484.

[31] J. B. Maller, "Cooperation and Competition," *Teachers College Contributions to Education* (1928), p. 384.

[32] C. Stendler and others, "Studies in Cooperation and Competition: I, The Effects of Working for Group and Individual Rewards on the Social Climate of Children's Groups," *Pedogogical Seminary and Journal of Genetic Psychology,* 79 (1951), 173–197.

individuals. The incentive condition of working for an individual prize was significantly more effective than when working for a group prize.

The superiority of individual motivation is due to the reality and personal appeal it provides. In individual competition the person's status and ego are constantly under observation. Even in group-versus-group competition, individuals often single out certain of their schoolmates whom they wish to surpass rather than try to exceed some impersonal group norm or standard. Competition as a member of a group against another group is less personal.

Self-rivalry. Striving to improve one's record is the most acceptable form of rivalry. In such a case individual initiative is at a premium. One may also take advantage of the motivational effects of competition without introducing suspicious attitudes that may be evident when one individual competes against another.

Accurate records of an individual's progress and opportunity for comparison with his own previous record of attainment give personal meaning to his work. In some cases a pupil may make conspicuous improvement in terms of his ability and background. His improvement may suggest he has made actual gain in those abilities in which he was deficient but as a slow learner was unable to compete successfully with other pupils. If he makes noteworthy gain over his previous record, it should be recognized.

taking advantage of the competitive tendency

A desirable modification of the competitive situation exists when pupils are organized into groups or teams and where the varied abilities of all contestants are pooled. The individual of low ability has opportunity to win approval within his group through cooperation. The learner of high ability may gain approval of the group as a part of his reward in contrast to the triumph he may have gained over those in a competitive situation. It is possible that all members of a group may eventually recognize that good team work is more important to success than is the superiority of its individual members.

Cooperative stimulation is more effective when members of a group feel they will be benefited personally. Under highly organized conditions in which each member feels responsible for contributing to group goals, cooperation[33] may be fully as effective as competition. Democratic methods involve both competition and cooperation and require conditions under which each individual experiences maximum personal gain and minimum personal loss. When a pupil fails to win as a direct result of competition, his failure may be offset by his gain as an indirect result of

[33] H. E. Yunker, "Group Atmosphere and Memory," *Journal of Abnormal and Social Psychology*, 51 (1955), 17–23. In a learning situation stressing recall under varying conditions, Yunker found that group recall was superior to individual recall. He also found that cooperative groups were superior to competitive ones.

cooperation. The football player who competes unsuccessfully for the particular position he desires may still receive a reward when his team, through cooperative activity, gains victory.

Instead of regarding cooperation as a form of self-sacrifice, it is desirable to recognize the personal gain that is possible. The strongest appeal for a cooperative attitude is the gain to each member of the group. Cooperation in school is fostered when each individual feels he "belongs" and when all are encouraged to participate freely in activities. Mutual respect is encouraged when the school sponsors democratic methods in all forms of school life.

certain group effects

Whenever individuals are assembled, certain group effects exist even though no special effort may be made to create them. Two of the aspects are the influence of an audience and the effect of collective thinking.

influence of an audience

The presence of an audience may either inhibit or facilitate an activity. If the audience in some way causes the individual to be sensitive, the effect may be marked. Specialists of speech disorders note that the behavior of some stutterers is poorer when they are in a group situation than when they are alone. The same situation is observed in a classroom while pupils are reciting. In a study of the effects of an audience in a choice situation, Warner and Alper[34] found that the time required to make a choice was longest in the presence of an audience, shortest when no audience was present, and intermediate when the audience was seen. The effect of an audience would be expected to vary with types of task—whether they are simple or complex. Gebhard[35] found that individuals perform simple tasks more rapidly when they are in the presence of spectators than when they are alone.

An audience may have an inhibiting effect, particularly in situations in which an individual puts himself forward or even remotely becomes subject to possible criticism. On the other hand, it may have a beneficial effect on some individuals who rise to the occasion. Others become overstimulated and are thwarted.

effect of collective thinking

Collective thinking is involved when students work together on problems and projects as members of small groups. Some studies show that superior performance more frequently results when individuals

[34] Seymour Warner and Thelma Alper, "The Effect of an Audience on Behavior in a Choice Situation," *Journal of Abnormal and Social Psychology,* 47 (1952), 222–229.

[35] M. E. Gebhard, "The Effect of Success and Failure upon the Attractiveness of Activities as a Function of Experience, Expectation, and Need," *Journal of Experimental Psychology,* 38 (1948), 371–388.

select their own members on the basis of congeniality or common interests. Self-selected groups often cluster spontaneously about a student who has capacity for leadership. Such groups perform better than do groups that are appointed on an arbitrary basis. Groups similar in social class as a rule profit more by collective thinking than do those of varied composition.

Hudgins[36] tested the effect of group experience in problem-solving situations. Two comparable groups were formed, one of which worked singly and the other as members of small groups. Group members solved more problems than did those working independently. In a series of investigations Lorge[37] studied problem-solving efficiency of ROTC students when working independently and as five-member teams in situations involving different degrees of reality. Working in a laboratory situation represented one degree of reality; working in a field setting the other. The team approach produced uniformly superior results in both situations. This superiority is attributed to the fact that members of teams ask more questions and make more suggestions than do individuals working independently. Not only do teams acquire more information; they also suggest more hypotheses regarding possible solutions.

Collective thinking is also valuable when a group is working on principles and issues such as debating activity. The differences in the opinions and ideas of group members are usually reduced in situations that require collective thinking. In such situations, individual members tend to compose their differences and act with greater unanimity of purpose. Group thinking usually affects slow-learning individuals most favorably and rapid ones least. The able learner is aware of his potentiality as a pacemaker and is not motivated as much by the necessity of keeping up with someone else.

levels of aspiration

The individual's learning effort is continually affected by the nature and intensity of his motives. He gauges the difficulty of a learning task in the light of his ability to achieve. He places a valuation on such tasks in terms of his expectations of success or failure, which are relative to the height of his ambition and the extent to which he attains it. He works with greater effort toward a goal he believes he can reach than he does toward one he feels he is unlikely to attain.

[36] Bruce B. Hudgins, "Effects of Group Experience on Individual Problem Solving," *Journal of Educational Psychology,* 51 (1960), 37–42.

[37] I. Lorge and others, "Solutions by Teams and by Individuals to a Field Problem at Different Levels of Reality," *Journal of Educational Psychology,* 46 (1955), 17–24. See also I. Lorge and others, "Problem-Solving by Teams and by Individuals in a Field Setting," *Journal of Educational Psychology,* 46 (1955), 160–166.

The level of aspiration refers to the learner's desires and ambitions. In experimental situations the individual adopts a standard of attainment that is based partly on his experience with a task and partly on what he thinks he may be able to do in the future. On the basis of initial attempts in learning a task, he tries out his capabilities and sets for himself a certain level of attainment. His success or failure in reaching his goal affects his further level of aspiration.

In the level-of-aspiration situation, the individual's self-esteem and ego are threatened, because he not only must commit himself regarding his ambitions (sometimes in the presence of a group as well as the examiner) but must demonstrate his ability at each testing period. He is thus confronted with a compromise involving the possibility of either success or failure. If he sets his goal too high and does not achieve it, he is a failure. If he sets his goal too low, he may be using the mechanism of avoiding possibility of failure to attain the appearance of success.

Success and failure are generally determined on the basis of certain arbitrary criteria. Success is frequently defined as attainment in a testing situation equal to or above the individual's expressed level of aspiration; failure is attainment at a level below his aspirations. Standards may also be based on the performance of the individual in relationship to the group. Use of both individual and group standards affords a better basis for judging attainment than does either alone.

experimental results

Many experimental studies have been concerned with the relationship between the individual's success or failure and his level of aspiration. The purpose of some of these studies has been to compare the effect of unrealistic as opposed to realistic goals; in others the aim has been to show the effect of repeated scholastic failure.

unrealistic versus realistic goals

Clarke and Clarke[38] asked a large group of nine-year-old boys, who varied widely in physical ability, to predict performance on the basis of their results on two succeeding trials on a strength of grip test. The findings showed that boys who strive to attain higher goals (higher expressed aspiration levels) were physically superior to comparable ones who seemed unwilling to risk the possibility of failure and who thereby chose aspiration levels that assured some measure of continued success. Leshner[39] wished to determine whether aspirations expressed in realistic

[38] H. H. Clarke and D. H. Clarke, "Relationship between Level of Aspiration and Selected Physical Factors of Boys Aged Nine Years," *Research Quarterly*, 32 (1961), 12–19.

[39] Paul S. Leshner, "Effects of Aspiration and Achievement upon Muscular Tension," *Journal of Experimental Psychology*, 61 (1961), 133–137.

(expectant) terms exert an effect on muscular tension that is different from unrealistic (hopefully) expressed aspirations. He also wished to determine whether such influence is related to achievement expressed as either success or failure. Undergraduate students, assigned at random to four groups, were designated as *expect-success, hope-success, expect-failure,* and *hope-failure.* These students were given a series of tasks equal in difficulty. Before undertaking each task, they were asked to express their aspirations for the succeeding one. After performing the tasks, each individual was given a report of his achievement. Half of the group was given a *success score,* the other half a *failure score.* The results showed that whether or not a student's aspirations are realistic depends on his success or failure. The rate of tension was considerably greater for those who succeeded than it was for those who had been unrealistic. Tension levels, however, decreased with success and increased with failure regardless of aspirations.

Pennington[40] performed three experiments on college students to determine the effect of success and failure on their further aspiration levels. In the first experiment students predicted the letter grades they expected to make on the next day's mid-term test. Of the 99 who did not achieve the expected results, 34 percent lowered their next predictions of their marks on the final test; the remainder restated the same levels. Of the students who reached or exceeded the grades expected, 36 percent raised their next estimates; two percent lowered them; and the remainder kept them as they were.

In another experiment, students predicted their course grades at the beginning of the term and kept a record of their relative class standings throughout the term. Of students whose standings were below their expected marks, the majority lowered their predictions of success on the final test, the extent of reduction being related to their degree of failure to achieve the expected class standings.

In the third experiment, students predicted their grades at the beginning of the course and also just prior to the final examination. On the basis of the initial aspiration level indicated, success or failure on four tests given during the course was determined. Successful students did not raise their final grade predictions; but those who were unsuccessful either restated the first estimate or lowered it, the extent of decrease being related to the number of failures on the four tests.

In a similar study, Worrell[41] compared students' levels of aspiration with their academic achievement. Forty-two volunteer students in a liberal arts college were used as subjects. The college emphasized

[40] L. A. Pennington, "Shifts in Aspiration Levels after Success and Failure in the College Classroom," *Journal of General Psychology,* 23 (1940), 305–313.

[41] Leonard Worrell, "Level of Aspiration and Academic Success," *Journal of Educational Psychology,* 50 (1959), 47–54.

scholarship but did not reveal grades to the students; they were given only decile placement scores at the end of each school year. The aspiration level of each student was determined. The student's performance was then analyzed to show the discrepancy between his level of aspiration and his scholastic success. Students who kept their levels of aspiration close to previous performance and who believed they could not achieve much beyond those levels tended to be successful in scholastic achievement. In contrast, those who held an unrealistic view and perceived their levels as above previous achievement continued to attain low scholastic ratings.

A slightly different situation exists when students are asked to indicate their grade expectations in relationship to the grades they believed they deserved and the grades they actually received. Murstein[42] found that superior students showed no significant change in their predictions as a result of their performance during a semester. They believed they deserved high grades and received them. Lower-ability students also showed little change in their predictions as a result of experience. In their case, however, this consistency was unrealistic. Even after they had been made aware of their cumulative standings, they still believed they deserved higher marks. The superior student undoubtedly has greater insight into his capabilities and is better able to set realistic goals.

effect of repeated scholastic failure

Sears[43] studied the effect of success and failure in reading and arithmetic on levels of aspiration. Three groups were formed on the basis of previous achievement records. The *success* group had high records in reading and arithmetic. The *failure* group had low records in reading and arithmetic but was otherwise matched to the success group with respect to age, intelligence, and social class. A *differential* group, similarly matched in background factors, had *good* records in reading but *poor* ones in arithmetic.

Each pupil was given individually a series of tasks to perform in reading and arithmetic; and his performance on each task was immediately scored before the next one was undertaken. After each pupil was informed of his score on a given task, he was asked to predict it on the next. The results of the investigation were analyzed on the basis of the discrepancies between the scores predicted and those obtained.

Pupils in the success group showed a strong tendency to adjust their levels of aspiration within relatively narrow limits. Those who had a

[42] Bernard I. Murstein, "The Relationship of Grade Expectations and Grades Believed to Be Deserved to Actual Grades Received," *Journal of Experimental Education*, 33 (1965), 357–362.

[43] P. S. Sears, "Levels of Aspiration in Academically Successful and Unsuccessful Children," *Journal of Abnormal and Social Psychology*, 35 (1940), 498–536.

history of failure, in contrast, showed extreme fluctuations. In many cases, they set their goals unnecessarily low to establish a margin of safety against failure or persisted in striving toward excessively high goals they could not reach. Some pupils seemed to assume there was little use in trying, others that they were equal to any task. In the differential group, pupils set realistic goals in reading but set in an irregular, unrealistic manner their goals in arithmetic, a subject in which they had poor records. Their performance depended to a large extent on the conditioning effects of success or failure during previous school experience. Success had given one group confidence and ability to appraise its abilities. Failure had given the other group a feeling of frustration, causing its members to rationalize or overpersist in setting their goals.

importance of success

The individual's success in attaining his expressed level of aspiration has a positive effect; failure has a negative one. After success he raises his level of aspiration; after failure, he lowers it. If one's level of aspiration is much lower than is his potential achievement, he may regard comparatively low attainment as success when evaluated by group standards. On the other hand, if he sets his level of aspiration too high, he may have a feeling of failure in relation to his potential ability, although, relatively, he may have done well.

The nature of the task, however, is an important consideration. If it is too difficult, the individual may not experience failure, because he makes no effort to master it; if it is too easy, he may not be challenged to do his best. Consequently, he may not have a feeling of success, although he may have done relatively well on the basis of group standards. Since the level of aspiration is raised as a result of success and lowered as a result of failure, it serves to protect the individual against continued failure on the one hand and easy success on the other.

Pupils at the lower end of the scale of ability tend to aspire to attainment levels that are above their achievement possibilities. Those at the upper end of the scale tend to set their achievement levels below such possibilities. The differences between pupils of extremes in ability suggest that the pressure of the classroom setting has the effect of creating an imbalance in the level of aspiration situation. Social acceptability in the classroom requires a high degree of conformity to group standards. Low-ability pupils may feel compelled to seek goals they cannot reach. In contrast, those of extremely high ability may not feel encouraged in the pursuit of high levels of aspiration.

Effective motivation requires flexibility in the difficulty of school work so there will be tasks appropriate for learners of low ability as well as for learners of high ability. Much learning material lacks range of difficulty.

As a result, pupils at the extremes of ability are inadequately challenged. For some pupils school work is either too easy or too difficult.

The problem is to guard against rewarding the able learner too well and the inferior one too poorly, especially when inflexible requirements are stressed. The superior learner may accept high marks as superficial evidence of success without experiencing the genuine satisfaction of having met a real challenge. The inferior one may deserve commendation for struggling valiantly to solve problems that he cannot understand.

keeping the learner motivated

The problem of enlisting the learner's effort to achieve is not solved by applying a series of techniques to specific situations. Motivation is primarily the art of working effectively with individuals so that each is stimulated to attack his problems with confidence.

showing interest in the learner

Much may be done to make the classroom setting effective by showing a genuine interest in the learner. Attitudes of helpfulness result from a desire to understand the nature of a pupil's problems, the conditions of his home and community life, and his goals or ambitions. It is sometimes difficult to realize that pupils have individual purposes and are sensitive to the teacher's attitudes toward their aims. As a result of their limited experience, they may magnify the significance of difficulties and rebuffs and expressions of sympathy and kindness. The teacher who is interested in his pupils is a friend who seeks opportunity to encourage and cooperate.

encouraging self-reliance

Pupils are motivated when they are encouraged to depend on themselves in selecting responses and in assuming responsibility for results. Responsibility is cultivated when the teacher is sensitive to the pupil's effort and assists him in finding satisfaction by doing things for himself. He may influence the learner to take pride in his accomplishment by permitting him to complete at least a part of every task unaided.

restoring confidence

Restoring a learner's confidence is an important step in stimulating him to exert effort. Continued failure may have thwarted his hope of attaining success. The problem is to recognize whatever ability may be evident and to provide tasks that he can perform. Confidence in his worth is the foundation upon which to develop assurance that he may successfully undertake increasingly difficult tasks.

the teacher as critic

The teacher has the responsibility of serving in the role of critic, of indicating errors, and suggesting ways by which improvement can be made. The function of a critic should be primarily that of appraising performance. It is necessary to refer to instances of merit as well as to indicate errors. The positive approach of showing a learner a way out of his difficulties spares him the discouragement of condemnation. During the initial stages of learning a task, imperfect performance is usual. One should not confuse the learner or destroy his confidence by magnifying small errors before he has completed his task. When it is acknowledged that his theme or report represents commendable effort, there is a basis for tempering correction of errors.

Finally, pupils are motivated when classroom activities are directed enthusiastically and purposefully. If the teacher regards instruction as a cooperative enterprise and is appreciative of accomplishment, pupils will share his attitude and assimilate much of his confidence in the possibilities of improvement. Such a teacher will be tolerant of errors, seek to correct them impersonally, and lead pupils to expect success. Setting the stage for success is the keynote for motivation.

study questions

1. Evaluate the assertion that some kind of motivation is associated with every human activity.
2. Discuss some of the difficulties in determining the conditions under which a child will exert effort to learn.
3. On the basis of your knowledge of child development, suggest certain motivating devices that become (a) inappropriate after certain age levels and (b) significant only when certain age levels are reached.
4. There is a popular notion that to a child a reward may serve as a bribe and make him increasingly reluctant to act without it. Discuss the extent to which this criticism has a bearing on school practices involving rewards.
5. Discuss possible injurious effects of the wrong kind and amount of motivation. Compare the effects of overmotivation with those of undermotivation. Suggest several criteria that may be used in judging the value of a particular incentive.
6. Personal relationships with a certain pupil are cordial; but he resents being forced by the administration to enroll in your course, which does not interest him. He consistently refuses to participate and sits silently in class. He has mental capacity for satisfying low-grade requirements. Without administrative cooperation, you must face the perplexing motivation problem yourself. What are some of the first steps you would take?

7. Evaluate the statement "Cooperation does not have to beg for recognition in a cringing, humble manner. On the contrary, it may rightfully promise to contribute as liberally to an individual's personal gain as competitive activity."
8. To what extent may a learner's level of aspiration be regarded as a crucial point in the problem of motivation, regardless of the type of incentive? What is its significance in determining the amount and kind of motivation?
9. Is the motivation of effort to learn essentially new among modern ideas? To what extent does current interpretation of desirable motivation suggest a change of emphasis from "making the pupil learn" to "making him wish to learn"?
10. You may have expected from the discussion of incentives to learn of certain tricks or procedures helpful in making pupils wish to learn. Why do you suppose the author, instead, has sought to familiarize you with some conditions of motivation?
11. Certain individuals may be continually motivated by a sense of duty or responsibility whether they are interested in a subject or not. As commendable as such a spirit is, some critics suggest that it is essentially self-motivation and, therefore, not so desirable as is interest in the subject matter or ability to discover satisfaction of personal needs. Comment on the merits of this contention.
12. Although psychologists frequently suggest that interest and accomplishment are nourished by success, many students believe that the idea of success has been overemphasized, asserting that "most persons cannot attain, in our present social order, what has been considered success." Point out the fallacy in this reasoning.

emotional and social adjustment

9

Every person has basic needs that motivate his behavior. He feels entitled to security in the home, the school, and the community. When his expectations in life are threatened, he seeks ways either to modify his environment or to relate himself more satisfactorily to it. If he cannot meet his needs by socially approved methods, he may try unacceptable or even antisocial behavior. Some kind of adjustment will be made, either good or bad.

Personality adjustment is revealed by a variety of signs and symptoms, ranging from simple emotional behavior to the more serious personality disorders. The so-called "bad child" responds to some unconscious urge arising from inadequate adjustment by bullying, truancy, lying, or stealing. When a child steals, he may be motivated by an attempt to gain prestige or to overcome feelings of inadequacy or inferiority. Tardiness is characteristic of one who is unhappy at school or home. Behavior should be regarded as more than spontaneous effort to satisfy immediate desires. A reason exists somewhere behind one's act, and the act itself is directed by his motives.

The individual's choice of behavior may lie among several possibilities. A single dominating emotional state may be expressed in numerous ways. A child who is disturbed because of unsatisfactory play adjustments with his companions may seek forgetfulness in intensive effort toward high scholastic achievement. On the other hand, he may commit disturbing acts in the classroom to attract attention. He may also seek a solution to his problems by withdrawing from all but the most necessary contacts with others; or he may sit quietly in class as an unhappy and perplexed person.

Children as well as adults employ various devices for disguising their manner of adjusting to emotional and social problems. Individuals use such devices when obstacles that impede the solution of a problem cannot be removed or adequately solved by direct means. It is important to recognize these as means of adjustment. They may not be inherently undesirable but become so when used as substitutes for reality.

behavior problems

When an individual's acts affect the fulfillment of our own purposes, we frequently regard *his* problem as *ours,* judge its seriousness on such a basis, and solve it in accordance with our own standards. Obviously, our attempts fail, because we do not help him solve his problem as his own.

Behavior should not be regarded as desirable when the child is docile or tractable. Likewise, it should not be regarded as undesirable when he asserts himself against authority. Many specific acts, such as stealing, destruction of school property, inattention in the classroom, or impertinence, are symptomatic of efforts to adjust. The seriousness of such behavior should be judged not solely by adult standards but by the significance of the offense to the child's development. In the classroom, throwing spitballs may be a more heinous offense than is sitting quietly and avoiding participation because of timidity or shyness. The first type may be an irregular reaction to the tactics of an autocratic teacher; but the second often is given little attention, because it does not break out into the open. The seriousness of different types of behavior depends upon whose criteria are accepted. Certain kinds of behavior and attitudes regarding their seriousness may be examined. The following include representative types of behavior from Wickman's[1] classic list:

Sexual irregularity
Cheating
Masturbation
Impertinence, defiance
Obscene notes, talk
Cruelty, bullying
Quarrelsomeness
Lack of interest
Truancy
Laziness
Selfishness
Smoking
Inattention

Fearfulness
Enuresis
Domineering
Interrupting
Whispering
Tardiness
Dreaminess
Slovenly appearance
Imaginative lying
Overcritical of others
Unsocialness
Shyness

[1] E. K. Wickman, *Children's Behavior and Teachers' Attitudes* (New York: The Commonwealth Fund, 1928).

The ranking of these various kinds of behavior tends to represent the attitude of the teachers used by Wickman. The teachers were inclined to rate as very serious such behavior as heterosexual activity, untruthfulness, cheating, lying, stealing, masturbation, disobedience, and impertinence. They were most concerned about the child who displayed some kind of aggressive or disturbing behavior. The mental hygienist, on the other hand, believed that shyness, daydreaming, or fearfulness were a menace to the individual's full development. In general, his emphasis was upon withdrawing or recessive personality traits.

Using Wickman's study as a frame of reference, numerous studies have been conducted, a principal objective of them being to check the validity of the original findings and to vary the procedure to include teachers at different educational levels. Stouffer[2] found that the correlation between the rankings of seriousness of behavior by elementary- and secondary-school teachers was .88; between the rankings of the secondary-school teachers and the mental hygienists, .49. On the other hand, the correlation between rankings of the seriousness of behavior problems by elementary-school teachers and mental hygienists was .61. The elementary teachers tended to be more concerned with withdrawing types of behavior, whereas the secondary teachers were more concerned with problems related to classroom management. Hunter's[3] study indicated the same trends, although his coefficients of correlation were somewhat smaller. In his investigation, aggressiveness was still rated to be more serious by teachers than it was by mental hygienists. Porter[4] collected data from several groups, including high school and college students, the purpose being to determine whether students change their attitudes toward child behavior as they become older and more mature. Both groups believed that the most serious behavior problems involved moodiness, unhappiness, stealing, being disliked by others, fighting, and truancy. There was, however, a marked decline in the frequency of choosing punishment as a means of discipline as students advanced from senior high school to senior college.

An attempt has also been made to determine the reactions of teachers to behavior problems, especially as they affect teaching efficiency. Weathers and Phillips[5] determined the reactions of 200 classroom

[2] G. A. W. Stouffer, "The Attitudes of Secondary School Teachers toward Certain Behavior Problems of Children," *School Review*, 64 (1956), 358–362.

[3] E. C. Hunter, "Changes in Teachers' Attitudes toward Children's Behavior over the Last 30 Years," *Mental Hygiene*, 41 (1957), 3–11.

[4] Robert M. Porter, "Student Attitudes toward Child Behavior Problems," *Journal of Educational Research*, 52 (1959), 349–352.

[5] Garrett Weathers and Beeman N. Phillips, "Some Reactions of Classroom Teachers to Problem Behavior in School," *Educational Administration and Supervision*, 43 (1957), 129–139.

teachers who were enrolled in a teacher-training department. These teachers believe there has been, during recent years, an increase in behavior problems, which has caused some teachers to leave the profession. The teachers also believe that much problem behavior is caused by large classes, inadequate teacher personality, and poor teaching techniques. They recognize, however, that some problem behavior is a part of the normal process of growth and development and should not be regarded seriously. The most significant result of the study seemed to be the need for administrative assistance in coping with behavior problems. In D'Amico's[6] study, a major purpose was to determine pupil behavior problems that were encountered by teachers during their first year of teaching. Types of problems that occurred most frequently, as reported by the teachers, were those that could be designated as the classroom management problems of careless work, inattention, and interruption. These problems occurred more frequently in the early than in the upper grades.

The net effect of recent studies of behavior problems has been a tendency for the difference[7] between teachers and mental hygienists to be less marked. Despite this trend towards closer agreement, however, attitudes of teachers continue to differ from those of mental hygienists, the two groups representing different ways of viewing the same problems. The mental hygienist tends to think of the cumulative effect of children's acts upon themselves. His experience has brought him into contact with mentally ill adults, adults suffering from irreparable emotional and social maladjustments and adults whose inability to lead normal lives is traced to childhood experiences.

The mental hygienist believes that shyness, daydreaming, or fearfulness are a menace to the individual's full development. He regards lack of interest, impertinence, cheating, and resistance to authority as relatively susceptible to re-education. In general, his emphasis is on withdrawing or recessive personality traits. He is most concerned about the individual who is unhappy or depressed, suggestible or weak in volitional development, asocial, easily discouraged, sensitive or morose. He believes that each undesirable act of a child is symptomatic of an unsuccessful attempt toward adjustment but that it is not necessarily

[6] Louis A. D'Amico, "Characteristics of ITTP Teachers and Some Pupil Behavior Problems They Encountered Their First Year of Teaching," *Educational Administration and Supervision*, 46 (1960), 5–10.

[7] Harry Beilin, "Teachers' and Clinicians' Attitudes toward the Behavior Problems of Children: A Reappraisal," *Child Development*, 30 (1959), 9–25. See also John C. Glidewell and others, "Screening in Schools for Behavior Disorders: Use of Mothers' Reports of Symptoms," *Journal of Educational Research*, 56 (1963), 508–515. Their findings indicate that a mother's report of symptoms provides a useful index of a child's mental health from the point of view of teachers.

evidence of basic personality disorder. He feels that many impulsive or transitory acts regarded as serious by teachers may be brought under effective control with no threat to personal development.

adjustment and educational progress

Our primary concern for behavior problems grows out of their relationship to the learner's educational progress. Studies of the relationship between a learner's adjustment and his achievement are generally limited to descriptive methods that use correlation and comparative-causal patterns. For example, measures of pupil adjustment are correlated with measures of achievement. Also, pupils having poor adjustment are compared with pupils having good adjustment.

Factors involved in adjustment of first-grade children were identified by Hammond and Skipper.[8] Effort was made to determine the relationship between adjustment and such factors as attendance at kindergarten, scores on readiness tests, and chronological age. Rating scales of adjustment were completed by each child's first-grade teacher at the end of the first six weeks of school. A significant relationship was shown between adjustment status and scores on readiness tests. Williams[9] studied elementary-school children with I.Q.s of 130 or above. Achievement was measured by standardized tests; personality traits were measured by the California Personality Inventory and the Classroom Adjustment Scale. A group of randomly selected classmates was used for comparison. The findings were analyzed to determine the extent to which the pupils were working up to expected achievement levels. More than *four* out of *five* children who were rated high in total acceptance were achieving within or above expectancy. On the other hand, more than *three* out of *five* who were rated low in total acceptance were achieving below expectancy levels. Astingdon[10] obtained data on a large number of English boys in a county borough in a study of personality qualities associated with academic success. His data were based on teacher ratings, classmate ratings, and a questionnaire. For comparative purposes, boys in a grammar school within the same borough were evaluated on the same qualities. Characteristics rated by classmates as well as by teachers included persistence, independence, dominance, interest, and

[8] Sarah L. Hammond and Dora S. Skipper, "Factors Involved in the Adjustment of Children Entering First Grade," *Journal of Educational Research*, 56 (1962), 89–95.

[9] Meta F. Williams, "Acceptance and Performance among Gifted Elementary School Children," *Educational Research Bulletin*, 37 (1958), 216–220.

[10] E. Astingdon, "Personality Assessments and Academic Performance in a Boys' Grammar School," *British Journal of Educational Psychology*, 30 (1960), 225–236.

emotional stability. Academically successful boys received significantly higher ratings than did unsuccessful ones on traits of independence, persistence, and interest. Successful boys also tended to be more stable emotionally than were the unsuccessful.

Studies of delinquents reveal similar trends. Glueck's[11] studies in the Boston public schools showed that 41 percent of the delinquents were two or more years educationally retarded as compared with 21 percent of the nondelinquents. Approximately 40 percent of the delinquents were also rated as "poor" in scholarship as compared with eight percent of the nondelinquents. Litwack[12] determined differences between recidivists and nonrecidivists in a reformatory. Among other differences, the nonrecidivists tended to reach higher educational levels. Dinitz[13] compared students who were regarded as insulated against delinquency with those who seemed inclined toward involvement with the law. The data were based on the California Test of Personality, the California Mental Maturity tests, and the Stanford tests in reading and arithmetic. The potential nondelinquent boys made higher reading and arithmetic scores than did boys designated as potential delinquents.

Probably the most pointed research concerning adjustment and educational achievement is that designed to discover the causes of reading difficulties. Tarblett's[14] findings indicated that poor mental health and reading retardation were closely associated. Retarded readers were significantly different in behavioral immaturity, interpersonal skills, social participation, satisfying work, and adequate goals. Grau's[15] data suggested that reading difficulties can cause emotional disturbances, and emotional difficulties in turn can produce reading problems. Spache[16] found that retarded readers tend to be more hostile and aggressive toward others than are children having normal reading ability. Personality patterns identified with reading failure included attitudes of hostility and resentment. Krippner's[17] study showed that reversals of words and letters characterized the reading process of boys diagnosed as socio-

[11] Sheldon Glueck and E. T. Glueck, *The Delinquent in the Making* (New York: Harpers, 1952).

[12] Laurence Litwack, "An Examination of Ten Significant Differences between Juvenile Recidivists and Nonrecidivists," *Journal of Educational Research,* 55 (1961), 132–134.

[13] Simon Dinitz and others, "Delinquency Proneness and School Achievement," *Educational Research Bulletin,* 36 (1957), 131–136.

[14] B. E. Tarblett, "Poor Readers and Mental Health," *Elementary English,* 35 (1956), 69–76.

[15] Albert F. Grau, "The Emotional World of the Non-achiever," *Journal of American Optometric Association,* 27 (1957), 523–531.

[16] George Spache, "Personality Patterns of Retarded Readers," *Journal of Educational Research,* 50 (1957), 461–469.

[17] S. Krippner, "Sociopathic Tendencies and Reading Retardation in Children," *Exceptional Children,* 29 (1963), 258–266.

pathic. Other characteristics included poor comprehension, slow reading rate, and negative attitudes.

The studies that have been reviewed strongly indicate that personality adjustment and educational progress are interrelated; but the studies do not differentiate between causes and effects. Emotional and social maladjustment contribute to educational retardation; learning disabilities also contribute to personality disorders by frustrating the individual's efforts in learning situations. The problem is further complicated by the fact that some individuals suffering from emotional or social disorders[18] may compensate for their limitations and become superior achievers. Roswell and Natchez[19] have called attention to the difficulty of determining whether maladjustment precedes or follows reading problems. Another approach to the complex relationship between adjustment and educational achievement is to determine whether or not the individual's achievement is enhanced when his adjustment is improved—a subject to be considered in a later section.

relationships between students and teachers

The extent to which a learner works in harmony with classroom purposes may hinge upon the attitude the teacher creates. It is axiomatic that pupils respond more favorably for a teacher whom they like than for one they dislike. His every word and act affect each pupil, often in different ways, creating attitudes including the negative ones of antagonism and unhappiness.

The teacher is influenced, likewise, by pupil attitude and behavior. Certain groups stimulate good teaching more than others. It is no less true of teachers than of pupils that attitudes generated by the classroom setting influence the quality of teaching as well as the pupil's work. The classroom organization is a unique situation, representing not only the influence of two levels of maturity, one upon the other, but the impressions that each person creates.

Relationship between pupils and teachers, as expressed in opinion studies, has been a popular subject for investigation. Studies now include high school and college students as well as elementary-school pupils.

what students like and dislike in teachers

Approximately 14,000 letters on the subject of "The Teacher Who Has Helped Me Most," written by pupils in grades one through twelve were

[18] Arthur S. Tamkin, "A Survey of Educational Disability in Emotionally Disturbed Children," *Journal of Educational Research*, 54 (1960), 67–69.

[19] Florence Roswell and Gladys Natchez, *Reading Disability: Diagnosis and Treatment* (New York: Basic Books, 1964).

analyzed by Witty.[20] The most desirable traits (in order of frequency) were (1) cooperative, democratic attitude, (2) kindness and consideration for the individual, (3) patience, (4) fairness and impartiality, (5) sense of humor, (6) good disposition and consistent behavior, (7) interest in pupil problems, (8) flexibility, (9) use of recognition and praise, and (10) unusual proficiency in teaching a particular subject.

In a further study, Witty[21] approached the problem from the standpoint of the negative or undesirable traits of teachers. His survey, based on 33,000 letters, shows that the teacher least liked by pupils (1) is unstable and irritable, (2) is arbitrary and dictatorial, (3) shows favoritism, (4) assigns unreasonable homework, (5) ridicules pupils in the presence of others, (6) is "cross" and unfriendly, (7) is impatient, and (8) is pedantic or dull. There was overwhelming indictment of the bad-tempered teacher by the youngest group and of the unfair teacher by the oldest group. Favorable comments of the youngest group were: "She never makes fun of any pupil before the class." "She never tries to make a monkey out of you." "Miss X's class is just like one big happy family." "She likes every one of us. You can tell it not by what she says but by what she does." "She doesn't talk to us like children."

More than 800 English children in primary and secondary schools ranked on specially prepared scales items that were descriptive of the "good teacher."[22] These scales were organized so as to sample these hypothesized areas of the good teacher's classroom behavior: *discipline, teaching,* and *personal qualities.* The findings differed somewhat for pupils at various age and grade levels. Pupils in the junior schools, where formal teaching tends to be common, stressed the good teacher's discipline, especially his firmness. Fourth-year secondary-school students, especially boys, emphasized the good teacher's personal qualities, including cheerfulness, even temper, and sense of humor. All children, regardless of age, sex, or maturity, however, evaluated most highly the "good teacher's" teaching, which they probably regarded as a means of satisfying their need for achievement.

College students share many of the same attitudes toward teachers with students in the lower educational levels. Bradley[23] asked college students to list what they liked and disliked about their teachers and their teaching. The most frequently-mentioned quality was teaching efficiency, which included careful preparation, clear explanations, exact-

[20] Paul Witty, "An Analysis of the Personality Traits of the Effective Teacher," *Journal of Educational Research,* 40 (1947), 662–671.

[21] Paul Witty, "Evaluation of Studies of the Characteristics of the Effective Teacher" in *Improving Educational Research* (American Educational Research Association, 1948), pp. 198–204.

[22] Philip H. Taylor, "Children's Evaluations of the Characteristics of the Good Teacher," *British Journal of Educational Psychology,* 32 (1962), 258–266.

[23] G. H. Bradley, "What Do College Students Like and Dislike about Teachers and Their Teaching?" *Educational Administration and Supervision,* 36 (1950), 113–120.

ness, effective questioning, and use of outlines and summaries. The next quality in order of importance was personality. The students liked the teacher who is emotionally mature, cheerful, friendly and one who "accepts us as mature men and women." Draper[24] administered a checklist during a period of several years to classes in an "introduction to education" course. The outstanding factor contributing to an instructor's success was his knowledge of subject matter and skill in its presentation. Among the qualities of a good college teacher were: accurate evaluation of the student's work and recognition of him as an individual. These students liked especially the teacher who knows his field and is enthusiastic about it. They disliked most the teacher who assumes an attitude of superiority.

The opinion studies conducted at the various educational levels indicate that students are not so unlike adults as often supposed. Their complaints against teachers include few criticisms different from those one adult might level against another for similar behavior. Whereas adults tend to express their opinions freely, students accept "authoritarian" teaching, though sometimes in silent rebellion. They recognize their immaturity and welcome the experienced leadership of older persons. Their reactions toward teachers leave one convinced, however, that they react unfavorably to arbitrary domination, unfair treatment, and failure to respect them as individuals.

student and teacher interaction

Student and teacher interaction includes not only student evaluation of teachers but teacher evaluation of students.

evaluation of teacher effectiveness

Evaluations of teacher effectiveness often include student ratings, which are sometimes compared with those of school officials. Symonds[25] compared ratings of pupils with each other and with those of the principals. The coefficients of correlation between pupil ratings ranged from .70 to .80. Those between pupil and principal ratings averaged approximately .60. In Bush's[26] study, student opinions concerning discipline were compared with supervisor ratings. The criterion of satisfactory discipline was the extent to which the classroom was a self-regulating unit. The coefficient of correlation between supervisor and student ratings was .90. Thus, teachers who managed their relationships with

[24] Adam M. Draper, "Student Views of the Qualifications of Their Teachers," *Journal of Higher Education*, 22 (1961), 338–341.

[25] P. M. Symonds, "Characteristics of the Effective Teacher Based on Pupil Evaluations," *Journal of Experimental Education*, 23 (1954–55), 289–310.

[26] R. N. Bush, "A Study of Student-Teacher Relationships," *Journal of Educational Research*, 35 (1942), 645–656.

students well were considered good teachers by both supervisors and students. Students who were superior in scholarship tended to give teachers a higher rating than did students who were low in achievement. Many students considered the teacher at fault for their own poor scholarship; but it was significant that their success was also associated with the teacher's effectiveness. They respected teachers who, through cooperation of the group, could maintain discipline.

An attempt has also been made to determine the characteristics of effective teachers as compared with their less effective colleagues. In Symonds'[27] study, a detailed analysis was made of teachers who ranked high and teachers who ranked low. Teachers who were rated superior were inclined to like children; those rated inferior tended to dislike them. Superior ones were inclined to be personally secure and self-assured; whereas inferior ones seemed insecure and to suffer from feelings of inferiority. The superior teachers appeared to be integrated; the inferior ones tended to be personally disorganized. Heil and Washburne[28] compared pupil achievement under the most effective teachers with pupil achievement under the least effective. They were able to identify teachers whose pupils typically made superior scholastic gains. The most effective teacher tended to be reasonably warm and sympathetic toward others. He was also *self-severe* and *methodical,* set high standards for himself, and then proceeded to achieve them. He also required the same standards of excellence from his pupils.

Student evaluations of teacher effectiveness are frequently as valid as those of school officials. The effective teacher is not only a person who maintains desirable personal relationships with students but possesses abilities and skills that contribute to the students' scholastic success. The learner likes a classroom to be well organized, subject matter to be presented in the light of definite aims, and each person to be engaged in some profitable activity. The entire classroom setting contributes to success and is an impelling force in a learner's outlook.

teacher evaluation of students

Experienced teachers are reasonably skillful in evaluating student achievement. They are less effective in evaluating other aspects of student personality. Leton[29] determined the relationship between teachers' ratings and student scores on the California Psychological Inventory. The rating scales were designed to measure the traits and qualities included in the inventory. The highest coefficients of correlation between

[27] P. M. Symonds (25).

[28] Louis M. Heil and Carleton Washburne, "Brooklyn College Research on Teacher Effectiveness," *Journal of Educational Research,* 55 (1962), 347–351.

[29] Donald Leton, "Personality Ratings of High School Students," *Journal of Educational Research,* 56 (1962), 160–163.

teacher ratings and scores on the inventory were shown in intellectual achievement, efficiency, sociability, and responsibility, indicating that teacher ratings are most useful in those personality traits that are associated with academic achievement. Williams and Knecht[30] asked teachers to rate high school students on the trait of "likability." The relationship between teacher ratings and student ability and achievement was then determined. The student's achievement, as shown by grade-point average, was more closely associated with his degree of "likability" than it was with his ability as measured by tests. Almost identical findings were obtained by Ryan,[31] who found that teacher ratings of high school students tended to represent little more than "imperfect reflections" of academic performance—that is, they may be given "after the fact" of grades. It seems possible from these studies, however, that trait ratings may involve personality characteristics which in themselves affect scholastic achievement.

The studies that have been reviewed suggest that there are certain differences between student ratings of teachers and teacher ratings of students. Students are inclined to consider personality characteristics as well as efficiency when rating teachers. They tend to be concerned with all factors that contribute to a satisfying learning situation. Teachers, on the other hand, are inclined to use the learner's academic performance as a frame of reference in evaluating his various traits.

Some evidence suggests that teachers tend to favor students who possess qualities and traits similar to their own. Hamlish and Gaier[32] tested the hypothesis that similarities between teachers and students affect student marks. The procedure consisted of asking students and teachers to describe themselves in terms of personality traits. The teachers also described the personality traits of the students. On the basis of the results they concluded:

> Students receiving high marks describe themselves in terms more like those which teachers used to describe themselves than did students receiving low marks. Conversely, students receiving high marks were described by the teachers more in terms of the teacher's self descriptions than were students receiving low marks.

Two other studies show similar trends. In a study by Russell and Thalman,[33] a definite positive relationship was obtained between the

[30] J. R. Williams and W. W. Knecht, "Teacher Ratings of High School Students on 'Likability' and Their Relation to Measures of Ability and Achievement," *Journal of Educational Research,* 56 (1962), 152–155.

[31] F. J. Ryan, "Trait Ratings of High School Students by Teachers," *Journal of Educational Psychology,* 49 (1958), 124–128.

[32] Irma Hamlish and Eugene Gaier, "Teacher-Student Personality Similarities and Marks," *School Review,* 62 (1954), 265–273.

[33] Ivan L. Russell and W. A. Thalman, "Personality, Does It Influence Teacher's Marks?" *Journal of Educational Research,* 48 (1955).

mark a pupil received and the personality rating the teacher made. Battle[34] determined the effects of similarities and differences in value patterns on the interrelationships of pupils and teachers as revealed through teachers' marks. His findings also support the idea that pupil patterns of values tend to be directly related to the level of pupil achievement as expressed by teachers' grades.

The results of these studies may suggest that a teacher is better able to understand those students who have personality traits and interests similar to his own and thus can more readily contribute to their success than he can to those students who have dissimilar qualities and traits. Likewise, it is possible that students work more harmoniously with a teacher who possesses many of their own traits and values. Nevertheless, the evidence suggests the possibility of bias. Nunnery and Gilliam[35] found that secondary-school teachers knew more about the background of students who had high intelligence than they knew about students who had low intelligence. They had more knowledge of those who made high grades than they had of those who made low grades. They also had more information about students who were well adjusted than they had those who came from homes of high social class than of those who came from a low social class.

understanding behavior

Children who have learning difficulties and those who are aggressive are identified readily. Many others, however, have problems that require special techniques. A study of these, even though they may not be applied, affords a basis for understanding a learner's problems.

techniques

The purpose is to describe some of the more promising techniques that may be used in school situations. These include *observations and checklists, questionnaires and inventories, expressive techniques,* and *sociometric techniques.*

observation and checklists

Pupil behavior may be observed on the playground, in the halls, the gymnasium, the lunch room, and in both formal and informal group

[34] Haron J. Battle, "Relation between Personal Values and Scholastic Achievement," *Journal of Experimental Education,* 26 (1957), 27–41.

[35] Michael Y. Nunnery and Robert J. Gilliam, "A Study of Secondary School Teacher Knowledge of Pupils as Related to Selected Pupil Characteristics," *National Association of Secondary School Principals Bulletin,* 46 (1962), 101–107.

activities. Such observation is more accurate when a checklist[36] is used, because it provides a systematic method of recording. Another means of increasing the accuracy of observation is to make a list of extreme traits, such as that used in the Psycho-Educational Clinic at the University of Wisconsin. This list consists of two classes of traits, aggressive and recessive, as follows:

Aggressive	Recessive
1. Angers easily	1. Overconscientious
2. Temper tantrums	2. Emotionally inadequate
3. Uncooperative	3. Overexuberant
4. Sex irregularities	4. Whiner
5. Enuresis (bed wetting)	5. Pessimistic
6. Uncontrolled bladder or bowel	6. Suspicious
7. Truancy, unexcused absences	7. Plays by himself
8. Cheats	8. Avoids others, unfriendly
9. Resents correction	9. Shunned by others
10. Destructive	10. Over-religious
11. Overcritical of others	11. Daydreams, preoccupied
12. Irresponsible	12. Plays with younger children
13. Impudent, defiant	13. Physical coward
14. Quarrelsome	14. Selfish
15. Cruel to animals	15. Feigns illness
16. Irritable	16. Too submissive
17. Belligerent, bossy	17. Depressed
18. Bully	18. Overdependent
19. Vindictive	19. Sullen
20. Steals	20. Nervous tensions, tics
21. Dishonest, untruthful	21. Bites fingernails
22. Marked change in personality	22. Fearful, timid, shy
23. Negativistic	23. Worries
24. Runs away from home	24. Jealous
25. Seeks attention	25. Cries easily

By keeping a record over a period of several weeks, one can observe behavior tendencies that are consistently exhibited. Tendencies that are apparent will be checked frequently.

questionnaires and inventories

Questionnaires and inventories are designed for a wide range of ages and grades and afford a convenient means of discovering symptoms of emotional and social problems. The California Test of Personality[37] (grades K–3, 4–8, 7–10, 9–16, and adults) yields fifteen scores, including self-reliance, sense of personal worth, sense of personal freedom, feeling

[36] Gene R. Medinnus, "The Development of a First Grade Adjustment Scale," *Journal of Experimental Education,* 30 (1961), 243–248. This is a standardized scale for use by parents and teachers.

[37] L. P. Thorpe and others, *The California Test of Personality* (Monterey, California: California Test Bureau, 1939–53).

of belonging, withdrawing tendencies, nervous symptoms, and total personal adjustment. The Children's Personality Questionnaire[38] (elementary-school children) is an instrument designed to measure fourteen personality factors. Some are temperamental factors; others are factors that are learned or are influenced by the environment.

The Heston Personal Adjustment Inventory[39] (9–16; adults) provides measures that include analytical thinking, confidence, and emotional stability. The California Psychological Inventory[40] (ages 13 and over) yields eighteen scores, such as dominance, capacity for status, sociability, social presence, and a sense of well-being. The Ego Strength Q-Sort Test[41] (9–16; adults) yields six scores, including ego status, social status, and good mental health.

The Syracuse Scales of Social Relations[42] (elementary, junior high, and senior high school) consist of a series of social situations, each of which elicits responses calling for a psychological need. In one situation the student is asked to rate his classmates as kind and sympathetic friends on whom he could call in time of difficulty. The results may be presented graphically, showing degrees of acceptance or rejection. The Vineland Social Maturity Scale[43] is a guided interview conducted by a person who knows something about the behavior of the individual (from birth to maturity). It is unique in that it is neither a test, rating scale, nor questionnaire. The behavior is described in terms of self-help and self-direction concerning such problems as eating, dressing, walking, talking, social relations, and occupations. It can be used as a basis for discussing an individual's behavior with parents and teachers and in informing them of stages of expected development. Doll has prepared for parents a simplified form of this scale, with illustrations, and verbal descriptions, which provide norms of social competence for various age levels.

An instrument for analyzing personality and interest problems is the Mooney Problems Check List[44] (grades 7–9, 9–12, 13–16, adults). The examiner totals the number of problems checked by the student in each general area. Its value lies in the extent to which it increases understanding of student problems. It is also a means of identifying interests. It

[38] R. B. Porter and R. B. Cattell, *Handbook of the IPAT Children's Personality Questionnaire* (Champaign, Illinois: I.P.A.T., 1960).

[39] Joseph C. Heston, *Heston Personal Adjustment Inventory* (New York: Harcourt, Brace and World, 1940).

[40] Harrison G. Gough, *The California Psychological Inventory* (Palo Alto, California: Consulting Psychologists Press, 1956–57).

[41] *The Ego Strength Q-Sort Test* (New York: Psychological Corporation, 1956–58).

[42] E. F. Gardner and G. G. Thompson, *Syracuse Scales of Social Relations* (New York: World Book Co., 1959).

[43] Edgar A. Doll, "Vineland Social Maturity Scale, 1935–53" (Minneapolis, Minnesota: Educational Test Bureau, Educational Publishing Co., Inc.).

[44] Mooney Problems Check List (Chicago: Science Research Associates, 1956).

is a descriptive, and to some extent, an analytic instrument; but it is not diagnostic in the sense that it identifies causes.

expressive techniques

The purpose of expressive techniques is to obtain, by indirect means, insight into an individual's personality. These reduce conscious control by him over his behavior and reveal responses reflecting his characteristics. Expressive techniques include *finger painting, drawing, interpretation of pictures, story completion,* and *play.*[45]

A child using the finger painting technique, for example, may reduce feelings of guilt about messiness by playing freely with the paint. He may make a smear he designates as an enemy or a "boogie man." Then he may remove it and thus take a step toward eliminating his fear. In using the drawing technique, a child may be encouraged to make numerous drawings, the interpretations of which are dependent upon repetitions of items as well as upon his comments during the process.

A method used with young children is the interpretation of pictures, which are sometimes mounted so they appear to be photographs. The child selects one for his own story. He may be asked to pretend, for example, that the person in a picture is having difficulty with his school work and he is asked to compose a story that explains the origin and nature of his problems. Children who have learning difficulties often project elements of their own history when composing stories.

The story-completion method is frequently used in interview situations. The following story themes are typical: "A boy goes to school. During recess he does not play with the other children but stays alone in a corner. Why?" "A boy is having a fight with his brother. Mother comes. Then what happens?" He may be told a folk tale and asked to retell it. Changes from the original representation may indicate personality trends. A variation of this technique is to tell a story illustrating certain emotional stresses or attitudes. Thereupon the child is asked to indicate his feelings about the story and his reactions to certain characters or events. In responding to this technique, a child reveals information that would not appear in response to direct questioning.

Play is a particularly appropriate medium for study because of the child's spontaneous interest. It is possible with play to duplicate with dolls and toy furniture the life situations of children. Through such means, reactions to parental rejection, sex, over-solicitude, and fear attitudes may be observed. When a family situation is duplicated, a child may differentiate individual members from the others, as for example, spank, bury, or crush the dolls.

[45] Haim G. Ginett, *Group Psychotherapy with Children* (New York: McGraw-Hill Book Co., 1961). The techniques for administering and using most of these are described in considerable detail in nontechnical language.

sociometric techniques

The need for sociometric techniques grows out of the interpersonal relationships of pupils as well as those between pupils and teachers. In discussing the importance of the learner's status in classroom situations, Prescott[46] says:

> Peer group belonging and standing influence greatly each child's concept of himself, and consequently, his self-confidence and level of aspiration, not only in peer group play but in other school activities. Furthermore, rejection, isolation, and "fringe" experiences give rise to strong and persisting emotions which often preoccupy the child in the classroom when he might be learning other useful things. They also lead to compensatory or attention-seeking behavior that is sometimes disturbing to the work of the classroom. Or, in gifted children, they may lead to preoccupation with academic tasks that result in unbalanced development and failure to acquire the skills of getting along with others that are requisite for later vocational and social success.

Sociometric techniques are based on the assumption that the individual can best be understood as a member of a group and that the group can best be understood by a study of those composing it. These techniques involve the measurement of pupil relationships showing the patterns of attraction or rejection of one person to another. Pupils are asked to select preferred companions in certain school situations frequently including first, second, and third choices. The results may be depicted in a sociogram that reveals the group structure and serves as a guide for subsequent steps in the investigation. The sociogram enables the teacher to analyze the relationship of one pupil to another. Sociometric techniques aid in identifying children chosen frequently and those who are left out. They are most accurate for children who are located at extreme positions on the scale of acceptability.

The first step in making a sociometric analysis is to choose practical situations for working together on committees or developing projects in small groups. If tensions exist among class members, one may ask for the names of persons with whom a pupil would prefer not to work or sit. Criteria sometimes used for social acceptance include choice of working companions, designation of friends to receive Christmas gifts, election of club officers, and lists of best friends and class leaders.

The results of a sociometric analysis are presented in Figure 20, which shows the degree of *acceptance, isolation,* and *rejection* of pupils in an elementary-school class. It will be noted that pupil twelve is a "star" whereas pupils two and six are isolates. Pupil twelve is the most popular member of the class, is average in ability, and is a good worker. Pupil two has long been handicapped by reading difficulties. He is "clearly outside the class" and pupil fourteen is a highly controversial person.

[46] Daniel Prescott, *Factors Affecting Learning* (Pittsburgh: University of Pittsburgh Press, 1958).

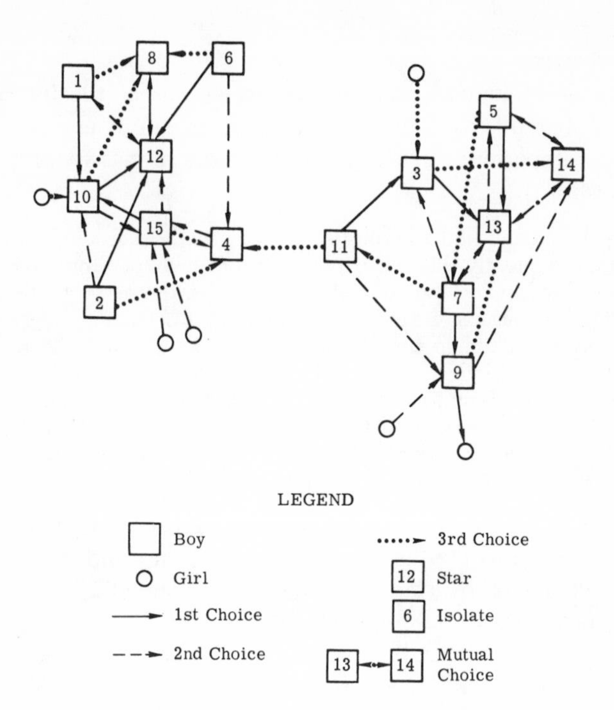

Figure 20. From Louis M. Smith, "Group Processes in Elementary and Secondary Schools," *Dept. of Classroom Teachers,* Amer. Educ. Res. Assoc., NEA, 1959.

In a study of fifth-grade children in 30 classrooms having an average enrollment of approximately 30, Gold[47] discovered that only two classrooms contained no children who might be designated as isolates. The range of isolates in a single classroom was 0–6; the percentage of isolates varied from 0–19; and the average number of isolates in a classroom was 2.4.

After a sociometric analysis has been made, assignments may be made of classroom tasks in order to bring certain individuals into a more favorable relationship with their classmates. Selection of pupils based on sociometric techniques may be used for grouping the children according to their needs and potentialities.[48] Social isolates may be placed in groups that provide opportunities for friendship and participation; others may be placed where there are opportunities for leadership. The techniques may also provide a basis for distributing leadership positions in all groups.

[47] H. A. Gold, "The Classroom Isolate: An Additional Dimension for Consideration in the Evaluation of a Quality Education Program," *Journal of Experimental Education,* 31 (1962), 77–83.

[48] K. M. Ecansm, "Sociometry in School: II. Applications," *Educational Research,* 6 (1964), 121–128.

evidence of improvement

The findings of studies designed to determine improvement resulting from understanding a learner and his problems are generally favorable, although the criteria used for evaluation are frequently based on subjective estimates. There is also the limitation that the improvement that is noted cannot be considered apart from other factors such as increased maturity, home, or other influences.

In an experimental study of low scorers in both achievement and personality, Seeman and Edwards[49] tested the value of half-hour play sessions during a four-month period in relationship to reading ability. The mean gain of the experimental group on the Gates reading test of approximately seven months was significantly greater than the mean gain of the control group. However, pretest and posttest records on the Tuddenham form of the Reputation Test and the Rogers Personality Test did not indicate significant differences for the experimental group. It is possible that therapy ameliorated conflict arising out of learning situations without a more generalizing effect. Talmadge[50] tested the effect of special teaching techniques with emotionally disturbed children who suffered from central nervous dysfunctions. The experimental group was taught reading by kinesthetic and auditory aids; the control group was taught by conventional methods. Children in the experimental group gained more than a year in reading skills during a three-month period as compared with a gain of four months by the control group. Case studies illustrated the relationship between reading improvement and emotional adjustment. McCleary[51] found that regrouping of the members of a high school class, based on data obtained by use of a sociometric technique, favorably affected the attitudes of pupils toward each other.

In a comprehensive study, Ojeman and Wilkinson[52] measured the effect analyzing and interpreting pupil behavior had on achievement. Two groups of pupils were selected and matched on such factors as chronological age, scholastic record, intelligence quotients, and general adjustment. In the experimental group significant data were compiled and the investigators analyzed each pupil's problems. On the basis of this analysis, suggestions were made to the teachers for interpreting the

[49] Julius Seeman and Benner Edwards, "The Therapeutic Approach to Reading Difficulties," *Journal of Consulting Psychology*, 18 (1954), 451–453.

[50] M. Talmadge and others, "Study of Experimental Methods for Teaching Emotionally Disturbed, Brain-Damaged, Retarded Readers," *Journal of Educational Research*, 51 (1963), 311–316.

[51] L. E. McCleary, "Restructuring the Interpersonal Relations of a Junior High School Class," *School Review*, 64 (1956), 346–352.

[52] R. H. Ojeman and F. R. Wilkinson, "The Effect on Pupil Growth of an Increase in Teacher's Understanding of Pupil Behavior," *Journal of Experimental Education*, 8 (1939), 143–147.

problems of each pupil. For the control group, no such provisions were made. Significant differences were found in grade-point average in favor of the experimental group. This group also showed differences in two other aspects of improvement: their attitudes toward the school improved and their personality conflicts declined.

Informal methods used by teachers in effecting improvement in the adjustment of pupils would be a contribution to knowledge. The most important outcome of such efforts probably would be the changed attitude of teachers during the process. Baruch[53] found that a program designed to help teachers recognize, prevent, and reduce maladjustments resulted in improvement of personalities of both teachers and children.

achieving emotional and social maturity

Some individuals achieve a high degree of emotional and social maturity at an early age; others remain immature in many traits throughout their lifetime. The most practical basis for evaluating maturity is to compare an individual's qualities with the qualities commonly possessed by well-adjusted persons.

Children are found at varying stages of development toward emotional and social maturity. It is necessary to take into account a child's age and the normal range of personality development characteristic of similar children. The desirable traits and qualities to be suggested should be regarded as idealistic standards of maturity; we may expect only a partial approach to such standards. A child may be regarded as achieving satisfactory adjustment when his behavior reflects progress toward attainment of the following:

1. *Good sportsmanship*
   The child is a good winner and a good loser. He works and plays in accordance with rules and notions of fair play. His attitude is neither extremely dominating nor submissive.

2. *Acceptance by other children*
   Other children are happy to include him in games and activities. He is interested in participating and understands the use of necessary social manners. He possesses the art of mingling harmoniously with his associates.[54]

3. *Objective viewpoint*
   He can look at himself without prejudice, accept criticism without resent-

[53] Dorothy W. Baruch, "Procedures in Training to Prevent and Reduce Mental Problems," *Journal of Genetic Psychology*, 67 (1945), 143–178.

[54] D. H. Stott, *The Social Adjustment of Children* (2nd ed.; London: University of London Press, 1963). In this book, Stott outlines a number of criteria by which the social adjustment of children may be evaluated.

ment, and does not expect success in all activities. He does not demand undue attention but in the classroom takes his turn as a matter of course.

4. *Happiness in school*
   The work of the classroom and other school activities interest him. He is happy and cheerful in most situations. He enjoys the stimulation of school activities and does not attempt to avoid social contacts and responsibilities.

5. *Poise and confidence*
   He can express himself without timidity in the classroom and in the presence of groups of pupils. In class he voluntarily asks questions if he does not understand or if he wishes further development of a subject.

6. *Concentration*
   He is able to discover sufficient meaning in school tasks to give them attention for reasonable periods of time. He is capable of working at one task at a time, without yielding to the distraction of conflicting purposes. When reciting, he does not resort to evasion to conceal lack of preparation or try to divert discussion into interesting but irrelevant channels.

7. *Self-responsibility*
   He solves his own school problems, without leaning excessively upon others for guidance. He knows the satisfaction of achievement through personal effort and does not wish recognition for accomplishment other than his own. He regards schoolwork as his personal responsibility and requires no pressure from others. He is punctual in his appointments. He is generally willing to accept responsibility for errors, without making excuses.

8. *Interests*
   He has interests outside school, as well as in some extracurricular activities. He is generally regarded as a busy child, making constructive use of free time.

9. *Realistic attitude.*
   He faces problems squarely, without unwholesome use of withdrawing types of behavior, such as daydreaming or avoidance. He is able to secure satisfaction of wants through acceptable ways of reacting to reality and has no need of pseudo-adjustments.

10. *Initiative*
    He participates in originating and developing ideas and is willing to make changes. He volunteers suggestions for increasing the value of classroom work and makes effort to promote it.

11. *Sex viewpoint*
    He is guided by common proprieties regarding sex and maintains a wholesome point of view. His interest in the opposite sex is characteristically mature at adolescence, and he seeks opportunity for companionship with both sexes. Adjustment at this stage is an important factor in ensuring well balanced adult emotions.

12. *Ethical standards*
    He has principles of rightness and wrongness in personal conduct, espe-

cially with respect to cheating, lying, and stealing. His methods of attaining his purposes do not require dishonesty.

The course of emotional and social development is characterized by the appearance of certain traits and the decline and disappearance of some behavior problems. Certain aspects of the individual's personality and specific behavior traits are temporary and disappear with increase in maturity. It is important to regard emotional and social development as a process of outgrowing many types of behavior as well as of developing increasingly mature personality patterns.

Certain criteria may also be used in evaluating the mental health of a classroom situation. These criteria, like those for achieving emotional and social maturity, represent stages of progress in attaining mental health goals. Menlo[55] has outlined four criteria which may be used in evaluating mental health within a classroom group as follows:

1. *The amount of acceptance or rejection within the group*
   This refers to the extent of positive or negative affect in the classroom, or the degree of friendly versus unfriendly atmosphere. This is the kind of thing teachers find out by doing a sociometric study on how much class members like each other, how much they think others like them, how much they like the teacher, how much they think the teacher likes them. The assumption here is that the predominance of accepting attitudes and behaviors is healthier than the predominance of rejecting ones.

2. *The amount of cooperative action or aggression within the group*
   This refers to the extent of active or passive movement with or against others, or the degree of helping versus force, threat, coercion, or harm. Teachers find this out when they ask students questions on how much they perceive themselves, other children, and the teacher as either being pushed around or pushing others around. The assumption here is that the predominance of cooperative action is healthier than the predominance of aggressive action.

3. *The amount of involvement in or withdrawal from the class process*
   This refers to the extent of active or passive movement toward or away from others or the degree of participation versus self-isolation and escape. Teachers assess this when they look for how much children appear to be, or feel they are, a part of the classroom experience. Here the assumption is that the presence of student involvement is healthier than the presence of withdrawal.

4. *The amount of feeling of comfort or anxiety in the class*
   This refers to the extent of "at ease" or tension, or the degree of calm versus nervous feelings and behaviors. One way teachers evaluate this is by providing opportunities for students' expressions of happiness or unhappiness with respect to classroom procedures, other students, the teacher, and the general class situation. The assumption is that a predominance of feelings of comfort is healthier than one of anxiety.

[55] Allen Menlo, "Mental Health Within the Classroom Group," *School of Education Bulletin,* University of Michigan, 32 (1960), 121–124.

the teacher's own adjustment

Children reflect the emotional and social traits of their teachers. If the teacher is irritable, unfriendly, and careless, they show similar characteristics. If he is calm, sympathetic and understanding, they exhibit little fear, are considerate of others, and do their work in a businesslike manner. Pupil reactions reveal the importance of a teacher's own adjustment.

Many of the teacher's adjustment problems arise from his relationships with pupils. Washburne and Heil[56] show that a teacher's personality has a measurable effect on pupil progress. Levin[57] found a significant relationship between the extent to which pupils described a teacher as *warm* and *friendly* and the amount of self-initiated and required work. Anderson's[58] studies indicated that teachers who met aggression with aggression incited increasing resistance. Kounin and Gump[59] show that children who have punitive teachers tend to manifest more aggression in their misconduct and to be less concerned with learning than do students who have nonpunitive teachers.

The fact that a teacher was maladjusted during his childhood does not necessarily imply that he will affect the adjustment of children unfavorably. If he was denied affection during childhood, he may have a better understanding of what it may mean in a child's life. Teachers are subject to the usual types and varieties of personality adjustments. There seems to be no "perfect teaching type" of personality. The following criteria may be used by a teacher for his own evaluation.

understanding children

The varied aspects of child adjustment require that the teacher be alert to any conditions that contribute to understanding. Trying to understand children is preferable to judging them arbitrarily and imposing adult

[56] Carleton Washburne and Louis M. Heil, "What Characteristics of Teachers Affect Children's Growth?" *School Review*, 68 (1960), 420–428. See also Robert F. Peck and James V. Mitchell, "Effect of Teacher's Mental Health on Pupil Learning" in *What Research Says to the Teacher* (Washington: American Educational Research Association, N.E.A., 1962).

[57] Harry Levin and others, "Studies of Teacher Behavior," *Journal of Experimental Education*, 26 (1957), 84–91.

[58] H. H. Anderson and others, "Studies of Teachers' Classroom Personalities: III, Follow-Up Studies of the Effects of Dominative and Integrative Contacts on Children's Behavior," *Applied Psychology Monograph*, 11 (1946).

[59] Jacob S. Kounin and Paul V. Gump, "The Comparative Influence of Punitive and Nonpunitive Teachers upon Children's Concepts of School Misconduct," *Journal of Educational Psychology*, 52 (1961), 44–49. See also C. M. Christensen, "Relationships between Pupil Achievement, Affect-Need, Teacher Warmth, and Teacher Permissiveness," *Journal of Educational Psychology*, 51 (1960), 169–174.

standards. Relationships with children normally inspire trust and confidence.

Since ability to maintain harmonious relationships with pupils contributes to teacher effectiveness, any instrument that will assist in prediction is helpful. One is the Minnesota Teacher-Attitude Inventory,[60] which is valuable in predicting at the beginning of the prospective teacher's professional training the reactions pupils will make to him after he has taught several years. By knowing a person's score on the inventory, it is possible to predict with some degree of accuracy the kind of emotional and social climate he will create in the classroom. It is useful[61] in differentiating between teachers who get along well with pupils in interpersonal relations and those who do not.

self-analysis

Jersild and Lazar[62] studied the responses of more than 200 teachers who had undergone psychotherapy. An attempt was made to determine changes in their attitudes and in their manner of reacting to problems of anger, competition, anxiety, sex, acceptance of others and themselves. As a basis of comparison, their responses were compared with those of a control group that had not undergone therapy. Teachers who had the benefit of therapy showed greater improvement than did those who were used as control. The most significant outcomes of therapy were those they experienced in the privacy of their own lives—"subjective reality."

Successful teachers study themselves objectively and are interested in discovering improved methods of adjusting to others. They also seek adequate means for solving their own personal problems. Personality and adjustment inventories reveal details of behavior characteristic of desirable and undesirable tendencies. Without taking such inventories, one may discover through their analysis a profitable basis for improvement. In self-evaluation one may consider the manner in which he accepts failure, is tolerant, responds to criticism, or adjusts to social activities. One interested in improving his personality should consider the impression he makes on people. He may discover in himself the defects he is most inclined to notice in others. He may, for example, reprimand children for restlessness when he himself lacks tranquility.

professional improvement

Teaching should be regarded as something more than the use of the same instructional materials from year to year in much the same manner.

[60] Anthony C. Riccio and Herman J. Peters, "The Study of Values and the Minnesota Teacher-Attitude Inventory," *Educational Research Bulletin,* 39 (1960), 101–103.

[61] Barry C. Munro, "The Minnesota Teacher-Attitude Inventory as a Predictor of Teaching Success," *Journal of Educational Research,* 58 (1964), 138–139.

[62] Arthur Jersild and Eva A. Lazar, *The Meaning of Psychotherapy in the Teacher's Life and Work* (New York: Bureau of Publications, Teachers College, Columbia University, 1962).

New knowledge and its application as well as improved instructional techniques continually make their appearance. Those interested in their teaching fields seek opportunity for self-improvement by attendance at professional meetings, advanced study at college or university, professional reading, or personal research. The teacher's example stimulates the learner's own efforts for self-improvement.

socialization

If one is to maintain emotional balance on a normal adult level, he should have contacts with mature individuals. The teacher needs the experience of contact and competition on a higher plane than that of the childhood environment to which the classroom often accustoms him. Knowledge of people in the community and of the problems they confront contributes to an understanding of teaching problems. His attitudes are also liberalized through travel, extensive reading, hobbies, and participation in community activities.

personal health

Teaching is a profession in which minor impairment of health is likely to be reflected in the performance of classroom duties. In many occupations lack of maximum efficiency affects objective output; but in the classroom, emotional states accompanying poor health are readily transferred to pupils who may respond in the form of inferior work, indifference, or irritability. Pupils are attracted by radiant health; it suggests a dependable source of power and strength. Consequently, the teacher's health should be carefully conserved so that a reserve of energy may be accumulated for unexpected situations. Proper food, rest, recreation, and sleep obviously are important. He may well set as his goal a condition of health sufficient to ensure the feeling that he has more than adequate force and vitality to meet the demands of each day of work.

study questions

1. Narrate experiences that you have had with children whose behavior in your presence has revealed (a) rationalization, (b) overcompensation, or (c) other behavior mechanisms.
2. Reconcile the statement that children are not born bad with the frequent observation that undesirable behavior appears among some children in certain families and not others.
3. On the assumption that behavior is adjustment to satisfy personal purposes and demands made by others, outline appropriate adult attitudes toward behavior problems.
4. Evaluate the assumption that the home is the ideal place for rearing children. Characterize various types of home as sources of emotional problems.
5. Outline procedures for helping a pupil adjust to a new school or neighborhood.

6. Describe some of the critical periods of emotional adjustment through which children pass before achieving adulthood. Why is chronological age an unreliable index of emotional maturity?
7. Outline various disciplinary problems that you have observed in school and analyze them as symptoms of (a) chronic emotional distress, (b) conflict with inflexibility of the school program, (c) developmental difficulty, or (d) lack of intellectual stimulation, particularly at the upper extremes of ability.
8. Describe experiences in which behavior problems have been precipitated by an immediate incident but upon analysis have proved symptomatic of one or more remote adjustment difficulties.
9. Suggest potential conflicts resulting from adult domination which fosters juvenile delinquency.
10. Compare the emotional influence of different kinds of teacher—dictatorial, sentimental, indifferent, and intellectually zealous—upon pupils you have known or upon yourself.
11. Some educators recommend case studies of every pupil. Suggest outcomes that may be desirable and undesirable from the standpoint of (a) pupil, (b) teacher, (c) school administrator, and (d) parents.
12. Outline a basis upon which an administrator may unostensibly (a) appraise a teacher's mental health and (b) eliminate causes of many undesirable symptoms. What is a desirable attitude toward a teacher emotionally unsuited for his work?

implications of learning theories

10

The discussion up to this point has been concerned with the course of learning and with the conditions under which it proceeds. We shall now consider the nature and process of learning. How may learning be described and what is the nature of the learner's progress during practice?

In studying the learning process, the psychologist has used both animals and human beings as subjects. In using animals he can readily devise techniques for studying various factors involved in the learner's progress. He can also provide obstacles, the reactions to which enable him to formulate principles that govern behavior in dynamic situations. But most important, through experimentation with animals, he is able to try out numerous techniques, some of which may be adapted to human beings. He conceives of his work with animals primarily as a means to the arrangement of more elaborate learning situations in which human subjects demonstrate greater insight and intelligence.

background of theories

Ideas about the nature of learning have long been a part of the literature of psychology and philosophy. Learning theories as we know them today, however, are products of this century and reflect psychological techniques used in experimental study. The purpose here is to review in historical perspective certain experimental techniques that have been useful in studying the process of learning and that have provided a basis for theory. These techniques include *trial and error, conditioning, memorization,* and *structured, goal-seeking* types of task.

trial and error

One of the earliest types of experimental work associated with learning theory was conducted by E. L. Thorndike,[1] who studied the behavior of animals in problem boxes. In such situations the animal tries first one and then another mechanism in a box until finally he releases himself, and food or some other reward is provided. He is again placed in the same situation, and a repetition of random responses occurs; with practice he narrows the range of exploration and eventually is capable of releasing himself quickly on one trial.

In circumstances such as the problem box presents, the animal exhibits all of the characteristics of trial-and-error behavior. He, supposedly by chance, makes successful responses that serve as a guide for further success until a solution is found. It is also assumed that unsuccessful responses indicate what to avoid just as the successful ones point in the direction of what to do. On the assumption the animal is incapable of analyzing the problem and reacting intelligently to it, trial and error tends to be the principal learning method.

At a later stage in his study of learning, Thorndike[2] used trial-and-error verbal situations, employing human adults as subjects. In one of these situations students were asked, after seeing a particular word in a series, to select any number between 0 and 10. Certain of these numbers were predetermined as either the right or wrong association. The purpose was to determine the effect of informing the learner of the correctness of the word-number associations upon his subsequent recall. In general, reward (informing the student that he was right) produced uniformity of response—causing the same response to be repeated. On the other hand, failure (informing him that he was wrong) did not eliminate erroneous responses even up to chance expectation. In a simple situation such as this the first responses are made on a trial-and-error basis; but with positive knowledge of results the individual soon learns to make the correct word-number association.

Another trial-and-error type of learning situation, which has afforded a basis for theory, is the maze, especially when animals are used as subjects. Because of its numerous pathways, the maze affords a systematic method for studying the acquisition of correct and the elimination of incorrect responses. When using this type of learning situation, the investigator can readily plot the learner's progress as practice continues. For example, he can record the number of errors made on the first trial,

[1] E. L. Thorndike, "Animal Intelligence," *Psychological Review Monographs,* 2, No. 8 (1898).

[2] E. L. Thorndike, *Human Learning* (New York: Appleton-Century Co., 1932).

the second, third, and so on. A record of the time required for each successful running of the maze can also be kept. In addition, he can determine the number of trials needed to meet a criterion of efficiency.

In using the maze with animal subjects, the learner's initial responses are made on a trial-and-error basis. As practice continues, the animal proceeds to fixate the correct and eliminate the incorrect responses. The situation differs, however, when certain types of mazes are used with human subjects who may be able to analyze their structure at the beginning and thus reduce random effort. Maze learning, however, whether it be with animal or human subjects, tends to be a measure of the learner's ability to profit by his successes and errors, which are initially made on a random basis.

Learning situations such as those described are widely employed in the psychological laboratory. Instead of increasing the complexity of mazes for animals and human beings, there has been a tendency to use the simpler kinds.[3] Through the use of simple types of task using various forms of reinforcement it is possible to determine the influence of significant variables, capable of being objectively evaluated, which when considered together form a basis for theory.

conditioned response

The conditioned response discovered by Pavlov[4] is based on the belief that both animals and human beings tend to respond to particular stimuli in certain ways. The technique of conditioning demonstrates that these same responses may be evoked by substitute stimuli. Pavlov discovered, for example, that the sight of meat would cause the salivary-gland reaction in dogs. If at the time a dog saw the meat a bell was rung and this association of meat and bell occurred a number of times, the bell itself would cause the salivary-gland reaction even though the meat was absent. The conditioned stimulus—the bell—becomes a substitute stimulus for the unconditioned stimulus—the sight of meat.

The essential requirement for developing conditioned responses is to provide a basis for association of stimuli and to apply the principles of frequency and recency of practice. Conditioning is a simple learning technique and requires little conscious control or awareness of responses that may occur. Indeed, it is frequently best developed in a quiet, serene atmosphere where stimuli act upon the learner. But this in itself does not limit its effectiveness in acquiring habits and in influencing emotional responses. Many undesirable responses, such as fears or negative atti-

[3] Howard H. Kendler, "Stimulus-Response Psychology and Audio-Visual Education," *Audio-Visual Communication Review*, 9 (1961), 33–41. See also W. F. Hill, "Contemporary Developments within Stimulus-Response Theory," in *N.S.S.E. Yearbook* (1964).

[4] I. Pavlov, *Conditioned Reflexes* (New York: Dover Press, 1960).

tudes, may be developed by conditioning. Consequently, the technique of reconditioning or the acquisition of new conditioned responses may be needed for their elimination.

The technique of producing learning by conditioning continues to be an important area of research activity but with emphasis upon "instrumental" as distinguished from "classical" Pavlovian conditioning. Experimenters using this technique study a variety of problems extending from simple eyelid conditioning to problems involved in discrimination learning. Proponents of conditioning believe that it affords a basis for studying most problems in learning. Some investigators,[5] notably Guthrie,[6] emphasize conditioning without reinforcement, whereas others, including Spence[7] and Skinner, believe that learning includes both conditioning and reinforcement.

The conditioned response as discovered by Pavlov was not a new concept but rather an aspect of Aristotle's principle of contiguity in space and time and its further development by the association school of learning. Associationism postulates that items of information learned together will be recalled together and that the larger the number of associations developed in studying a body of subject matter the greater will be the probability of completeness and accuracy in recall. In studying large bodies of material it affords a basis for developing a cross-index file that assists revival of important items.

memorization

The process of memorization is one of the oldest and most common techniques used in studying the learning process, particularly when employing verbal tasks. As a means of providing active learning situations (as distinguished from recall of what may already be known) laboratory materials tend to be artificial and often meaningless. In the laboratory, the procedure consists of selecting certain materials, providing standardized conditions of practice, and measuring the learner's efficiency in their recall. Inasmuch as such tasks possess little inherent meaning in themselves, rote learning methods are encouraged, if not required. Also, because of their artificial nature, the learner obviously is motivated by external means such as knowledge of progress or some form of reward.

When meaningful materials are used in laboratory situations, they tend to consist of passages whose contents are not likely to be familiar to the learner. The student may study, for example, a selection of prose under

[5] Morris L. Bigge, *Learning Theories for Teachers* (New York: Harper & Row, 1964).

[6] Edwin R. Guthrie, *The Psychology of Learning* (rev. ed.; New York: Harper & Row, 1952).

[7] Kenneth W. Spence, *Behavior Theory and Learning* (Englewood Cliffs, New Jersey: Prentice-Hall, 1960).

controlled conditions and then be required to reproduce its essential substance. But whether using meaningless or meaningful material, stress is placed on the fidelity with which the learner is able to recall the significant items.

structured, goal-seeking situations

Learning theories and experimental techniques were strongly challenged when the contributions of German psychologists, notably Köhler, Koffka, and Lewin, were widely publicized in psychological literature. Gestalt psychology, with which these theorists are associated, is based mainly on experiments in perception that emphasize the fact that the stimulus situation to which a learner responds is always structured. The learner does not respond effectively to separate items of a stimulus situation but rather to a pattern of events. Learning is a dynamic process based on the individual's previous experiences that are interwoven with those of his present and related to his particular goals. The individual's experiences in turn result in additional insights, understandings, and attitudes. Learning is regarded as a developmental process, which proceeds from simpler to more comprehensive meaningful wholes.

Perhaps the most significant of the experimental work of these psychologists was that by Köhler,[8] who devised problem situations and studied the behavior of chimpanzees in seeking a solution. In some of his learning situations, bananas were hung from the ceiling of a room as an objective. On the floor of the room tables and boxes of varying sizes were provided. Sticks that could be pieced together as a means of reaching the bananas were available. The problem of the chimpanzees was to use the table, the boxes, and sticks in attaining the objective. Records were kept of the methods used as well as the results. These indicated that some animals demonstrated exceptional ability in attaining their goal—the bananas.

Unlike trial-and-error, conditioning, and memorization methods, the experimental situation provided a goal and the means for its attainment. The learner could survey the situation and perceive relationships between means and ends. It was in this kind of learning situation that "gestalt" psychology or the more general "field concepts"[9] were conceived and developed. Out of it came concepts such as goal seeking, insight, and interpretation of total situations in describing the nature of learning.

techniques and theories

The techniques that have been reviewed become more meaningful when they are considered in their relationship to certain broad schools or theories of learning. In *trial-and-error*, *conditioning*, and *memorization*

[8] W. Köhler, *Gestalt Psychology* (New York: Horace Liveright Co., 1929), p. 299.

[9] K. Lewin, "Field Theory of Learning" in *Psychology of Learning*, N.S.S.E. 51st Yearbook (1942).

situations the learner exhibits many of the characteristics of sheer repetition. One notes the gradual fixation of successful responses and the elimination of the unsuccessful. The most easily observed conditions are the effects of practice together with some form of reward, which presumably establishes connections between stimuli and responses. There is also the tendency for one to analyze behavior according to numerous elements and for success in one aspect of behavior not to be accompanied by equal success in another. Consequently, a basis is formed for theories that are *stimulus-response* in nature and *atomistic* in method.

In contrast, where the investigator devises a problem situation so that the learner is encouraged to perceive relationships between a goal and the means for its attainment, the stage is set for a different description of the learning process. Under such conditions the learner is stimulated to make his own discovery. He has opportunity to survey the situation as a whole and become actively involved in a task that permits initiative and flexibility of response. When the learner is capable of mastering such problem situations, his behavior is characterized by *goal-seeking* and *insight*. One who describes learning in this manner will also emphasize the *purpose* and *meaning* of any task used for experimentation. Thus, a basis is formed for theories that are *cognitive* in nature and *wholistic* in method.

The two broad groups of theorists differ not only with respect to their views concerning the nature of learning but even more in their methods of investigation. Stimulus-response theorists are primarily interested in analyzing and studying behavior;[10] the cognitive group are interested in the more subjective and complex mental processes. Some distinguishing characteristics of the two groups of theories will be considered.

distinguishing characteristics of theories

Some of the issues that are involved in the two groups of theories are illustrated by contrasting situations as follows: (1) specificity versus flexibility of response, (2) parts versus wholes, (3) trial and error versus insight, and (4) incidental versus purposive behavior.

specificity versus flexibility of response

According to the stimulus-response view, when a given stimulus is presented, it is assumed a certain response will be evoked and repetition of the stimulus will call forth the same response as before; a connection is formed between a stimulus and a response. In contrast, proponents of

[10] Wells Hively, "Implications for the Classroom of B. F. Skinner's Analysis of Behavior," *Harvard Educational Review,* 29 (1959), 37–42.

cognitive theories suggest that a given stimulus is not necessarily followed by a particular response. The individual never confronts a learning situation without some kind of experience that determines the stimuli to which he will respond. Thus, the emphasis shifts from the *stimulus* (emphasized in stimulus-response theories) to the *learner,* who is the principal element in the learning process.

parts versus wholes

The most readily recognized difference between the two groups of theories is the emphasis placed on parts as compared with wholes in a learning situation. The stimulus-response theorist is interested in an analysis of the elements of behavior; the cognitive theorist decries analysis and insists that the individual reacts to the whole—and this whole is different from and greater than the sum of its parts.

A simple example is found in arithmetic. The cognitive school would contend that the learner, in considering a division problem, does not react to the numerical signs and digits as separate and independent elements. He responds to a division problem—$75 \div 25$—as a situation that has meaning and he does not separate the numbers from the division sign. If he is ready to study this aspect of arithmetic, he interprets the problem as an exercise in division and he proceeds to solve it as such. It is the total situation that has meaning for him.

trial and error versus insight

Another basis for cleavage between the two groups of theorists is whether learning takes place by trial and error or by insight. In most trial-and-error situations, there is limited opportunity for the learner to survey the total problem and react intelligently to it. With practice, however, he narrows his range of exploration, eliminates errors, and fixates correct responses. In trial and error, his progress tends to be gradual and continuous until mastery is achieved.

When learning by insight, on the other hand, he may view the problem in its totality. Supposedly, there is sudden understanding of the problem, and the solution is reached quickly. The learning process may be analyzed by stages that are scarcely perceptible even to the trained observer. First, there is a need to solve a problem. Second, the learner surveys the problem, becomes aware of the obstacles, and develops a tentative means of solution. Third, insight occurs at the point at which he definitely performs the acts necessary to solve it. After the problem is solved, further practice, as implied in stimulus-response doctrine, is regarded unnecessary.

In trial-and-error situations, progress is characterized by both correct and incorrect responses; possibilities for correct responses only during initial trials are limited. When he learns by insight, the learner's behavior is based on a pattern of ideas or on all the elements included in a problem. Persistent and uninterrupted responses are made toward a goal —the solution. Instead of reaching a solution after many random attempts, the learner responds to total situations and not to numerous, successive, independent stimuli.

incidental versus purposive behavior

Inherent in stimulus-response theory is the assumption of a predetermined task where the learner's responses tend to be restricted by the learning situation. The learner may have no purpose other than to meet the requirements built into the task, be made aware of his progress, and receive a reward. Under cognitive theory, in contrast, the learner's goal and understanding of the task are important factors that contribute to efficiency.

implications for teaching

The broad aspects of changing learning theory have been generally accompanied by parallel trends in instructional practice. Judd,[11] in summarizing a century of psychological applications to education, in 1925 stated that there was in many institutions "not so long ago a wholehearted acceptance of the psychology which regards the process of learning as nothing other than the memorization of authoritative statements." Efforts to make such applications have been evident through the years.[12] Psychologists[13] who are most active in formulating theories, however, are reluctant to extend their applications to situations other than those in which they are developed. Nevertheless, it is in the laboratory setting where certain variables and conditions can best be

[11] Charles H. Judd, "A Century of Applications of Psychology to Education," *Teachers College Record*, 22 (1925), 771–781.

[12] For example, see Caswell and others below:

H. L. Caswell, "Practical Application of Mechanistic and Organismic Psychologies to Curriculum," *Journal of Educational Research*, 25 (1934), 16–24.

Morris Bigge, *Learning Theories for Teachers* (New York: Harper & Row, 1964).

B. R. Bugelski, *The Psychology of Learning Applied to Teaching* (Indianapolis: Bobbs-Merrill, 1964).

H. J. Eyesnek, "The Contribution of Learning Theory," *British Journal of Educational Psychology*, 30 (1960), 11–21.

Travis L. Hawk, "School Practice and Certain Principles of Learning," *Elementary School Journal*, 64 (1963–64), 36–41.

J. B. Murray, "Review of Learning Theories," *Catholic Educational Review*, 63 (1965), 20–27.

J. G. Woodworth, "Some Theoretical Bases for a Psychology of Instruction," *Canadian Educational Research Digest*, 26 (1965), 514–526.

[13] K. W. Spence, "The Relation of Learning Theory to the Technology of Education," *Harvard Educational Review*, 29 (1959), 84–95.

controlled and consequently where theories may be derived. An obvious need is that such theories be further tested in the broader setting of the school curriculum. In any case, their value for the educator lies in their possible implications rather than in their direct applications.

What would be the nature of teaching if one adhered to the stimulus-response rather than to the cognitive view of learning? Would there be many or few learning objectives? How would course materials be organized? Would there be many or few learning activities? Would drill or meaning be emphasized? What kinds of test would be used for evaluation? The implications of learning theories point to these and other questions.

many versus few objectives

Under stimulus-response theory there would be many learning objectives related to specific elements in a course of instruction. In an English language course, for example, the objectives would be linked with each aspect of subject matter, which might be the elements of grammatical structure such as nouns, pronouns, tenses, moods, verbs, and adjectives. The learner would be made aware of the kind of proficiency expected in each of the elements. Little would be overlooked as far as objectives are concerned.

According to the cognitive view there might be one major learning objective defined—for example, the ability to communicate efficiently in oral and written composition. The elements of grammatical structure may be practiced separately but would be related to their use in communication.

small versus large units

According to the stimulus-response view the curriculum would be organized into many short, intensive courses and studied more or less independently. Under a cognitive view there would be a few basic courses scheduled over an extended period of time and interrelationships of subject matter would be emphasized.

The stimulus-response theorist would organize a course into a number of small divisions, the cognitive group into a few large divisions. The former would also organize material in considerable detail, providing a blueprint for all significant items. In contrast, the latter would provide the learner with only a broad outline in the belief that he should assume some responsibility for its development. Under the first theory the learner would regard a course of instruction as a task to be mastered as outlined; under the other it would be regarded as one to be developed.

Educators have been very much aware of learning theory in curriculum planning. Current types of organization, such as the *integrated* curriculum, *core* curriculum, *fusion* courses, and *broad* subject-matter fields, imply cognitive viewpoints. The aim of such forms of organization is to encourage the learner to study materials, not as independent entities, but as parts of larger wholes where transfer is more readily achieved.

few versus many activities

According to the stimulus-response view there would be few activities but they would be repeated in numerous learning situations. In a college history course, for example, the activities might be limited to lectures and reading source materials. There might be several objectives for this particular course, representing certain kinds of proficiency desired in its various parts; but the same activities would be used for their attainment. In contrast, under a cognitive view the learner in the same course might engage in varied kinds of activity such as reading source materials, listening to lectures, participating in discussion, working on problems, and taking field trips. The purpose would be to study subject matter in various ways, resulting in different kinds of response. Under a stimulus-response view, memorization and assimilation of information would be emphasized. Under a cognitive view, application of information to problem situations would be stressed.

drill versus meaning

For the stimulus-response theorist, learning is a specific process that is made up of numerous connections between learning materials and the individual's responses. In arithmetic, for example, there would be one connection between 3 plus 4 and another between 3 plus 10. Each of these connections would require specific practice for mastery. The function to be improved is isolated and practiced until the desired degree of mastery is achieved.

Extensive research on arithmetic has been performed to determine if learning takes place more effectively by drill or by meaning. In stimulus-response theory there is the assumption that arithmetic may be analyzed into a number of relatively independent elements of skill or knowledge and that the pupil should master these elements whether he understands them or not. He should learn them in the form in which they will be later used. There is also the belief that he will learn them most effectively by formal repetition.

Cognitive theory, in contrast, emphasizes the meaning aspects of arithmetic. Should arithmetic be taught so that it makes sense to the child or should he learn principally by drill? In essence this is what is meant by the *meaning* versus the *drill* theory of learning arithmetic. Under the meaning theory, teaching emphasizes understanding of the basic concepts of arithmetic through independent discovery rather than through skill in computational exercises. In measuring understanding, the learner is expected to answer a variety of questions that are different from, but belonging to the same general class as, those practiced during instruction.[14]

numerous test items versus major problems

According to stimulus-response theory a test would consist of numerous items as illustrated by conventional objective examinations. It would also include short-answer items in which responses could be evaluated objectively. Such tests would be based on the assumption that improvement of behavior can be effected by changes in its separate elements and that evaluation may be made by the process of adding discrete achievements.

Under a stimulus-response view, tests would be planned to emphasize measurement of each unit of material independently. In preparation for tests the learner would tend to regard each unit as separate from every other and adjust his study methods accordingly. The testing program would not require him to maintain a continuing relationship with previous units as a course proceeds.

The cognitive theorist would regard behavior as a unit of activity where the learner reacts to the varied aspects of a significant problem. A test would consist of a few major problems, frequently those for which all the information needed for solution is provided. Problem situations may also require the learner to draw on a wide range of learning experience in seeking a solution. In a particular instance he would react to broad areas of learning material rather than to detailed items of information implied under stimulus-response doctrine.

Instead of testing over single units of material and evaluating them independently as in stimulus-response theory, the learner would be expected to reorganize and unify learning materials as he advances through a course. Each test would include previously acquired concepts or principles and incorporate them in a new setting. Such cumulative testing would provide the learner with opportunity to demonstrate improved quality of performance at each stage of his progress. This plan is sometimes referred to as the "snowball" method of testing as contrasted with the "stone" method under stimulus-response theory.

other implications

Table 2 shows the two groups of theories under which are listed a number of additional implications, some of which overlap with those

[14] Evan R. Keislar, "The Development of Understanding in Arithmetic by a Teaching Machine," *Journal of Educational Psychology,* 50 (1959), 247–253. See also David Rappaport, *Understanding the Meanings in Arithmetic* (Chicago: Science Research Associates, 1959).

Table 2. Implications of Theories

Stimulus-Response Theories	Cognitive Theories
Rote learning	*Logical learning*
Course of instruction organized in advance	*Course of instruction developed as learning proceeds*
Logical organization of curriculum	*Psychological organization of curriculum*
Transfer of training based on specific elements	*Transfer of training based on generalization and transformation*
Abilities: reproduction and recognition of information	*Abilities: interpretation, application, and inference*
Accuracy and specificity of response	*Understanding information and principles*
Motivation: extrinsic	*Motivation: intrinsic*
Nature of guidance: direct	*Nature of guidance: indirect*
Consumers and scholars in the traditional sense	*Productive scholarship and creativity*
Subject-matter centered	*Learner-centered*
Authoritarian methods	*Democratic methods*
Programmed instruction	*Independent exploration and discovery*

already discussed. The reader will think of others that might be included.

developing a teaching philosophy

Learning theories and their implications provide reference points for developing a teaching philosophy. One can judge for himself the extent to which his philosophy leans in the direction of stimulus-response or cognitive viewpoints. He cannot rely solely, however, upon theoretical concepts. His philosophy is influenced by many factors. Certain of his ideas may result from an analysis of the learning process in the laboratory, some from everyday teaching experience, and still others from a study of expert opinion. His convictions and beliefs grow out of a blending of many observations and experiences, including how he himself learned and was taught in school and college.

In time, the teacher may be expected to have certain views about the nature of learning, the function of drill, the method of organizing learning materials, the value of different types of learning activity, and the kinds of test that are used for evaluation. He may also hold certain views about the significance of interests, the part played by incentives, and the influence of emotional and social adjustment on learning.

One interested in developing a teaching philosophy will find it helpful to consider two factors: the definition of learning and teaching methods.

the definition of learning

Is learning a matter of memorizing the main ideas of a textbook? Does it consist of assimilating the subject matter of a course and expressing it in one's own words? Is it ability to apply principles to new situations? Does it mean being able to use information in solving problems or in reaching decisions? Some teachers are satisfied when their students demonstrate familiarity with a wide range of information at examination time. Others insist the learner has not really learned until he can translate his ideas into practical application. It may be assumed that some responses operate on a memory level whereas others require reasoning and reflective thinking. In considering the nature of learning one may use as a frame of reference the views of the two extreme groups of theorists.

teaching methods

After one has reached a decision about the definition of learning, he should develop some convictions about the effectiveness of teaching methods. In reaching a decision he may consider two types of method, which are implied by the two major groups of learning theories: those that center on the teacher and those that center on the learner. This classification enables one to evaluate the extreme types and identify their differences and similarities.

Under the first classification instruction centers on what the teacher does: his directions, explanations, illustrations, demonstrations, interpretations, and points of view. In college or university a principal activity may be the *lecture* interspersed by questions and discussion. The *demonstration* may be used by the teacher to develop skills as in physical education and music or to illustrate principles as in biology and physics. As an activity, *discussion* may center on either the learner or the teacher. It may be planned for small groups for the purpose of exchanging and clarifying ideas. In most cases, discussion is rarely an activity in its own right but, rather, is associated with the teacher's leadership where the learner asks questions, ventures opinions, takes issue with viewpoints, or requests elaboration. The teacher stimulates the questions and usually approves or provides the answers.

Activities that tend to draw the learner into a more active learning role than those centering on the teacher include problem approaches such as the *project, the case study, laboratory work, independent study,* and various types of *group discussion* and *group-study procedures.* Instead of assimilating the discussion or interpretation provided by the teacher or textbook, the learner is encouraged to derive his own generalizations, principles, or interpretations. He moves from relatively passive learning situations to relatively active ones.

Teachers are not expected to use exclusively either teacher-centered or learner-centered methods; but they may tend toward one or the other as their typical practice. Some characteristics of the two types of method will be outlined.

teacher-centered methods

One who believes that learning takes place effectively by teacher-centered methods first defines and outlines the abilities he wishes to develop. Learning materials are also outlined systematically into major and subordinate topics, providing the learner with a blueprint of a course.

Learning activities tend to be restricted in number. The learner is required to do the assigned reading, perform exercises for particular topics, and to be ready to answer questions raised in class.

The tests stress recall, a premium being placed on the accuracy with which the learner is able to reproduce or recognize the material. They measure the kinds of abilities that may be evaluated objectively whereby correct and incorrect answers are indicated. Short-answer examinations and objective tests of the true-false and multiple-choice types are used frequently.

In motivation, emphasis is placed on incentives such as praise and reproof, knowledge of progress, competition, rewards and punishments. Since teacher-centered methods presuppose a predetermined task, there is minimum recognition of interests; the learner is motivated by external means.

The teacher occupies a focal position in the learning program. Activities of a class tend to center on what he does. In its extreme form teaching consists primarily of imparting information together with insistence that the learner master it. Memorization and assimilation of material tend to be the principal learning methods.

learner-centered methods

One who believes learning occurs effectively by learner-centered methods stresses abilities involved in reasoning and problem solving. The information acquired by the learner through his reading and study is used in solving problems or in answering questions; it is not acquired primarily for its recall.

Instructional materials may be carefully prepared, but the outline made available to the learner is not fully developed. The learners themselves are stimulated to assist in developing the various topics or units.

The students are encouraged to ask questions and to draw upon their experience and observation in developing the varied aspects of a particular body of subject matter. They may seek information from a variety of sources such as books and encyclopedias and interview persons in positions of authority for pertinent material. They may also organize themselves into groups with similar interests and develop certain units where a free exchange of ideas is encouraged. At the end of their work on a particular topic, they may draw conclusions and evaluate what they have accomplished.

Evaluation situations emphasize problem solving. Instead of numerous short-answer items, an entire testing period may be devoted to the solution of a few major problems. Such problems likely will be new in the sense that they have not been used previously. The learner, however, is expected to draw upon his experience in solving them.

Two aspects of motivation are emphasized. One is the importance of meaningfulness of the learning task itself. A large part of the motivational problem is solved when materials make sense to the learner. The other is that thorough learning is its own reward and reinforces the individual's efforts.

Learner-centered methods also include recognition of behavior disorders, provisions for remedial measures, and the means for establishing harmonious relationships between the learner and teacher. The emotional and social climate of the classroom is regarded as an influential part of the setting for learning.

Other earmarks of learner-centered methods are: The teacher permits the learner to choose his projects and the subjects of themes for his compositions and allows flexibility in the type and scope of his reading. The teacher regards his own most important work to be that of providing materials appropriate for the learner, of stimulating him to develop his own solutions, and of rewarding him for unique responses. The major responsibility is placed on the learner.

Consistency is an important criterion in formulating a teaching philosophy. Does the teacher have one view about the nature of learning and another about the nature and function of tests? Is his method of motivating students consistent with his views about the manner in which learning proceeds? If his philosophy were formulated, it would be possible to determine the extent to which he recognizes or violates in practice the implications of any views he might hold.

The acid test of a teacher's philosophy lies not so much in what he says about the kinds of learning he believes are developed in his classes as in the types of tests or other means of evaluation he uses to measure learning. These are the most tangible kinds of evidence for judging what learning means for a particular teacher.

study questions

1. Give what you consider a workable definition of the learning process. In doing so, take into account learning in varying situations and at different levels of response.
2. Discuss the two major groups of learning theories under the following headings: (a) what each of the groups of theories means, (b) how they are similar and different, and (c) what their implications for teaching are.
3. How does one develop a teaching philosophy?
4. How does one's teaching philosophy influence instructional activities?
5. Comment on this statement: "A person cannot have one philosophy of learning and another of testing."
6. Write a paper of approximately six pages showing how certain learning principles are recognized or violated in a teaching situation with which you are familiar.

author index

subject index